Confucian Ren and Feminist Ethics of Care

Confucian Ren and Feminist Ethics of Care

Integrating Relational Self, Power, and Democracy

Lijun Yuan

LEXINGTON BOOKS
Lanham • Boulder • New York • London

Published by Lexington Books
An imprint of The Rowman & Littlefield Publishing Group, Inc.
4501 Forbes Boulevard, Suite 200, Lanham, Maryland 20706
www.rowman.com

6 Tinworth Street, London SE11 5AL

British Library Cataloguing in Publication Information Available

Library of Congress Cataloging-in-Publication Data

Names: Yuan, Lijun, 1951- author.
Title: Confucian ren and feminist ethics of care : integrating relational
    self, power, and democracy / Lijun Yuan.
Description: Lanham : Lexington Books, [2019] | Includes bibliographical
    references and index.
Identifiers: LCCN 2018048423 (print) | LCCN 2019006219 (ebook) | ISBN
    9781498558198 (Electronic) | ISBN 9781498558181 (cloth) |
    ISBN 9781498558204 (pbk.)
Subjects: LCSH: Confucianism. | Feminist ethics. | Caring.
Classification: LCC BL1853 (ebook) | LCC BL1853 .Y83 2019 (print) | DDC
    170.951—dc23
LC record available at https://lccn.loc.gov/2018048423

In memory of my parents

Contents

Acknowledgments

I have worked on this book for more than a decade, mainly by myself to its completion. Although I did not receive many comments from others, since a very small number of scholars have done such a huge comparison, I sincerely thank the following persons who have inspired and encouraged me to accomplish this significant work. First, I owe a deep thank-you to Alison M. Jaggar, who always inspires me into lifelong engagement with a feminist pursuit for women's equality and a complete theorizing of gender justice and care. Next, I am very grateful to Craig Hanks, who encouraged me and generously assisted with the first draft abstract of the book proposal. He encouraged me to deepen every thought and argument through the book. I also thank Vincent Luizzi and Audrey M. McKinney for their constant support. Vince gave me his consistent support during my decade's work. Audrey helped me with my academic achievement in general; in particular, she commented on and edited my early version of China's aging as part of chapter 7. I also thank all those who expressed interest and supported my project for a decade! Lastly, I express my gratitude to Jana Hodges-Kluck and her team at Lexington Books. This book would not have been possible without their diligent work and their insights on the value of it.

Introduction

The primary purpose of this book is to contribute to an ongoing discussion of various concepts of self and the ways in which concepts of selfhood shape women's views of their relationship to the communities in which they live. This is a practical approach to applied ethics; I am especially interested in how ancient philosophical traditions affect contemporary Chinese society by tracing how certain concepts of selfhood underlie women's subordinated status.

Confucian and feminist ethics of care both emphasize people's interdependency and positioning, *ren* and *care*, respectively, as the most fundamental value of their ethical theories. Both argue that the concept of *care* as a theory and practice can extend to the public domain to accomplish its task of taking care of all people in need. Nevertheless, there are significant differences both historically and conceptually between the two theories. I will explore and clarify whether the Confucian notion of selfhood, because of its deep commitment to social harmony and hierarchy, excludes a serious engagement in the social ideal of equality and in gender equality in particular. I will also explore the ways in which attention to the Confucian notion of selfhood can enrich the feminist notions of reciprocity and self-other relationships. The book makes a significant contribution to the comparative study of the two scholarly traditions. It exhibits many important unique features: first, it is a comparative approach at its best. The book is to inquire the complementarity of Confucian and Western feminist ethics of care as applied to the situation of women in contemporary China: the feminist approach can help Confucianism avoid its excessive commitment to social harmony which would exclude any serious engagement in the gender equality, while Confucianism can enrich the feminist notion of reciprocity, which is crucial to the gender equality. Second, this book combines the theoretical and practical dimensions. On the one hand, it does not merely aim to produce a theoretical construction of an idea of gender equality; on the other hand, it is not meant to be a merely sociological survey of women's situation in contemporary China. Rather, the book aims to draw on both Chinese (particularly Confucianism) and Western (particularly feminism) resources to develop a unique conception of gender equality which is both theoretically innovative and practically effective not only to explain but also try to improve through critical scrutiny the women's situation in care practice in contemporary China.

Sixty years ago, China was one of the poorest countries in the world, populated mostly by peasants in rural areas, and still suffering from internal turmoil and international humiliation for more than a century. Today, China is a rapidly modernizing economic dynamo with exponentially escalating global influences. China has witnessed an expansive increase in income inequality since the late 1980s when reform was introduced. As the income gap widens, the prereform "classless" society of China is becoming stratified. A certain degree of inequality and stratification is justifiable in a market environment for the sake of economic incentives.[1]

As a woman studies scholar and a philosopher, I see how important the international women's movement and feminist concepts of women's equality are on women in China. The UN Fourth World Conference on Women convened in Beijing in 1995 helped China make gender equality a basic national policy. The policy has supported gender mainstreaming under which millions of Chinese women grass root activists and academic women studies scholars work to promote women's social status through gender justice strategies and protection of women's rights. Although the government has adopted some effective policies in securing economic growth and securing employment through creating jobs and employment policies for both men and women, job and income gaps are increasing.

According to Bohong Liu, the former director of the Women Studies Institute of China, one example of the gap is that the government invested 4,000 billion yuan for the development of 10 industries and created 40 million jobs. Most of these industries are male-dominated and controlled work forces. These investment strategies confirm full employment for men but lack employment opportunities for women. The government's macro-economic policies still lack gender awareness. She also claimed that gender segregation in the labor market is closely related to stereotypes in education and training. For instance, although the percentage of female university students rose to 49.9 percent in 2008, girls still predominantly study social sciences while boys study engineering and technology. These apparent choices by girls and boys are closely linked to cultural stereotypes, gender biases in the education system, gaps in public services and family polices, and women's lack of public participation in decision making at the macro-level.[2]

In *New Masters and New Servants* Yan (2008) examines the experiences of the rural Chinese women who migrated to cities in search of economic opportunities and personal fulfillment during China's reform era. Yan explores a vexing question of why these women failed to find their fair share in the fast-growing gains of urban life. Issues of gender and class have been neglected in post-Mao modernization. Under post-Mao policies, rural China is reconceptualized as the polar opposite of the modern, civilized city, and rural youth migrate to the city in hopes of defining their own "personhood" or "*suzhi*," but find only low-class positions open to "surplus rural labor." *Suzhi (human quality)* plays a key role in the discourse of development in post-Maoist China. A resolution passed by the 12th Party Congress in 1986 declared the importance of "the moral *suzhi* and the scientific and cultural *suzhi* of the Chinese nation."[3] The concept was comprehensively connected with modernization by the 15th Party Congress in 1997. The concept of *suzhi* acts as an inducement and a limitation for rural Chinese women who seek to escape their poverty. They learn that they lack *suzhi*, and, thereby, desire to develop greater *suzhi*.

As Jacka notes in *Rural Women in Urban China* (2006), the rural/urban dichotomy echoes the traditional Confucian distinction between the ruled, those who use their muscles and are without education, and the morally superior rulers, those who use their minds and hearts. In my view, the Maoist effort to reverse the Confucian order during the ten-year Cultural Revolution by sending young intellectuals to the countryside for reeducation from the poor and lower middle-class peasants was a national failure. Confucianism reemerged within post-Maoist modernization and has been reshaped within the discourse of development. The emphasis on *suzhi* is a direct extension of the Confucian notion of self-cultivation.[4]

How is urban women's social status in recent decades? We may hear stories that many urban Chinese women express anxiety about becoming a "leftover" woman if they are not married by their late twenties and early thirties. In *Leftover Women*, Fincher points out China's gender income gap has increased substantially in the last twenty years: "In 1990 the average annual salary of an urban woman was 77.5 percent that of men. But by 2010 the gap relative to men had widened by 10.2 percentage points, with urban women's average income just 67.3 percent that of men, according to demographer Isabelle Attane's analysis of figures from the All-China Women's Federation and NBS."[5] Also, China's urban employment rate for women aged twenty to fifty-nine fell to a new low of 60.8 percent in 2010, down from 77.4 percent twenty years earlier. "The 2010 rate was 20.3 percentage points lower than that of men, whereas in 1990 urban women's employment rate was 14.5 percentage points lower than that of men. That is, while gender gaps in employment are narrowing throughout much of the world, China's gender gap has widened significantly over the past two decades."[6]

In "Gender Equality in China's Economic Transformation," the authors analyze the status and implications of gender inequality during China's economic transformation through a careful examination of the three areas, employment opportunities, income, and unpaid labor, from a gender perspective.[7] The authors indicate that gender disparity has increased in employment opportunities. Compare the Fifth National Population Census in 2000 and Sixth National Population Census in 2010: "the gap between the labor force participation rates of men and women was 11 percentage points in 2000, and it grew to 14.5 in 2010. Although the labor force participation rates of both men and women are declining, women's participation rate is declining at a higher speed." In 2010, 27 percent of Chinese women who dropped out of the labor force reported their reason as "taking care of families," but only 2 percent of unemployed men reported the same reason.[8] According to the data from three national surveys of women's social status in China, the gender disparity in income in the labor market has been expanding from 1990 to 2010. The authors further indicate that the average income of urban women, as a percentage of that of men, dropped from 77.5 percent in 1990 to 67.3 percent in 2010. The increase in income disparity in rural areas has been even greater than that in urban areas. The average income of rural working women was 79 percent of that of men in 1990. This number plummeted to 56 percent in 2010.[9] Gender disparity in unpaid care work is also severe. Data from the National Bureau of Statistics time-use survey shows: the traditional gender stereotype of "men working outside and women staying at home" still affects modern family life. Women spend almost triple the amount of time men spend on unpaid work every week. This phenomenon is more prominent in rural areas: "it is clear that women—especially rural women—perform most of the unpaid work."[10] In addition, unpaid care work clearly affects women's individual rights, capabilities, and autonomy. These authors emphasize that women used to "hold up half of the sky" in the planned economic era but they are now the most unpopular and discriminated against in the market economy. "Changes in economic and public policies in the past three decades of the market-oriented reform have accelerated the marginalization of women in the labor market and exacerbated gender inequality."[11]

The rehabilitation of Confucian tradition raised new challenges for Chinese feminist thinkers. Can a Confucian ideal of reciprocity help women realize their equality? What is the hope for Chinese women seeking a social ideal of equality given the growing gender gap in the current economic development of China? I believe that Confucianism cannot help unless it is integrated with feminism. An urgent need of a comparative study between their notions of self and reciprocity demands this research. In this book I will examine three argumentative clusters of debates and explore how the concept of self affects women's equality through a comparative study between the Confucian and feminist notions of relational self, reciprocity, and relevant issues regarding the social idea of equality in a caring democracy.

I will reveal and examine the links between political and ethical consider-ations of sex/gender equality. Specifically, I will explore whether traditional Confucianism has the resources to argue for sex/gender equality in its univer-sal *ren* or *care*. I will do so by placing the Confucian tradition in dialogue with contemporary work on the ethics of care. Many scholars argue that the golden rule of reciprocity at the heart of Confucianism does not ground any views of gender inequality and oppression of women, but there is a lack of analysis of why its practical implementation could not be achieved in Confu-cian society. That is, if Confucianism does not support gender inequality, why have existing Confucian societies practiced such inequality? How might we reclaim equalitarian aspects of Confucianism? I propose that we place recent work on feminist critical care ethics in dialogue with early Confucian *ren*.

First, postmodern critiques of "essentialism" remind us of the danger of generalization about men and women: exclusion of the powerless, the op-pressed, and the disabled. The idea of the situated self should be brought into consideration of partner relationships between men and women. As long as we know who gained priority and who remained disadvantaged, Chinese women can raise their consciousness through visiting the debate of meanings of democracy, caring responsibility, power imbalance of people's relations, and so on. I try to reveal why gendered stratifications perpetuated so deeply in today's China through the influences of Confucian culture tradition based on a cosmological vision of *ren* with *dao* and ontological oneness as a whole that is the unity of heaven, earth, and humanism. I also attempt to argue that we might reclaim Confucian egalitarian aspects to develop its openness for gender equity with integration of feminist critical care ethics. I will bring up a debate about people's livelihood as *Minben* and autonomy in democracy: Qi Liang makes a distinction between *Minben* (people oriented) and *Minzhu* (democracy); he argues in three points that the thought of *Minben* fails to build a democratic politics in China (Qi Liang 1995, 1998), but Zhang sees *Minben* as a prerequisite so that to deny it does not make *Minzhu* a complete theory. How should we interpret alternative meanings of democracy associat-ed with Confucian *ren* and ethics of care? Joan C. Tronto's *Caring Democra-cy* (2013) provides provocative thoughts with her argument of "care with" for such issues. Before we move to a comparison from the Confucian original tradition of *ren* to recent critical ethics of care in today's market globaliza-tion, we have to consider what we had in a democratic practice during Chi-na's May Fourth Movement in 1919, and why Mao's democratic centralism dominated in China for three decades (1946–1976). I will expand these con-siderations in the first two chapters.

Second, the issue of sex equality has become more complicated in the contemporary world. A phenomenon known as the feminization of poverty is evident in China as Chinese women were encouraged to go back home and perform the role of domestic caregiver under the influence of Confucianism. The cultural representations of femininity definitely affect women's lower political authority and economic ability to compete in job markets. These culture, politics, and economy combine together to impact women's roles and strengthen the traditional view of women as inferior to men. I argue that gender role ethics cannot be separated from concerns of political authority and that feminist inspiration encourages women to be aware of inequality among diverse groups of people. To know how feminist theorists have been examining gender role stereotypes and continue to focus on analyzing implicit injustice in gender division of labor in recent endeavors will be a necessary step in making a close comparison of Confucian gender role theory and ethics of order through a dialogue with feminist critical ethics of care. I will present and interpret feminist perspectives on issues of gender difference and equality, and how the ethics of care emerged and have developed toward a democratic care as an inclusive approach in chapter 3.

The next question is about the links between political and ethical considerations on sex/gender equality. The defenders of Confucianism interpreted the concept of self as universal among men and women, and reciprocity is a feature of the self. But there is a precondition necessary to actualize the selfhood: the political authority, or, using feminist words, "the personal is political." Without political power, women cannot establish the authority to speak up for their own needs and interests. The underrepresentation of women in top decision-making roles illustrates the scale required to achieve sexual equality. Political authorities tend to silence women's voices if they are in conflict with social norms and the authorities' goals of keeping social stability. I argue that the golden rule at the heart of Confucianism has a wonderful expression of partnership between men and women, but practical implementation could not be achieved because it excludes women's voices. In chapter 4, I compare three meanings of notions of reciprocity: they are Confucius' golden rule, Kant's categorical imperative, and de Beauvoir's reciprocal claim, and trace their implications and influences in Chinese women's status and inferiority. In order to have different voices out in a gendered stratification society, we must appeal to both rights-based gender justice approach and caring relational-based care ethics.

This combined methodology has been a highlight in reading feminist critical ethics of care. In chapter 5 I will examine these methodological issues and the combined approach raised by Virginia Held in her 2006 book, *The Ethics of Care: Personal, Political, and Global*. Virginia Held offers a balancing approach to "fairer caring" and "caring justice," meshing them together as inseparable but emphasizing caring relations as a wider framework into which justice should be fitted. Thus, care should be the priority in a more comprehensive moral theory while the concerns of justice must not be overlooked. I will interpret Held's thoughts and arguments of how justice and care integrated for each other, and why the ethics of care will work out a better way regarding many ethical issues. I will compare feminist care ethics with Confucian golden rule of reciprocity, evaluate the difference and strength of each, and how they may learn from one another.

For a methodological comparison, when we evaluate Confucian *ren/care* ethics, we should recognize the distinctions between *Minben* and *Minzhu*, but I argue that a combined approach of both might provide insights against paternalism and hierarchy, which is necessary to analyze the complexity of gendered stratification in today's China, toward a social ideal of equality for all who are in need of care and who should also share equal responsibility to join care. At the end of this chapter, I will critically evaluate Held's *caring justice/justice care* and Tronto's *caring democracy*, the two meeting in a conjunction of Confucian vision of *ren* and notion of nested caring reciprocity.

Next, chapter 6 continues on meta-ethical issues about human nature, the will of heaven, and how people should identify themselves with heaven's will in Confucian deep belief: the belief of profound, loving fibers under the sky and above the earth, living in a great harmonious country with peace and serenity—without gender discrimination. The mysterious Chinese respect for nature, represented in the relationship between heaven and earth, could be comprehensively understood as a guide to living well if we learn to govern ourselves with a *ren*/goodness that originates in heaven but can be brought into identification with a person's natural body/mind. Mengzi's theory of extensive virtue in four sprouts will be examined in comparison with Hume and feminist theorizing. We will see that today's feminist ethics can learn from the ancient discussion of how caring relations may expand from the personal realm into communities and the world.

Chapter 7 is about how to look up the idealist concept of selfhood in Confucianism while overcoming the exclusion of women in issues of aging and gender. Confucianism summarizes the importance of human virtues into the *ren* (benevolence or goodness): the *ren* being the most important and supreme virtue to follow at all times. If *ren* calls for the liberation and equality of women, then *ren* is still being followed. *Ren* and *shu* (sympathetic understanding or reciprocity) should not be mutually exclusive but harmoniously collaborative. "What makes our world valuable to us is, above all, love that is gladly embraced."[12] *Ren* represents a valuable love that would not allow women to be subordinated. I will examine China's retirement policy for women as effective care practice to reach integration of Confucian *ren, yi, li, zhi, xin,* and feminist *caring justice* as *sharing care/responsibilities* for all.

This book includes seven chapters in three parts. Part I, Ontological Oneness, examines strengths and weaknesses of early Confucian ethics on women, and a debate of *Minben* and *Minzhu*. Part II, Methodological Dimensions, explores feminist critiques of ethics of gender difference and equality in the development of care ethics. It also reexamines Confucian golden rule or reciprocity in methodological dimensions compared with feminist integration of the justice/care dichotomy and caring democracy for inclusive methodology. Part III, Meta-Ethical Matters, investigates meta-ethical issues in *ren/ care* ethics: the extension of virtues in Mengzi in comparison to Hume and feminism, and the integration of the idealist concept of selfhood and nonideal social contexts in feminism and Confucianism.

The design of this research concludes three strategies: a solid reading and interpretation of the original Confucian ethics of *ren* regarding notions of self and reciprocity; an interpretation of feminist notions of selfhood and challenges to various traditional notions of self, in particular, an examination of how the feminist notions of reciprocity fit into the Confucian concept of reciprocity; and an analysis of the impacts of Confucian and feminist concepts of selfhood and reciprocity on women's roles and clarification of the contributions of each for women's equality in care practice. All these areas demand a deep interdisciplinary understanding of the central concepts through the original languages, Chinese and English. I understand that a philosophical work on women's equality through notions of selfhood and reciprocity is not only an investigation of women's experiences but also a broader vision of the interconnected political, economic, and cultural analysis. Profoundly, I feel the difficulties of such a complex comparative study between these two traditions in scholarship. All my current and previous work of more than a decade has provided me a solid base for a continual investigation of selfhood, reciprocity, gender justice/care, power, and democracy in China, the United States, and other parts of the world.

Hopefully, this book will be a unique contribution to understanding the importance of cultural contexts in seeking gender equality in a caring democracy. I argue that we need to integrate feminist theories of global justice/care with traditional Confucianism, since both traditions emphasize caring relationships in humanity and interdependency between social individuals within and beyond their communities in a global scale. Importantly, it will enlarge our philosophical visions of how cultural traditions can be undeniable sources for strengthening contemporary social ideas of humanity, democracy, equality, and freedom for all.

NOTES

1. Yan Hao, *China's Growing Middle Class in an Increasingly Stratified Society*, EAL Background Brief No. 307 (Singapore: East Asian Institute, National University of Singapore, 2006).

2. Bohong Liu, "Seeking Development Alternatives in Meeting Challenges of Global Economic Crisis," apww.isiswomen.org/index.php?option=com...view (2010).

3. Hairong Yan, *New Masters, New Servants: Migration, Development, and Women Workers in China* (Durham, NC: Duke University Press, 2008), 112.

4. Tamara Jacka, *Rural Women in Urban China* (Armonk, NY: M.E. Sharpe, 2006), 5.

5. Leta Hong Fincher, *Leftover Women: The Resurgence of Gender Inequality in China* (London: Zed Books, 2014), 36.

6. Fincher, *Leftover Women*, 36.

7. Bohong Liu, Ling Li, and Chunyu Yang, "Gender Equality in China's Economic Transformation" (Beijing, China: United Nations System in China, 2014).

8. Liu et al., "Gender Equality," 13–14.

9. Liu et al., "Gender Equality," 20.

10. Liu et al., "Gender Equality," 26.

11. Liu et al., "Gender Equality," 28.

12. Richard W. Miller, *Globalizing Justice: The Ethics of Poverty and Power* (New York: Oxford University Press 2010), 260.

I

Ontological Oneness

Chapter One

Strength and Weakness of Early Confucian Ethics on Women

What is the most critical issue of applied ethics in today's nation-crossing world? Most likely, safety/security is not on the list of serious theoretical concerns. Surprisingly, many ethical theories and schools of moral reasoning do not pay sufficient attention to such basic issues; instead, they would rather focus on more abstract, theoretical, principle-oriented questions, such as how can we categorically and consistently entail that lying is always wrong no matter what, or how can the notion of impartiality be worked out through a maximizing principle of utility to benefit all individuals who have unalienable rights to seek their own interests, and so on. As Ruth Groenhout (2014) describes it, philosophical explorations of moral/ethical theorizing in ethical education remain mainly in the three categories of consequentialist, deontological, and virtue theories. This triadic structure covers the intellectual territory, while other approaches are marginalized as not fitting or not fitting well into this "Standard Taxonomy" (ST). [1] Fiona Robinson (2011) further argues that a feminist approach to human security in care ethics can play a crucial role in changing the world for the better. [2] Joan C. Tronto also made a comprehensive exploration of two decades on a theory of democratic care that distinctively improves visions of caring as the highest moral value toward a decent, safe, and collaborate society. [3] Confucian ethics started such significant inquiries of human existence, interacting with nature, heaven, earth, and all humans more than three thousand years ago. Among a variety of schools, Confucianism, beginning with its first master, Confucius (Kongzi), advocates that all living things within the world are subject to heaven's will toward oneness. A holistic *ren* humanity thus guides all levels of thinking for human livelihood—from surviving to thriving in openness—through constructive processes toward an idealist perfection of truth, goodness, and beauty. This chapter observes that Confucian *ren* tried to play a magnificent role in bringing peace and compassionate care back to the turbulent society during the Warring States period of China, and *ren* governance kept growing until the beginning of the twentieth century. *Ren* features openness nurtured by the way of heaven, and is compatible with contemporary feminist care ethics, but is different from issues on the feminist political agenda, such as antisocial hierarchy, gender role stereotypes, and strife for women's equality.

HUMAN SECURITY AS A
PRIMARY CONCERN OF ETHICS

When we rethink human security, security is usually understood in military terms in the field of international relations, which is not what care ethics is; "security" is also applied to health and food, and the survival and sustainable development of a community's livelihood, and so on. "Thus, the 'national' and 'human/social' understanding of security express starkly contrasting conceptions of global relations, interfaces between state and civil society, and the role of the state."[4] As we will see, a feminist care ethics has special visions on security, and its perspective is inherently critical "insofar as it reveals relations of power that are normally hidden from view and provides a method of analyzing the ways that these relations are connected to people's security."[5] Confucian ethics also provides valuable visions on human security since it starts its notion of *ren/care* or benevolence by denying the idea of military ruling or of governing a country with force, instead affirming the original idea of ruling the country with a culture of love and learning to be moral as in the earlier Zhou dynasty three thousand years ago.

Contemporary care ethics and traditional Confucian ethics have commonalities in terms of important aspects in understanding human relationships such as empathy, sympathy, enjoyment of responding to other's needs, reciprocity of social psychology, virtuous conduct, and so on. With all these sharing ideas and concepts, they distinguish one from another in their uniqueness of different aims and approaches of social and political theorizing. The care ethics focus more on women's experiences relating to their everyday life such as nursing the young and old, domestic responsibilities, and conflicts of double shifts in the workplace and household. Feminist theorists of care ethics have realized through analyzing women's experiences that unbalanced power in people's relationships kept pushing back women's pursuit for gender equality due to the devaluation of care as a moral concept compared to justice accepted as the most valuable concept in moral theorizing. Hence, Virginia Held argues in her book *The Ethics of Care* (2006) that care as a moral value should be prioritized as a companion to justice; the two should go together dynamically and become a matter of priority to each other in different situations or contexts.[6] Fiona Robinson (2011) also argues how to hold the value of security as the core of care ethics. Stephanie Collins reconfirms that feminist care ethics is about the integration of care and justice (2015). Both care ethics and Confucian ethics would not fit in the ST, but the two ethics have emerged in recent decades and incited intense issues about whether they belong to virtue theories or variants of virtue ethics so they can be included in one of the ST categories. This big question has provoked scholarly research interest and engagement in Confucian ethics studies (e.g., Ames 2011; Angle and Slote 2013; Shun and Wong 2004; Van Norden 2007; Yu 2007) and in care ethics studies (e.g., Collins 2015; Groenhout 2014; Held 2006; Tronto 2013). Since the big question has left out the important uniqueness in both care ethics and Confucian ethics that is far beyond a field of personal virtue ethics, I simply prefer not to be involved in those details of debates in each position. In this chapter, I try to clarify questions related to, but different from, the ones usually entangled with complexities belonging to virtue theoretical details. Here I am asking whether Confucian ethics, especially in Kongzi, Mengzi, Laozi, Zhuangzi, Xunzi, and Hanfeizi (before Qin, prior to 221 BCE), expressed biases and sexist assumptions regarding sex/gender inequality. Then I ask whether early Confucian ethics can develop potential themes to overcome its bias and sexism, so that it is available to join a critical analysis of nonidealist gender reality that contributes to a model of social equality in an idealist sense. Three notions are examined: "天人合一: Tian ren he yi" (Identity of Heaven and Humanity), "阴阳互补: Yin-yang hubu" (Yin and Yang complementarity), and "内圣外王: Neisheng Waiwang" (Inward Sageness, Outward Kingship). These notions are associated with sexual morality, and they went through transitions of meaning beginning with original texts of *Zhouyi* and *LiJi* (*The Records of Rites*) in Eastern Zhou, passing through the Spring and Autumn Period, the Warring States Period, and into the Qin and Han dynasties.

INTERPRETING THREE NOTIONS OF
CONFUCIAN ONTOLOGY OF ONENESS

The above three notions of heaven, earth, and humanity as oneness in identity, yin-yang complementary, as well as sageness of rulers in governance are the foundations of Confucian ethics that can be traced back to the beginning of Chinese civilization. According to Li Zehou, Chinese civilization five thousand years ago originated with two main characteristics: one is tribe systems based on family clans' blood links; another is Shamanism rationalization that would be a very important source for understanding the history of Chinese thoughts and philosophy in social and political constructions.[7] Briefly speaking, a Shaman was believed to be an ancient mathematician. Shaman masters could draw maps for river channels associated with irrigation plans as well as predict natural phenomenon such as thunderstorms, wild fires, storm winds, and so on by making eight trigrams and using their magical skills (see *Zhouyi*). We may ask how the Shamanist culture immerged with the history in a form of rationalization and became a key to exploring early Confucianism and its development toward a state ideology.

During the Shamanist rationalization, ruling kings and Shamans played a governing role in demonstrating subjective powers available through the practical use of mathematics. But how could such powers, which apparently derived from heaven's will and divine revelation, come to be combined perfectly with human activities? Here, humans must perceive divine orientation in heaven's will and bring human activity into an identical relation with them. This is the work of the Shaman in early dynasties, as historical and anthropological records show.[8] Shamanism is also expressed in terms of Shamanistic Rituals and Rites during sacrifices to the divine, which show tremendous reverence and faith in heaven's kindness and mercy. But heaven's mandate must be realized through human identity with it and accomplished through human endeavor, which is why there is a Chinese saying, "谋事在人，成事在天" (humans can plot events but heaven decides their results)—a dialectical idea that expresses a power relation in the achievement of identity between heaven and humanity. Li Zehou interprets the original Confucian *ru* (儒) as "reverence," which is not a religious doctrine as would be found in Western Christianity but a psychological feeling of coexisting with the divine. That is to say, the magic force of Shamanism is gradually turning into moral magic. This is the sense in which the *de*, or virtue, as an inward, inherent character, becomes the first demand of a political ruler. In short, this inward magical force, virtue, becomes a requirement of all sons of heaven, who must work hard to possess this inherent virtuous character and manifest it in all of their conduct.[9]

These demands of being virtuous restrict rulers to keeping self-sacrifice and self-control during important events of sacrifice and ceremonies, and so on. The force of *de* also transformed into outward *li*, while keeping a magical force in the ruler's governing, using their self-affirmation. A Chinese historian Moruo Guo explains that *li* was transformed from records that express objective aspects of *de*. All proper styles of behavior of people possessing *de* were selected as *li* for generations to follow, clearly concentrated on one word, "reverence."[10] Although *li* originated from Shaman rationalization, it went through a long history to include all details about human propriety and behaviors in everyday life comprehensively.

LiJi prescribes all secular events in social, political, and ethical areas into arrangements of hierarchy in accord with Shamanist ritual decorum: the rigid distinctions represented in the forms, postures, countenances, garments, and so on as very concrete rules of norms, called *li shu* (ritual mathematics), meaning varieties of orders, procedures, conducts, and regulations. All of them seemed too complicated to remember such as "Jing rites in three-hundreds and Qu rites in three-thousands."[11] These ritual rules restricted a person's life, both private and public, from the royal court down to local offices and hierarchical orders, including all social relations, such as ruler and ruled, husband and wife, parents and children, brothers, and equals. All relations covered with *de*; virtuous governing became *li* governing too; since *li* connected with Shaman rationalization, *li* itself became rationalized as well and connected to the heaven's way and *dao*.

In Zehou's Li interpretation, Shamanist rationalization, on the one hand, went through three aspects to its completion: they are Shaman connecting with history, *de* connecting with *li*, and Shaman identity connecting with the divine holiness. On the other hand, moral oneness as the root of Chinese civilization is always being followed, and follow-up ethical assumptions emerged as the three notions of the identity of heaven and humanity, yin-yang complementary, and inward-sageness with outward-kingship. Sage kings such as Yu and Rao, who knew heaven's will in helping people control water for irrigation, performed "kingship" as "the identity of heaven and humanity." Similarly, Shaman masters could predict nature's phenomena to help people overcome natural disasters. Therefore, Shaman masters and sage kings became identical. Sageness was an expansion and enlargement of Shamanism; sageness became "the idealist model for later Confucian schools to worship and respect."[12]

The sageness in Kongzi's *Analects* highlights his idea of self-cultivation, emphasizing the king's internal perfection of *ren* governing, love of learning, six arts to squarely strengthen stability, and prosperity of the king-land. In Mengzi, a strong defender of Kongzi, we see not just a faithful continuation of Kongzi' thoughts of *ren, yi, li, zhi,* and *xin* and self-cultivation of internalizing the king's sageness, but also a development of expanding the sageness inside out to reach the public performance of *ren* governing. Both Kongzi and Mengzi advocate personal psychological entailment of empathy and reciprocity in relational-self considerations to reach out in social connections; Mengzi, in particular, focuses on advising rulers to be extending their internal *ren* to reach out for people's needs to be met. Therefore, You-lan Feng, the world's best-known expert of Chinese philosophy, comments that "Kongzi as a master of cultivating characters through six arts. . . . Mengzi, on the other hand, carrying out Kongzi's personal perfection of virtue to rulers' governing behaviors."[13] Furthermore, Xianglong Zhang argues that the Confucian way of heaven is distinct from the original found in the culture of the Zhou dynasty and different from Western conceptual metaphysical principles. Rather, it can only be understood as a possibility of knowing capacity, that is, one enters into a contextual envisioning at the proper time, sustaining that ultimate capacity up to a point of illumination, which is "a kind of 'categorical intuition' for event advancing."[14] According to Zhang, "the way under heaven" in principle refers to six arts of learning to be moral through self-cultivation. Such thoughts in politics are fundamentally open and inclusive and should not lead to any fixed forms of government. In Zhang's summary, to Kongzi, *ren* is not just a moral character but is far more beyond that: *Ren* would be a fundamental moral ontology/methodology or sincere attitude to treat the ultimate reality. Therefore, "Achieve the way of *ren* is understanding heaven; practice way of *ren* is matching the way of heaven."[15]

YIN-YANG AND GENDERED RELATION

Among three notions in the above, the *yin-yang* doctrine is the key to understanding Confucian views of gender stratification. Several classic readings of *Zhouyi* or *Yijing, LiJi*, and passages in *Analects*, *Mengzi*, and *Xunzi* must be sources of early Confucian views of gender, starting with female relating to male but gradually formulating a mainstream Confucian ethics of women's supreme virtue theory, defined in early Han, Dong, and Zhongshu's cosmology, systematically describing the relationship of both hierarchy and interdependence between *yang* and *yin* and husband and wife; the *yang* or husband is the norm and the lead for the *yin* or wife to follow: "What is constant about the heavens and the earth is that there is a *yin* and then a *yang*. *Yang* is the heavens' virtue and *yin* is the heavens' punishment."[16] Dong's *yin-yang* doctrine set a significant tone toward a hierarchy and unequal treatment of men and women for generations to follow and reinforced his ideas in various stereotyped discriminations against female/women in their systematic applications in society.

Zhouyi or *Yijing* (the Classic of Change) is generally regarded as the first and most important text philosophically and is cherished in both Confucian and Daoist traditions. *Yijing* is a collection of the wisdom of generations of sages; originally, it was a manual of divination devised by Fu Xi and King Wen, combining eight trigrams into sixty-four six-lined figures known as hexagrams. Its main aim is to clarify the *dao* of tian (the heaven, the sky, nature) and *di* (earth) including the *dao* of sage in its practical applications.[17]

Eight trigrams represent almost all powers in nature, the heaven, earth, fire, water, mountains, wind, thunder, and lake. The sixty-four hexagrams elaborate on these eight images as they occur in various combinations with one another. "The commentaries (Yizhuan), transmitted along with the text (Yijing), became the basis for the development of the cosmological and metaphysical speculation emergent in the early Han dynasty."[18] Given this explanation, we can see the original *Yijing* produced in the Zhou dynasty was about seven hundred years before the Han era; but the *Yizhuan* were written some six hundred years after the *Yijing*, and the differences between the two could play a significant role in Confucian views of gender.

Reading *Yijing*: "The movement of *qian* [*yang*] create the male, and the movement of *kun* [*yin*] complete the female."[19] "The correlation of one *yin* and one *yang* is *dao*."[20] "*Qian* is productive because when it is still, *qian* is pure and focused, and when in motion, it is straight without limitation. *Kun* is procreative because when it is quiet, *kun* is closed, and when in motion, it is open into a vast field."[21] The correlation of the functions of both *qian* and *kun* explains the correlation with *tian* and *di*, their change, and continuity with four seasons—so the significance of *yin* (female) and *yang* (male) with the sun and the moon and beauty and goodness. These comprehensive principles offer an easy and simple way for people to recognize and follow the highest excellence (*de*). In the *Yijing*, we have expression of unique contributions in Chinese philosophy: the correlation of yin-yang as complementary, the oneness of ontology in a triadic identity of heaven, earth, and human *dao*, harmoniously ordered under the governess of *de*, nurturing and embracing needs of all people and living things under the sky.

Yufu Li (2015) raised a similar point in an article "Research on Female Ethics of Zhouyi" (originally in Chinese); here is the author's English introduction: "Zhouyi includes Yi Jing and Yi Zhuan, which with different values of female ethics . . . Yi Zhuan tends to the social ethics that women are inferior to men and it finds out the foundation of the women social ethics from the heaven-human relationship by ontology as well."[22] Li urges us that "We should make a distinction between Yi Jing and Yi Zhuan in order to accurately grasp the female ethic view."[23]

Yizhuan obviously expressed early Han perspectives on the original *Yijing*. It became a more assertive assumption of all female-essential character of submissiveness, from natural softness, receptiveness, and openness transmitted to female's humility and should follow the male's lead and needs as a servant figure. I argue that the highlights of a female's submission at all times and places in contrast to male's leading roles such as creativity and dominion are not given in *Yijing*, which originally describes the observance of the nature, notably emphasizing the interdependence of *yin* and *yang* and complementarity between them when following the *dao* and governed by *de*. Rather the *Yizhuan* made those naturally observed correlations in nature, as described in *Yijing*, into a social, political power of differences between female and male an order of leading and following—a hierarchy of high and low. Sex and gender differences, as emphasized, consolidated, and updated in the Confucian *LiJi*, were presented as original meanings of the *Zhouyi*. The completion of *LiJi* was also the early Han's version but clearly a representation of early Confucian version of images of women, which was far from that of the *daoist* version of female virtue and social and political status for women.

In *Daodejing*, Laozi uses the image of mother representing *dao*, which is nameless, boundless, and unchanging in all changing things of the universe. The mystic *dao* shares similarity as the mystic female being the root of heaven and earth (Book 6). Understanding the correlation of *yin* and *yang*, Laozi suggests the superior power in *yin* in general and the female in particular.[24] Women, as female, are portrayed as the *yin*—the soft, gentle force of the universe; as images of valleys, water, and mysterious gates for the secrets of life. In Book 28 named *Know the Male but Preserve the Female*, Laozi makes a crucial point of *yin-yang* union and harmony: neither is to be understood as good or evil in itself, rather, good is the proper balance between *yin* and *yang*; evil is an excess of one of these over the other (see also Books 42 and 61). Paul Goldin makes a comment about Laozi's point in these passages, "The main point here is that the sage must recognize the value of the Female as well as that of the Male, not that the Female is inherently superior to the Male. The text stresses the Female only because it is more likely to be ignored than the Male."[25] Laozi wrote this advice for the ruler of men, using the female as an abstract reference to shed light on the complementary aspects of the universe. In my view, Goldin's comments sound mostly accurate but I think Laozi's notion of *yin-yang* beyond a meaning of complementary. The advantage and favor of *yin* or female (as one symbol of many elements of *yin*) are remarkably emphasized and Laozi has shown us no bias toward female moral values such as natural yielding and receptiveness to preserve life. To Laozi, the philosophy of yielding associated with female is the philosophy of *dao* that goes with a dialectic approach of *wuwei* and natural *simplicity*. These thinking patterns certainly led Laozi and other Daoist followers not to appreciate Confucian ethics based on *li* culture and complication of life.

LI CULTURE AND WOMEN'S SUBORDINATION

The Confucian *li* cultural philosophy overwhelmingly took place in most passages of *LiJi*: "the *LiJi* contains the earliest formulation of the Confucian code for women, what later became known as the sancong side (threefold obedience and four virtues)."[26] We read "The woman follows (cong) the man: in her youth, she follows (cong) her father and elder brother; when married, she follows (cong) her husband; when her husband is dead, she follows (cong) her son"[27] and "she was taught women's virtue (fude), women's speech (fuyan), women's appearance (furong), and women's work (fugong)."[28] A woman is expected to be a faithful and virtuous wife. She is expected to serve not only her husband but also all others in her family-in-law: "all her life she will not change (her feeling of duty to him), and hence when the husband dies she will not marry (again)."[29] There are paternalistic expectations in regulating relations of husband and wife: if a son has two concubines, one of whom is loved by his parents, while he himself loves the other, he should not dare to make this one equal to the one his parents love; "if he very much approves of his wife, and his parents do not like her, he should divorce her,"[30] and "No daughter-in-law, without being told to go to her own apartment, should venture to withdraw from that (of her parents-in-law). Whatever she is about to do, she should ask leave from them."[31] All the details of codification of women's marriage life set a tone of their submissive role and self-sacrifice for the others.

To summarize Confucian ethics of gender in terms of its strength and weakness: Confucian scholars did regulate women's daily life with moral codification during the pre-imperial era to constrain a female to a silent servant figure, limiting her space inside the home, playing domestic service to all family members wholeheartedly, being faithful to her husband, parents-in-law, and a loving mother in her care of her children, and home educating them with *li* cultivation and righteousness, and so on. All a wife and mother would be fit to do is to assist with the husband's leading role both at home and in public, maintaining ranks of hierarchy in social status; preserving harmony in domestic life and public affairs at royal court and local offices; and assisting with the cultivation of a peaceful, stable, and secure society.

Family filial piety, a son's loyalty toward his parents and ancestors, assisted by a wife's faithful service as caregiver to support the whole family at large, built up a solid base for the Confucian humanistic institution with a golden ethical rule of reciprocity. A son could become a father with privilege through a lifetime; a wife could become a mother-in-law to command her daughter-in-law; these social rule-performances could change for a sense of getting around and fitting one's name properly. The rectification of a name,[32] going along with the Golden Rule of reciprocity, established a common sense of social psychology of equilibrium. Most importantly, these social orders seemed to fit shamanist rationalization of social and political establishment of the sage-ruling culture: the culture inherited a deep belief of sage king ruling who would take care of all people's livelihood and bring about peace and prosperity for people. Taking care of people's livelihoods and security rightly represented heaven's will, and only the sage king, as a son of heaven, could rule and rule well the expansive family of state, because he alone would carry out a mission of benevolence with *ren*, *yi*, *li*, *zhi*, and *xin* (humanity, righteousness, rites or ritual, wisdom, and trust). These ideologies of comprehensive virtue were easily welcomed by farmers, landowners, craftsmen, merchants, teachers, officers, lords, and so on. Thus, the sage kings, as heads of families, provided examples for all families to follow, creating a benevolent ruling model for a feudal society, from the decline of the Eastern Zhou dynasty through the unification of mainland China in the short-lived Qin dynasty (221–207 BCE), culminating in the Han Dynasty (207 BCE–220

CE) as Confucianism rose to the status of a stable, state dominating ideology for centuries to come.

COMMENTS ON EARLY CONFUCIAN
REN ETHICS ON WOMEN

The Spring Autumn and Warring States eras (772–221 BCE) was the period of diversified perspectives and tolerant attitudes toward different schools of thoughts, and social and political theories. The main reason for keeping all differences in thoughts and ethical explorations was the openness of Confucian schools led by Kongzi, Mozi, Mengzi, Laozi, Zhuangzi, and Xunzi, through their serious debates about human nature, partial or impartial care, moral cultivation or profit driven priorities, and so on. Confucian masters did a good job of keeping these debates inside Confucian schools as a whole; furthermore, they reached out in confronting and exchanging ideas and having dialogues with different ideologies, such as Daoism and schools of logic, school of names, and so on. We may read *Zhuangzi*, the second master of Daoism, who was imaging a dialogue between Yanhui and Kongzi, making fun of these Confucian well-known figures. The powerful influence of Confucian masters, and the fact that their diverse, original, and scholarly texts could have survived over five hundred years or more, presents sufficient evidence of the openness and inclusiveness of Confucian ethics, the best possible ethical theory we could get during the declining period of the semi-slave and semi-feudal society of Eastern Zhou (770–256 BCE). Again, the strength of early Confucian ethics in general is its openness in embracing different scholarly perspectives, which made its contemporary reinvigoration in post-Mao China today possible (the anti-Kongzi political movement of the cultural revolution in the early 1970s having collapsed within only a few years). The early Confucian family-state ethics came back to embrace people's livelihood and interests and has been welcomed in people's hearts and daily lives.

On the other hand, an emphasis on the responsibility of rulers to take care of people's livelihoods does not seem to offer sufficient support for democratic ideas of individual autonomy in free speech or self-determination. Concepts of care in early Confucian ethics exposed its weakness of paternalism and its bias against female caregivers, exaggerating sex/gender differences in biology to the level of social, political, and ethical values, so that females and women as a group fell to the status of petty people, being evaluated as having less worth in a moral sense (the *Analects* 7.25; *Mengzi* 3B2). These fragments about women, with their bias against females, led to a robust view of women's threefold obedience and four virtues in the *LiJi* that demanded women's sincere service as caregivers. Self-sacrifice became a supreme virtue bound with female fate—a universal moral judgment upon a woman's whole life. This moral demand sounds not only unfair to all women but is also an injustice for a benevolent society to uphold. As Hu Shi pointed out, this looks like a biased single-sex morality that would be against Kongzi's own golden rule of reciprocity.[33] A moral person will not accept it if he or she is a sincere believer in reciprocity; this is the logical problem of Kongzi's idea of sympathetic understanding. Kongzi could reply to this charge by saying that he is talking about vertical reciprocity between parents and children: parents as a pair of partners take care of the next generation, just like their parents did for them. But this way of thinking about gender as a pair of parents ignores the gender distinction that Kongzi (in *LiJi*) had already emphasized when he distinguished between the *nei* (domestic) role of women and the *wai* (public) role of men. For a fair judgment toward gender, natural differences should not justify valuing one gender as a subject of respect and another as a subject of humility, the values prescribed to gender distinctions in the *LiJi*. Gender bias and the devaluation of females had already appeared in early Confucian discussions, but there was a transition of early Confucian views of women, gradually changing from discursive fragments to systematic regulations of women's behavior in the *LiJi*.

Consider another objection against criticisms of early Confucian ethics as "sexist": Paul Goldin claims that the early Confucian tradition conceived women as moral equals to men.[34] The evidences he tried to show are made up of two examples. One is Sun Pin's method of war in which Sun divides all fortresses into "male" and "female." The other is from Laozi's *Daodejing*, where female features, being soft as water, can adapt to any situation and conquer "hardness" by submitting, and so on. These two cases do not represent the core of Confucian ethics but pertain to its Daoist counterpart and its favorable idea of knowing the masculine but keeping the feminine (*Daodejing* 28). Nevertheless, it seems that Goldin read both early Confucian ethics and Daoist views of the feminine together, as they both cherish women's capability to adapt and give moral weight to women's submission. Goldin also argues that although women should follow their husbands, men were also allotted hierarchical social roles to fulfill, all the way up to the ruler, who in theory could not escape his obligations to heaven and the spirits.[35] Here, Goldin identifies women's and men's social roles with similar submissions within the social hierarchy, and therefore women and men had equal moral roles to fulfill. Obviously, he failed to see a gender difference between women and men within the hierarchy. According to the Confucian moral code, a woman's primary role is to serve her husband, who should be respectful as she should be humble. Without this moral distinction, there would not be any bias or sexism in early Confucian ethics. These sex biases are already embedded in *li* or ritual culture, as natural observances of heaven and earth, sun and moon, light and dark, male and female. Although Confucian masters remained open to Daoist thinking about femininity over masculinity, which emphasized the complementarity of yin-yang or harmony of opposites, neither Kongzi nor Mengzi accepted the idea of keeping femininity as an equal moral value to that of men. Their views of women did not elevate female attributes as formulated repeatedly in the *Daodejing*.

Regarding strengths of early Confucian thoughts of *ren*, *yi*, *li*, *zhi*, *xin*, and a comprehensive theory of benevolent, humanistic government, we need to see the openness, receptiveness, and inclusiveness in Mengzi's extension of personal virtues to public care of people's livelihood and prosperity. Mengzi's position is based on a relational self who, in social roles, upholds the rectification of names in order to meaningfully meet people's interdependency in life, survival, and thriving. This view may enlarge our vision for the integration of Confucian *ren* with contemporary feminist ethics of care. In chapter 6, we explore a nonsexist care ethics, comparing Mengzi, Hume, and feminism in order to extend virtue across genders, breaking up the division of labor, and reassigning equal responsibility of care to all people. Neither Kongzi nor Mengzi advocate ruling a country with military force or invading others' territories to gain benefits, and so on. Even during the turbulent Warring States period, they barely offer any efficient ways to solve problems of confronting powerful neighboring countries.

A focus of power relations became an attractive theme in Han Feizi's writing, who was a student of Xunzi and a most famous synthesizer of the Legalist school. Although he was a Confucian, Han Feizi incorporated the Taoist idea of *wuwei* into Legalist concepts of *shi*, *shu*, and *fa*. Within a position of authority (*shi*), the ruler masters governing practice (*shu*), including the promulgation of strict laws (*fa*); however, governing practice (*shu*) incorporates tactics and behaviors of nonaction (*wuwei*) for the ruler to be successful. No doubt the king of Qin adopted Han Feizi's method to build the first imperialist Qin dynasty, but it lasted less than two decades. Han Feizi created some brilliant ideas of how to deal with various obstacles confronting a ruler's authority to control a kingdom as a whole. "A truly effective government must be based on a firm grasp of the existing sociopolitical condition."[36] "[H]e did not believe that goodness by itself was sufficient to guarantee peace and prosperity."[37] While he rejected Confucian thoughts of goodness, benevolence, and care for all people, Han Feizi respected absolute power for the ruler in reigning, governing, and keeping order with strict punishment and rewards, banning all Confucian classics and schools of learning, unifying people's thoughts under the centralized authority of Qin State to conquer other states. In Han Feizi's talk of chains of authority, the top leader holds absolute authority without any bounds and is not subject to the same laws governing the people and ministers. Obviously, this could lead to issues of corruption and abuse of power, but Han Feizi did not offer deep concern about these issues, although he did not disagree with the idea that "it was better to have a good ruler in power than a bad one."[38] Most leaders, he felt, would "fall somewhere in between."[39] Considering the chaotic situation of the states involved in the Waning States period (475–222 BCE), it was very reasonable for Han Feizi to set his goal as to simply "determine which measures were the most effective way of insuring the continued survival of the state and furthering the public interests of the ruler and his people."[40] This brought to an end the one hundred schools of scholars that had flourished during the era of the Spring Autumn and Warring States periods, and ushered in a centralization of power under a single emperor or dictator. What would be the effect of Han Feizi's legalist practice upon what followed in Confucian traditions? At the beginning of the Qin reign, although all Confucian classics were burned, *li* culture was advocated by the new ruling elite, and the First Qin Emperor built stages with carved stones encouraging the chastity of women, one of them called 《会稽刻石》 (Huiji stone inscriptions), for the purpose of cultivating the local people.[41] Thus, according to Jiang, the dictatorship's institutions could be associated with *li* culture that would control women's sexuality and chastity.

Confucian ontological oneness and its cosmological envisioning of *ren*—following Zhang's argument that the way of *ren* is the way of heaven—helps us to understand why Kongzi's notion of *ren* has strong commitments to openness and inclusion for a possible gender interdependence approach to meet contemporary challenges of gender equality. Early Confucian concepts of *ren* definitely inspire feminist arguments for inclusive methodology in the concept of "care with" (Tronto 2013) and the claim that all people should share responsibilities to care for others. Since early Confucian ethics' strengths include being open and listening to different perspectives to enrich its own profound *ren/care* ethics, it is possible to integrate Confucian *ren* and recent developments in feminist care ethics. Together, feminism in alliance with Confucianism may demand elimination of sexist codes and biases against women caregivers as *ren/care* ethics call for joined efforts of all people, regardless of gender, age, race, class, sex-orientation, and so on in building a secure, stable, and democratic model toward a better global village.

NOTES

1. Ruth Groenhout, "Virtue and Feminist Ethics of Care," in *Virtues and Their Vices*, ed. Kevin Timpe and Craig A. Boyd (Oxford: Oxford University Press, 2014), 482–501, here 482.

2. Fiona Robinson, "Rethinking Human Security," in *The Ethics of Care: A Feminist Approach of Human Security* (Philadelphia: Temple University Press, 2011), 41–62.

3. Joan C. Tronto, *Caring Democracy: Markets, Equality, and Justice* (New York: New York University Press, 2013).

4. Robinson, *The Ethics of Care*, 7.

5. Robinson, *The Ethics of Care*, 8.

6. Virginia Held, *The Ethics of Care: Personal, Political, and Global* (Oxford: Oxford University Press, 2006).

7. Zehou Li (李泽厚), *Grand Viewpoints Remarks in Boulder Study Room* (波斋新说) (Hong Kong: Cosmos Books [香港天地图书有限公司]), 1999); 45.

8. Li, *Grand Viewpoints Remarks in Boulder Study Room*, 48.

9. Li, *Grand Viewpoints Remarks in Boulder Study Room*, 52.

10. Li, *Grand Viewpoints Remarks in Boulder Study Room*, 52n46.

11. Li, *Grand Viewpoints Remarks in Boulder Study Room*, 53.

12. Li, *Grand Viewpoints Remarks in Boulder Study Room*, 56.

13. You-lan Feng (冯友兰), *History of Chinese Philosophy*, (中国哲学史 上下二册), 2 vols., 16th ed. (Shanghai, China: Huadong Normal University Press [上海，中国，华东师范大学出版社], 2016), 1:74.

14. Xianglong Zhang (张祥龙), *Heidegger and Chinese Way of Heaven: Enlightenment and Communication in the Ultimate Envision* (《海德格尔思想与中国天道：终极视域的开启与交融》) (Beijing: Life, Reading, and New Knowledge Press, [北京: 生活 读书 新知 三联书店], 1996), 241–43.

15. Zhang, *Heidegger and Chinese Way of Heaven*, 248–49.

16. Robin R. Wang, ed., *Images of Women in Chinese Thought and Culture: Writings from the Pre-Qin Period through the Song Dynasty* (Indianapolis: Hackett, 2003), 68.

17. Wang, *Images of Women*, 25.

18. Wang, *Images of Women*, 26

19. Wang, *Images of Women*, 29.

20. Wang, *Images of Women*, 29.

21. Wang, *Images of Women*, 29–30.

22. Yufu Li (李育富), "Research on Female Ethics of Zhou Yi" (《周易》女性伦理析论), *Journal of Chongqing University of Sciences and Technology: Social Sciences Column* (《重庆理工大学学报：社会科学版》) (2015): 94–100.

23. Yufu Li, "Research on Female Ethics of Zhou Yi," 2015.

24. Wang, *Images of Women in Chinese Thought and* Culture, 7.

25. Paul Rakita Goldin, *The Culture of Sex in Ancient China* (Honolulu: University of Hawaii Press, 2002), 71.

26. Wang, *Images of Women*, 48.

27. Wang, *Images of Women*, 53 (Book Nine Jiao Te Xing).

28. Wang, *Images of Women*, (Book Forty-One Hun Yi), 60.

29. Wang, *Images of Women*, (Book Forty-One Hun Yi); 53.

30. Wang, *Images of Women*, 56.

31. Wang, *Images of Women*, 56–57.

32. Bojun Yang (杨伯峻), *Lunyu Yizhu* (论语译注, *Interpretations of Analects*) (Beijing: Zhonghua Shuju [中华书局, China Book Bureau], 1996), 134; 128 (*Analects* 13:3; 12:11).

33. Lijun Yuan, *Reconceiving Women's Equality in China: A Critical Examination of Models of Sex Equality* (Lanham, MD: Lexington Books, 2005), 34; Hu Shi, *Collections of Writings of Hu Shi, Series 6: On Issues of Chastity* (Hong Kong: Hong Kong Yuanliu Press, 1986), 50.

34. Goldin, *The Culture of Sex in Ancient China*, 2.

35. Goldin, *The Culture of Sex in Ancient China*, 70.

36. Philip J. Ivanhoe and Bryan W. Van Norden, *Reading in Classical Chinese Philosophy*, 2nd ed. (Indianapolis: Hackett, 2005), 312.

37. Ivanhoe and Van Norden, *Reading in Classical Chinese Philosophy*, 312.

38. Ivanhoe and Van Norden, *Reading in Classical Chinese Philosophy*, 312.

39. Ivanhoe and Van Norden, *Reading in Classical Chinese Philosophy*, 312.

40. Ivanhoe and Van Norden, *Reading in Classical Chinese Philosophy*, 312.

41. Xiaoyuan Jiang (江晓原), *Chinese People under Tensions of Sexuality* (性张力下的中国人) (Shanghai: Shanghai People's Press [上海人民出版社], 1995), 115–116 (《会稽刻石》).

Chapter Two

A Debate about *Minben* and *Minzhu*

Toward Caring Democracy

To inquire whether early Confucian *ren* is valuable for people pursuing a better society and to uphold *ren* ontology in ruling has always been a core issue in Chinese political debates. This chapter explores whether *ren* is or is not compatible with the social ideal of democracy and gender equality, thereby *ren* may support or hurt the value of democratic care. I will discuss the following issues associated with a theme of feminist caring democracy. The caring democracy cannot be easily defined and defended at the level of abstract thinking in Western philosophical domination, because the two words "care" and "democracy" have been understood and interpreted differently throughout history and in diverse cultural circumstances; but they have been adopted by both Confucian *ren* politics and feminist ethics of care based upon the ontological commitment that all human beings need care and interdependency to live as well as is possible. First, I explore whether early Confucianism can be taken as a democratic vision and be adopted in a democratic model of women's equality in their real life; this brings about issues of *Minben* (people-oriented) and *Minzhu* (democracy) in three sets of arguments. Hall and Ames, Qi and Zhang, and feminist ethicist Tronto confront one another in answering a central theme: should the Kong/Meng (Confucius/Mencius) original *ren* as the thought of being people-oriented be the prerequisite and foundation for the modern thought of democracy? Next, in consideration of Mao and post-Mao policy of women in China, how should we evaluate the strength of helping the most vulnerable women in order to support women's participation in economic development? I argue that although this policy might not have been a success in helping women's autonomy and raising their gender consciousness in the past,[1] the state should not

take a complete retreat from assisting women both politically and economically in these fast economic changes, because the robust stereotypes of gendered norms remain pervasive and deserve the state's special concerns.
Meanwhile the state should not repeat Mao's dominate slogan that women
can hold up half the sky, but rather should adopt an approach of intersectionality, demanding multiple ways of sharing responsibilities of both caring
domestically and publicly, which will promote gender equality as demanded.
Third, I continue to examine Tronto's vision of caring democracy that defends a key notion of "care with" based upon the fundamental idea of relational ontology and genuine humanity of people's interdependency to develop a political theory of democratic care to include all voices to be heard.
Such caring democracy truly admits that each of us, as a needy person, has a
right to receive care when needy, and to share equal responsibility of care
assignment for others presupposed by authentic *Minben*. I will respond to a
challenge about Tronto's arguments for her defense.

A NEED OF DEMOCRATIC SOCIAL SYSTEM

In the literature of Confucianism, many contributions are devoted to an idealist social and ethical annotation of Chinese tradition. For Kongzi, to realize a
harmonious and idealist society requires all individuals to overcome self and
perform the perfect roles in family, community, and the state by integrating a
small self into the big self as a whole of cosmological harmony. Such harmonious order depends on a hierarchy, different and unequal orders of the ruler
and the ruled, predetermined destinies, paternalistic decision making, and
various views of filial piety, which would support and justify the will of
heaven as a harmonious society with *Three Kangs* and *Five Norms*.[2] Family
security and social solidarity is the core in the consideration to realize the
Confucian ideal society. Thus, the enforcement of women's morality and
encouragement of women's self-sacrifice are the primary work in *LiJi* of
Confucian ethics. Neo-Confucianism did a perfect job of focusing on the
differences between the sexes and the supremacy of men over women, which
led to most Chinese families' belief that women should live on the virtue of
threefold obedience and three Gang (principles and rules of conduct) that
strictly regulated women's dependency on men. Although all individuals
including a king or an emperor should make sacrifice for the will of heaven,
women's self-sacrifice would be the highest, for women's position is the
lowest. Confucian *LiJi* (*The Records of Rites*), focuses on various regulations
of women's ritual activities. It was honored as the encyclopedia on women's
subjugation and it implies the meanings of a civilized woman in the Confucian world. Its pervasive influence on the Chinese is not only the concrete
actions of women's respecting men but also the internalization of sex in-

equality in both men and women, which encourages a tolerant attitude to the social abuse of women. This tolerance did not go away under the policy of women's equality from the top down in Mao and post-Mao times. The tolerance accompanying a popular expectation of family and social solidarity built conditions for the revival of the Confucian ideas of women in the post-Mao period. Besides all these impacts on women from Confucian resources, can Confucianism be any help in a democratic model of women's equality?

In *The Democracy of the Dead* (1999), Hall and Ames defend Confucianism as a democratic theory, because they think it is compatible with American Deweyan pragmatism.[3] They found common features in Confucianism and pragmatism, and shared thoughts between two perspectives. They claim that each of them holds a democratic vision.[4] Hall and Ames spell out six commonalities between pragmatism and Confucianism and I will focus on the last one, a democratic vision, because it is a provocative challenge to Huntington's allegation that "Confucian democracy is clearly a contradiction in terms."[5]

Hall and Ames point out two principle misunderstandings in Hustington's opinion. First, according to them, he fails to recognize that the Confucian idea of "authority" entails indispensable moral and aesthetic content. Confucianism is concerned with the self-cultivation of individuals, especially that of rulers and ministers. In the doctrine of "the proper use of names," a ruler must act as a ruler (being an exemplary person, a model of *ren*). If he does not, a ruler is not deserving of the name. This sounds like an idealist moral demand on a ruler rather than a solid law to implement. There were many bad rulers and despotic government in China, as the defenders noted. Nonetheless, they still believe that China discovered secrets of the immoral empire and such continuity could hardly be sustained by a succession of despots.[6]

Hall and Ames are correct in emphasizing upon the doctrine of names and a ruler being a moral leader, which is compatible with the idealist notion of "内圣外王: Neisheng Waiwang" (Inward Sageness outward Kingship). However, the Confucian expectation of a ruler of *ren* does not entail that a ruler actually is a king of sage and a king without abusing his authority. In response to this issue, I will discuss the distinction between *Minzhu* and *Minben* raised by a Chinese writer, Qi Liang, in *Critique of New Confucianism*[7] later.

The second misunderstanding, according to Hall and Ames, is the belief that somehow hierarchy is irreconcilable with democracy, because it identifies democracy with individualism and the mathematical notion of equality follows individualism. Hall and Ames express their appreciation of democracy in America in an earlier time, which includes important inequalities with respect to knowledge, virtue, and the burdens of responsibility, while it still holds the recognition of equality under the law.[8]

Here we can see two levels of recognition: abstract equality in principle and inequalities in the concrete situations of different people. Hall and Ames criticize how equality in individualistic terms is a quantitative notion. Such a notion militates against the notion of goods held in common and does not do a good job of maintaining order. On the other side, the Confucian community likes an extended family, with resolutely hierarchical relations. Since the conception of people is the performance of distinct roles and relationships, and these roles and relations are reciprocal, the hierarchical relations need not be as rigid and inflexible as is often thought to be. They even go further to suggest that the resources within Confucian classics could be used for the promotion of overcoming gender inequality for women and minorities.

Here, the issue is whether hierarchy can be conciliatory with democracy, especially in women's situations. In response to this issue, we need a comparative examination between Hall and Ames on one side, and Chinese scholars Qi and Zhang on the other. In Hall and Ames's explanation of the Confucian model of democracy, the classical source is *The Book of Documents* (eighth century BCE): The masses ought to be cherished, not oppressed, for it is only the masses who are the root of the state, and where this root is firm, the state will be stable. Also, in Mencius: Tian (Heaven) sees and hears as the people see and hear.[9] As Hall and Ames state, in Confucian society, the priority of morality over law as the principal means that insures social harmony is increasingly emphasized. Under this model, self-cultivation is radically embedded in communal roles and relations. From the emperor down to the common people, all should take self-cultivation as their root. Since the family is the model of social organization, personal identity is realized through the cultivation of those roles and relations that locate one within the family and community. Conceptually, there is no radical difference between a person's public or private life. The society as a whole is just like a big family, "The centrality of this familial model has significant consequences for the shape of Confucian democracy,"[10] which readily contrasts with the liberal democratic tradition in the West.

Hall and Ames are right to grasp the essence of the Confucian tradition: A ruler should take people's needs as the roots and consider those roots as the ruling guide. They take this idea as the most reliable resource of Confucian democracy; but Qi Liang would not call this a thought of democracy (*Minzhu*) and he makes a distinction between *Minzhu* and *Minben*. *Minben* is a commitment of taking people as roots of ruling. He argues that these two notions are fundamentally different in the modernization of democratic government.

THE DISTINCTION BETWEEN *MINBEN* AND *MINZHU*

In *Critique of New Confucianism* (1995), Qi claims that he differs from those new Confucians who consider Confucianism as a prescription of solving problems in the progress of China's modernization.[11] He thinks that Confucianism produced and maintained a base internally for the despotic culture and politics, hence, it is not helpful in changing people in a modern society. Qi also cites the *Book of Document* to show the idea of *Minben* (民本 people-oriented): take people as roots of ruling and be a virtuous king. Qi notes that those traditional defenders take the *Minben* as the *Minzhu* (民主democracy) and confuse the essential difference between the two.

According to Qi, there was no such thing as an aristocratic political system in ancient China like there was in Athens, which was the originator of modern democracy. Although there was an aristocrat class in ancient times in China that served the rulers, it was definitely not a force to restrict the ruler's authority. In the records of Chinese history, the supreme ruler alone, not a system of votes, decided every major affair of the state in the Western Zhou dynasty.[12] The issue of election was absolutely out of the question. The supreme rulers had complete authority without any restrictions. If the ruler happened to be a despotic one rather than a benevolent one, the only way to return the will of heaven was through revolutionary riots. Look at the turbulent situations of every power transition between generations and dynasties; there was bloody fighting and brutal violence for the birth of a new supreme power. Such revolutionary change of taking over the old reign was a vicious circle and could not solve the issue of social justice at all.[13] The arguments for the failure of the thought of *Minben* are as follows.

First, Qi points out that the thought of *Minben* is actually opposing the thought of *Minzhu* (democracy), because it holds the personality ruling by *ren* rather than ruling by law. Moral consciousness of the ruler relies on his self-cultivation, but in reality, this moral demand on the rulers easily failed, and corrupted rulers and officials were often more than the benevolent and good rulers in history.[14]

Second, the thought of *Minben* does not put the ruler and the ruled on equal ground but gives the ruler an absolute, supreme power. People could never be autonomous or have independent identities at all. Their fates were not in their hands but depended on whether or not the ruler implemented a benevolent governing. This expectation of a sage king actually nurtured a slave personality, enforced a consciousness of rulers' supreme power, and consolidated the dictatorship of political system.

Third, the thought of *Minben* is not consistent with itself, because it is used as a means to reach the aim of society's solidarity and safety, and to prevent the social order from breaking. The final goal is the enforcement of the ruler's reign, not the interests of the people.[15]

Thus, Qi claims: "The thought of *Minben* is fundamentally the opposite of democracy, because it emphasizes the sage of king as the Savior and supreme authority rather than the equal rights of ordinary people. The Confucian *Minben* possibly instructed wise rulers and upright officials, but it can never produce democratic politics of modern time."[16]

In his further reflection of the thought of *Minben*, Qi explains that *Minben* does not refer to the relationship between people but the relationship between people to gods. This relationship originated from the rebellious spirit of the people against theocracy and was the first awakening of people from mythology. The change from respecting gods to respecting humans was the first step of the thought of *Minben*. The next step was the idea of ruling with virtue or *ren*; *ren* was used to regulate social cast as an attitude of the ruler toward his subjects. *Ren* together with *li* (ritual regulations) became a powerful means to govern the state. "Respecting *ren*" was always associated with "protecting people."[17]

The so-called protecting people was based on a presupposition that those people should give respectful service to the ruler with loyalty and filial piety. Thus, the essence of "protecting people" or *Minben* was not only for the interests of people but also for the absolute supremacy of the ruler.

Ren, as an idealist imagination, was welcomed by people's expectation, and the thought of *Minben* easily convinced people to accept the unequal positions between people, the hierarchy of the ruler, the ministers, the officials, ordinary people, and slaves. This kind of *Minben* had nothing in common with the thought of democracy in modern political systems. This view is far from Hall and Ames's when they make the comment that "a Confucian democracy is not only possible, but presently plausible."[18]

Qi's critique of the thought of *Minben,* in my view, is quite convincing in exposing its hypocrisy when it is associated with despotic rule. There were many cases of tyrannical rule in the history of Chinese feudal society, and the thought of ruling with *ren* failed to restrict the authority of the tyranny but suppressed any possible resistance to the superior because such resistance would violate the norm of rites and would not be allowed. Thus, it is partially true in Qi's claim that "ruling with *ren*" is essentially against democracy.[19] However, Qi lacks an analysis of one element of *Minben*: ordinary people also need to perfect their goodness in their self-cultivation of virtues. In my opinion, Qi went too far in denying any possible compatible elements between people-oriented *Minben* and modern democratic *Minzhu*; furthermore, his version of *Minzhu* was only conceived in a narrow sense concerned with individual autonomy and the practice of politics. In recent discussions, Zhang more helpfully shows that while there may be opposition between the two notions, there is also some compatibility. Although Qi does not expand his thought to the issue of women's situations under the rule of *ren*, he does mention that women's equal rights with that of men and women's participa-

tion in politics should be included in the progress of China's modernization.[20] I will add that the necessary social condition for women seeking
equality is the democratic social system with a principle of equal concern and
respect to all individuals. We should not expect a social hierarchal system
with a benevolent ruler to nurture such social condition, but the thought of
taking care of people's needs as roots of his ruling could provoke insights for
a better governance.

In their argument that hierarchy is not irreconcilable with democracy,
Hall and Ames emphasize two necessary observations regarding equality:
"Not only Confucianism, but pragmatism as well, requires hierarchical relationships of parity rather than relations of abstract equality."[21] But these
inequalities did not cancel the recognition of "equality before God and under
the law."[22] This idea should be further clarified with its counterpart of "hierarchical relationships," but there is a lack of such analysis in reading Hall and
Ames.

It is true that the notion of equality on a high abstract level cannot and
should not rule out the unequal circumstances in people's concrete situations.
On the other hand, these factual differences should not be taken as evidence
to prove some humans as superior to others and perpetuate the inferiority of a
certain group, such as women or small men in the *Analects* 17.25. Unfortunately, the thought of *Minben* in Confucian tradition, as Qi exposes, cannot
entail the recognition of abstract equality in principle (Zhang holds a different view on this). Without this recognition, people easily believe their unequal positions cannot change and women who are doing care labor should
unconditionally obey men who are breadwinners.

SOME COMMONALITY BETWEEN *MINBEN* AND *MINZHU*

According to Zhang (2016), in contrast to *Minzhu*, the traditional *Minben*
with almost three thousand years of perfection has a great advantage of being
authentic in language and political orientation, conceptual refinement, and
completion. "Although there was no democratic social system in ancient era,
there were rich thoughts resisting dictatorship or tyranny."[23] These thoughts
would be compatible with the modern Western democratic principles of people's involvement in politics. After the opium War in 1840, people-oriented
thoughts evolved into different schools under the influence of Western culture. More Chinese thinkers welcomed the Western ideas of *democracy* and
sciences, trying to achieve reformation in political systemic changes to reject
the old and weak system of feudal dynasties. As Zhang pointed out, these
thinkers expressed an effort to combine the modern *Minzhu* and the traditional *Minben* since they desired to hold a political value of equality for all and a
view of people's sovereignty. Nevertheless, the combination of the two could

have enriched anti-dictatorship thinking and helped to establish a firm grip on political reform from the perspective of people-oriented thinkers. Zhang realized that the two notions are not exactly from the same root, but neither are they that far apart. The Confucian position of *Minben* focuses on how the sage government accomplishes a mission of realization of common good for people under heaven's will, but the *Minzhu* emphasizes people's participation in ruling, to protect individuals's rights, autonomy, equality, and freedom. After clarifying the different roots in these two positions, Zhang emphasizes their commonality in serving the people's interests: on one hand, the Western democratic elections and presidency obtained legitimacy of the political idealist vision of common goodness under heaven from the Confucian people-oriented thoughts in the circle of Chinese politicians; on the other hand, the Confucian idealist vision of common goodness under heaven gained complementary strength from the Western democratic thoughts of people-involved politics—the long-standing thoughts such as "listen to people, serve the people, and take care of people's needs," and so on. As *ren* governance gained world support, the two notions of *Minben* and *Minzhu* supported people's livelihoods. Nevertheless, Zhang insisted that there must be some kind of rending and retrofit from the *Minben* to *Minzhu*. To me, it seems that the Confucian *Minben* could be a kind of prerequisite to the modern democratic thoughts as the firm foundation of Confucian *ren* governance and could inspire feminist exploration of care ethics. Nevertheless, the feminist blueprint of women's equality, in my opinion, include at least four types of challenges on their agendas while they examine all traditional theories on gender and politics: they are against dictatorship, social injustice/ inequality and hierarchy, challenging gender roles or division of labor, and paternalism. These challenges from feminist analyses appear through these chapters but I now want to turn to Tronto's analysis of caring democracy that can help in understanding a mistaken assumption of human nature as self-sufficient in seeking the true meaning of democracy.

SEARCHING FOR THE TRUE MEANING OF DEMOCRACY

Tronto redefines democracy as settling disputes about care responsibility since citizens in the United States feel the two deficits of care and democracy: care deficit refers to a shortage of care workers to meet the needs of American families in caring for the young, the elderly, the sick, and the infirm; the democratic deficit refers to the incapacities of governmental institutions to "reflect the real values and ideas of citizens."[24] In her vision, only a caring democracy, a democracy that emphasizes "caring with," can address both of these problems. Her next step is to connect the two in order to justify a synthetic approach of care ethics and political democratic theory; but connecting care with democracy must deny that care was private. She claims that "without a more public conception of care, it is impossible to maintain a democratic society."[25]

A feminist ethics of care has a different starting point: first, all humans are in relationships throughout their lifetime (not as if they were Robinson Crusoe); second, all are vulnerable and fragile, meaning that they rely on others for care and support; third, all are both recipients and givers of care—there are those who are the most needy and those who are the most capable of helping themselves and others. Being committed to the notion that all of us are both caregivers and care receivers in human relationships, the feminist care ethics is able to explain how individuals can balance autonomy and dependency in their lives. Tronto criticizes that most democratic political theories simply assume *the existence of autonomous actors* as the starting point for democracy. From this assumption, such thinkers see human dependency as a flawed condition or problem. But this assumption leaves unanswered the question of how infants go from being children to adults, from dependency to autonomy. As we recognize the extent of caring as a part of human life, "it becomes impossible to think politically about freedom, equality, and justice for all."[26] We have to redefine the elements of democratic life that make citizens equal.

Politically, first, the initial separations of life into public and private spheres remove some political questions from public consideration (they seem prepolitical); second, all relationships of care inevitably involve deep power differentials (seemingly antidemocratic, therefore excluded from public life), but a feminist democratic set of caring practices is aimed in part at reducing both these power differentials and their effects on people.[27] If caring is democratic then it must be inclusive: to include care as a public concern upsets the distinction between public and private life. The inclusion of care in public life forces a reconsideration of how to think about gender, race, class, and the treatment of "others." To be inclusive thus turns out to be more difficult than "add women and stir."[28] Care workers are disproportionately concentrated at the bottom of the economic scale, lacking basic benefits, and many of these workers are also marginalized by race and migration status; a democratic rethinking of caring practices would also require close attention to the dynamics of power in different caring settings. An important part of democratic caring concerns the breaking down of hierarchical relationships. One starting point for doing so is to undermine the logic of care as dyadic: to create opportunities to "triangulate" care also creates opportunities to break up a relentless hierarchy of power. The last point Tronto makes in defining a caring democracy is about "responsibility." In connecting care with responsibility, we can see some groups who may give themselves "passes" out of certain forms of responsibility, and Tronto proposes that we consider them as forms of *privileged irresponsibility*.[29] These forms could allow us to be better able to see how some people end up with less, and other people with far more. With her unique notions of "care with" and "responsibility assignment," Tronto provides insights of how we should reasonably challenge those long-standing traditions of social hierarchy and gender division of labor or roles.

The defenders of Confucian hierarchy use the notion of reciprocity to explain people's change in their role position. It is surely that the reciprocity relationships could happen in the relations between the ruler and the subjects and the husband and wife within power differentials. In those relationships, the hierarchy is rigid and inflexible. Nevertheless, Hall and Ames insist: "Confucianism offers important, largely unused, resources for overcoming gender inequities."[30] Evidence for this claim is two-sided: one is the lesson of liberal rights-based democracy; the Western means of becoming truly human perpetuates the old male prerogatives, as they say, "To be (fully human you must be (largely) male."[31] The other is the merit of Confucian and pragmatist equality, a qualitative notion that refers to one's self-cultivation. A self-realized person can be defined in terms of a dynamic balance of *yin* and *yang* characteristics.[32]

What does the qualitative notion of equality mean by Hall and Ames in the situation of women? It is hard to find their explicit analysis about its practice of women. According to them, the Confucian conception of the individual is dynamic, entailing complex social roles. "It is the quality of these roles that focuses one's identity, which is constitutive of one's self."[33] They go on to claim that such a conception of a person as a specific matrix of roles "will not tolerate any assertion of natural equality"[34] and "Person so understood in irrevocably hierarchical relationships that reflect fundamental differences among them."[35]

With a strong sense of fundamental differences and hierarchy in mind, how could the qualitative notion of equality work toward a sense of equality at a higher level? Hall and Ames explain as follows: First the dynamic nature of roles means that privileges and duties within one's community tend to be a lifetime, rather than a short time; second, one's duties and privileges can be balanced through changing one's roles. For example, a son's duties will be balanced by his privileges as a parent; similarly one's role as a benefactor during middle years will be paid back when one grows old. Therefore, they conclude, "A dynamic field of relationships over time produces a degree of parity in what is perceived as the most vital source of humanity—one's human relations."[36] This view resists "any assertion of natural equality," but as I understand, "equality" is not about "natural," but rather about a value from a judgment.

According to the above argument for the qualitative equality between people, all that matters is the reciprocity of relationship. It is in perceiving relationships and nothing beyond that. Does the reciprocity in this dynamic field of relationship matter in the relationship of the supreme ruler and the inferior ruled? It was presumed that the ruled must play loyal roles and give services to the ruler and that is the presupposition of being protected by the ruler. This hierarchy was rigid and inflexible enough to oppress the powerless. There were no means for those ruled to resist possible abusive power of the rulers, because the hierarchy in this harmonious order did not give the oppressed the right to break up the vertical relations even under a despotic ruling. There is no reciprocity in these two relationships since the hierarchy does not tolerate any equality between the two. The powerful superior class can always be the beneficiary in this dyadic relationship without enforcements of just laws. Hence, the defense for keeping a relation of social hierarchy does not seem to be sound.

Similar situations happened in the relations between wives and husbands: the rigid sex roles and the division of labor regulated each sex playing their roles appropriately. Most women played their roles best during their golden age. That did not mean that they would be protected when they grew old, as we see women's situations exposed by He.[37] There was no reciprocal relationship between wives and husbands in those cases. The qualitative service of young wives as benefactor did not guarantee they would be paid back when they were getting old. Why is a woman most likely the benefactor rather than a beneficiary in the devoted lifetime of caring for others? No satisfactory explanation can be found in Hall and Ames's argument about how to achieve real sexual equality in women's relevant situations, but only "fundamental differences among them."[38] We can ask in what fundamental sense should women and men be treated equally and share a qualitative equality in their lifetime. Should their gender roles assigned by social institutions matter in answering this question?

Nevertheless, feminist theorists explored sex/gender and society: As we will see in the next chapter, although female productive functions differ from that of male originally, social and cultural institutions created and changed sex/gender differences, and they are not natural. Tronto's challenge of social hierarchy and power differentials within gender relations help us further understand the hidden questions of privilege/disadvantage unasked and unanswered in Confucian ethics. In *Confucian Role Ethics: A Vocabulary* (2011), Ames does not raise these questions, as Bell points out in his review: "Most obviously, the role of 'wife' has evolved over time, and no doubt Kongzi would have been shocked by the 'modern' assumption that women can be men's moral and intellectual equals, both within the family context and in 'the community' at large . . . it is unclear how Confucian role ethics can help us answer the question."[39]

ON THE STATE POLICY OF RAISING GENDER
CONSCIOUSNESS AND EMPOWERMENT OF WOMEN

As I described in the introduction of this book, women's status regressed in the economic transformation in the post-Mao period. However, the open-door policy of the ruling party inevitably brought in a democratic air and open mind on women's issues. The international and national seminars, workshops, symposiums, hotlines, and so on, have raised deep questions such as what kind of help women need regarding issues of women's subordination. Women's self-consciousness and collective-consciousness on gender become more and more realized in meetings and in exploring women's issues. "Chinese women do need help,"[40] as Li Xiaojiang describes. The document of Protection of Women's Rights was passed and implemented by the government in 1992.

However, feminists should consider not only the state protecting women's rights, but also the negative side of its implementation. Some women scholars suggest that the state should completely retreat from intervention in the economic transition, and that women should fight for equality on their own. There emerged many strong women who managed both career and household labor successfully and became models of excellent contributors in economic development. Nevertheless, most women, especially women in poor, rural areas are not progressing in the feminization of agriculture, and women in urban areas are forced into early retirement at the age of forty-five to fifty-five. Gender gaps in jobs are rising.

Zheng's argument of women staying home[41] is popular in today's male-dominant society, and Mao's call for women's equality in production is out of fashion. Should the state take more action to protect women's interests in current economic changes? I argue for a need of state law and policy to support women's rights and interests for public jobs while avoiding the devaluation women's care work at home. The state protection should be a means to serve the goal of reaching gender equality. In order to reach this goal, the state intervention should be based on a democratic policy that includes women's voices regarding their interests and opposes Mao's dominant, centralized view of women.

THE CENTRALIZATION OF MAO'S POLICY OF WOMEN

Mao's view of women did help people to realize the significance of the power of the husband in Chinese society and immorality of men forcing women into subordinated positions. Mao's call for women's participation in production raised women's social status through their employment in public jobs, regardless of women's double burdens. From the feminist challenge of

Affirmative Action in the United States, male-biased norms are serious issues for those who set standards for qualification of employment. This challenge presents two aspects in theoretical examination of women's issues: discrimination of women and male-centered culture. To strive for women's equality, we must consider the two aspects together, which is also applicable in Chinese women's situations and recognized by Chinese women scholars.[42]

Mao's view of women focuses on the first aspect, discrimination of women in the traditional culture, but he never challenged fundamentally the male-centered norms except his view that recognizes the authority of the husband.[43] Instead, Mao moved his view and policy to women's equality in production, and he thought that only production could raise women's position. Mao created the Maoist theory that only class struggle and the success of the proletariat can bring women's final emancipation. Hence, he used his theory of continuity of class struggle and class analysis into women's issues and his dominant class approach blocked any discussion about problems in applying women's equality in production.

Why did Mao change his view of women from his original thought of seeking individual freedom during the May Fourth Movement (1919), to his late view of class theory that dominates all other issues (1966–1976)? When I examined Mao's philosophy of dialectical materialism and his political thought of democratic centralization, I realized that these two sources led him to his dominant/essentialist view of women's equality in production, which silenced other possible views of women's issues. To further trace the origin of these two sources, we need to look at the deep impact of Chinese traditional culture on Mao's thought and policy.

Mao was extremely familiar with Chinese classics of literature, history, and philosophy; he came from a peasant family and grew up in the social environment of a peasant community. He was the first leader to see the importance of the peasant issues during the National Revolutionary period after the May Fourth Movement. Mao repeatedly stressed the point that national revolution must rely on two kinds of people: peasants who consisted of more than 75 percent of China's total population and workers who were secondary in number. Mao showed his sympathy for peasants and decided to rely on them. He wrote:

> China is a semicolonial country that is economically backward. The major targets of the revolution in such a semicolonial country are the patriarchal class and feudal class (landlord class) in rural areas because they are the only solid foundation of the domestic ruling class and foreign imperialism. We cannot change the superstructure of the foundation without shaking this foundation. We must rely on peasants if we want to overthrow the landlord class.[44]

The majority of Chinese society, peasants and especially the poor peasants, was always the concern in Mao's thinking of national revolution. This accordingly consolidated what he inherited from the traditional culture: the idea of *Minben* and ruling by authority. Mao saw that many peasants' uprisings and riots happened in the corrupted dynasties and he believed that "the peasant uprisings and peasant wars constituted the real motive force of historical development in Chinese feudal society."[45] Hence, Mao used the peasants uprising as a criterion to judge who would be the heroes in the development of Chinese history, and he regarded his view as historical materialism. This view was challenged by Tang for its difference compared to Marxist view of historical materialism.[46] My concern here is the link between Mao's emphasis on peasants' issues and his belief of the idea of *Minben*.

Remember Qi Liang who makes the distinction between the idea of *Minben* and *Minzhu*. He gives three points in his argument for the failure of the thought of *Minben* to build democratic politics in China. His first point is: The *Minben* (taking people, most likely the poor peasants, as the roots of ruling) is not the *Minzhu* (advocating democratic principles of autonomy, equality, and freedom for all citizens); the former relies on the Confucian ethical canon of self-cultivation but the latter emphasizes an equal right for all individuals. The next point is the essence of the thought of *Minben*: It gives absolute power to the ruler, not the ruled; the supreme power of the benevolent ruler comes from the loyalty of the ruled and a firm belief of social hierarchy and natural difference, but democracy will challenge this belief and the so-called natural differences among people, leading to social hierarchy. The last point is different results in the two political thoughts: The *Minben* encourages better, wiser rulers to take care of people's interests and livelihoods, but provides no guarantee if the ruler happened to be a tyrant; the *Minzhu* emphasizes on the equal rights of ordinary people and improves democratic politics with people's participation. Although the so-called principle of equal concern and respect also has many problems and challenges during postmodern time, its fundamental difference from the *Minben* is the encouragement of individual autonomy, which is the most important element to establish the social ideal of sex equality.

Mao's political belief of *Minben* nurtured his political thought of democratic centralization, which was based on his dialectic method of Maoism. With this method, Mao arbitrarily explained when his party needed opinions from the masses and when the party's decision would be a centralization of those opinions. In fact, this centralization was submitted to the supreme authority of Mao himself: He became the infallible leader in Chinese democratic revolution at the end of the 1930s and 1940s as well as the socialist transformation period in 1950s and 1960s. The loyalty of Chinese people and the party consolidated Mao's absolute authority in ruling the country, until his death in 1976, the end of the Cultural Revolution. Under Mao's democratic centralization, the issues such as women's double days, how to choose a husband, and so on, were impossible to put on an agenda of women's

meetings organized by women federations. Mao's view of women's participation in production dominated through decades, and women were encouraged to make sacrifices in both public and domestic domains. Since they
could earn part of the family income in public jobs, women's voices appeared here and there but they were also burdened by double days. In reality,
women's status did improve through the participation of production, and
most importantly, social discrimination of women seemed to decrease with
the increasing number of women's participation in both the economy and
politics. According to Mao, "Enable every woman who can work to take her
place on the labor front,"[47] the top-down state policy followed effectively to
keep women's employment increasing in Mao's time.

Nevertheless, Mao's centralization policy of women's equality in production concealed complicated issues, and silenced women's voices under the
dominant view of class struggle and class analysis. To highlight, the issue of
equality must go together with the issue of democracy: without a democratic
exploration of women's issues, how can Chinese women make progress toward their equality in a post-Mao era?

INSEPARABLE RELATIONS BETWEEN
WOMEN'S EQUALITY AND DEMOCRACY

Since China opened her door to the world in the post-Mao era, Chinese
women have more opportunities and freedom to express their pursuit of
equality and development. As we see in today's market, economic changes
provided more chances to men than to women, and feminization of agriculture became recognized. Women will face more problems in the wake of
economic globalization, especially after China's entry into the World Trade
Organization (WTO) in 2001.

As three Chinese female experts on women's issues point out, although
the WTO will bring Chinese women opportunities and development, they
will face great risks and pay the price for greater reforms. They estimated
that women would have problems in employment, in health care, a decrease
in pay during maternity leave, and so on. According to their observance,
more men tend to shift to the nonagricultural trades while women became the
mainstay of farming. "With the decrease in value of farming products, wom-
en in rural areas will become poorer."[48]

How should the government and state deal with the gender imbalance in
the transition of economic development? Is that politically right for the state
to take a complete retreat from Mao's policy of women's participation in
production? Should the state continue to give women preferential treatment
such as maternity leave with full pay and other benefits in women's health
care? Should the state impose policies like Affirmative Action in the United

States to request employers to hire a certain number of women in their enterprises?

Peng Peiyun, the former president of the All-China Women Federation, comments that the economic development will not naturally bring women's development and progress at the same pace. "So necessary policies inclining to women should be adopted in order to gradually shrink the differences in development between the two sexes and to realize coordination and uniformity of economic benefit and social equality."[49] This is exactly what I agree with: the state should intervene in evaluating justice and equity of social development in current economic transformation.

Chinese women, particularly rural women in the poor areas, deserve the state's special concern on changing their status quo. New state policies inclined toward women should not just be a copy of Mao's policy but a set of multi-concerns of promoting women's position in fundamental ways. The most important concern in state policies must be a recognition of how to promote women's voices. In order for women's voices to be heard, several necessary steps can count as presuppositions of including women's voices: women's participation in government decision making, in various jobs that traditionally excluded women, and so on.

According to the survey conducted by the All-China Women Federation in 2000: Chinese Women's Status in Transformation, the gender imbalance is obvious in the last ten years compared to the first survey conducted in 1990. The number of laid-off women workers in state-owned enterprises was 18.9 percent higher than male laid-off workers. "Moreover, the income gap between women and men enlarged. Urban women's yearly income was 70.1 percent of men's, 7.4 percent lower than in 1990. Rural women's yearly income was just 59.6 percent of men's, where the gap widened too."[50] The more recent statistical data show that gender gaps keep rising (Fincher 2014; Liu, Li, and Yang 2014; Wei 2011).

Nonetheless, according to the survey, gender equality is still a growing, mainstream concern for people in China. People believed gender equality was actually an ideal for the most part in Mao's time. "Now, having experienced the shock from the social transformation and hardships of life, women do not rely anymore on preferential treatment and special care; self-strength has become their need and pursuit in life."[51]

This view seems to be an objection to the previous point of necessary state policies inclined toward women, and also an excuse for state retreat from any intervention in the economic operations and its result of women's unemployment.

My first response to the view of women's self-reliance points to a fact in the survey—a fact that must not be neglected, according to the survey— "Under the environment of a market economy, there are signs of returning of the traditional ideas on work division based on sex."[52] This traditional mode of thinking is mainly a rehabilitation of Confucianism. Its emphasis on family values and women's proper roles expect women to retreat from public participation. Hence, a viewpoint of "Working well cannot be better than marrying a good husband"[53] became popular in recent years. Women accounted for 37.3 percent among those who approved of this viewpoint. This shows, according to the survey, that some young women still place hopes of changing their fate on men and marriage and not on self-reliance.

I fully agree with the idea of women's self-strength, because it is the most important element in seeking their equality. Furthermore, we need to explore other accountable conditions to support women's self-reliance. Without attentive attitudes toward these accountable conditions, women's self-strength could be empty talk since most women are primarily caregivers or dependency workers without pay and their care labor is usually done in private settings.

Unfortunately, the current reviving of the traditional view of women does not encourage women's self-strength and independence. This social expectation and medium also influence women's "choices" to be caregivers at home and stand behind their husband's success. Besides these external reasons, women who believe in relying on a husband lack concern for developing gender consciousness outside traditional norms. These women are not aware of the social phenomena of Bao Ernai (keeping a second wife) and will easily become victims of rich men who are seeking the so-called perfect life of needing more than one wife in their golden age.

Obviously, the cultural tradition and social expectations contributed to beliefs of women's secondary position and dependence upon a husband. If the state really wants women to be strong and self-reliant, the state should create social conditions and policies for women's equality by correcting the historical discrimination against women.

Frankly speaking, Chinese government is facing a dilemma relating to women's equality. On the one hand, a pervasion of Chinese culture and tradition favors the idea of state solidarity and family stability, which requires women's sacrifice and their role of complementing men. The policy decision makers are overwhelmingly males. Most of them could not be immunized from those traditions and take the attitude of the state retreat, which neglects or even increases gender imbalance in the current market economy. On the other hand, Mao's policy of women's equality in production went through three decades and effectively changed women's images and social position in people's minds. Most people realized that individual freedom and equality would be an inevitably acceptable idea in the process of China's modernization. Women should be treated as equal to men and their equality definitely needs the state's special care because women cannot fight against an extremely obstinate patriarchy on their own. The male-centered culture would not allow or yield to women's equality; hence, the state should intervene to shrink the gender gap difference in hiring in the job-market through laws against discrimination and policies to keep gender balance.

My second response to the state retreat from Mao's policy of women's equality is for improvement of state policies inclining toward women and empowering women. Recall the state did interfere in the economic changes: the frequent residency check made migrant women's situations worse in their city.[54] The state has powers to limit people's preferences and to control the people's staying or moving to the urban areas. I suggest the state should work out more effective policies and programs such as "double learning," as in the 1980s, gender balance policy in the job market, and fundamental imposition of women's education, and so on.

While the state institutions should take care of women's special needs and interests, the state needs to recognize the distinctions between *Minben* and *Minzhu*. Any policies built on the idea of *Minben* are not sufficient enough to solve women's problems, because the state policies and caring for women's interests can only provide conditions for women seeking equality. Women also need a democratic social environment to express their issues in the practice of those policies. Only when the idea of *Minzhu* takes place in women's issues will women's equality make progress toward its full accomplishment. This accomplishment requires women's gender-consciousness, self-strength, and self-fulfillment.

My third response to the issue of state policies addresses the issue of methodology with respect to democratic initiatives that would incline women toward gender equality. Since state policies have risks of paternalistic management that would take control of women's minds (as has happened with Mao's class-based programs that silenced women's voices), a democratic method that will overcome paternalistic thinking is necessary. This means that women should be involved in policy decision making, in observance of the policy program running, and in adjusting and solving problems in the practice of gender equality. Women should be the subjects/agents of seeking women's equality, not just objects of the state policies. Women should have voices about what kind of equality they want and what policies can really help them to reach the goal of gender balance and equality. Women should have equal representation with men who strive for women's equality at top decision-making levels. And in matters of economic development, state policies with a democratic style cannot retreat from demands that women get equal footing.

After examining what state policies inclined toward women should be, we need to consider what Chinese women should do for their own pursuit of equality. Obviously, a better approach to reach sex/gender equality, as I reconceive it, should not be an essentialist method to represent voices of "the other." It should be an inclusive method that pays attention to women's specific experiences and sentiments about their life changes in various aspects of economic transformation. It should also be plural and opened to all possible voices of the oppressed, with consideration for all disadvantaged people.

TRONTO'S CARING DEMOCRACY AND CRITIQUES

Turning to Tronto's caring democracy, her contribution to merging democratic theory with feminist care ethics has inspiring thoughts in rethinking the genuine concerns of citizens in a decent society. In a review of Tronto's caring democracy, Jenkins raised two points, which followed Tronto's endorsement of caring: first is an ontological claim about humanity, asking democratic theorists to reframe the basis for equality of citizens.[55] Tronto roots equality in the inescapable and unversed nature of humanity as relational, vulnerable, and interdependent, and we all share existence as "care receivers."[56] The second point is that since we are equal in vulnerability, as a result, each of us has an equal right to have her or his needs publicly recognized and addressed. Jenkins denies that these two claims are conceptually groundbreaking. Jenkins criticizes that Tronto failed to adequately develop a clear definition of inclusion and at the same time to make it a prerequisite to a revolution of care. I see the point Jenkins made in this denial and he could be right about Tronto's lack of a clear definition of inclusion and making it "a prerequisite to a revolution of care,"[57] but I believe Confucian *ren* and the identity of heaven and humanity (天人合一) could be associated with Tronto's definition of inclusion. A book by Xianglong Zhang, *Thoughts of Herdger and Chinese Heaven and Dao*, clearly addressed a compatible link for Kongzi's *ren* as a preconceptual cosmos vision to support humanity's sustainability.[58] The *ren* governance philosophy such as listen to the people, serve the people, and take care of people's needs gained the support of most Chinese people, which is justifiable simply in the recognition of heaven's will, not in human being's conceptual definition. With a deep endorsement of this recognition, the two notions of *Minben* and *Minzhu* were associated with and supportive of one another's livelihoods. The above two points made by Tronto are significant contributions to her unique notion of "care with," which set up the foundation of her holistic analysis of why caring as the moral value is crucial to cross the private and public and to connect with democratic life and politics. Without a clear, simple endorsement to the fact of people's interdependence, there would be no way to link women's caring experiences of reproduction and household labor with a public conception of care and caring responsibilities; without a public discussion of women's overproportionately burdened domestic labor, the complicated issues of women's inequality could not be exposed and addressed. The second point is that each of us has the right to publicly address our needs as a care receiver, which leads to the notion of "care with" or shared responsibilities that is more groundbreaking than the first. As a caregiver, as most women usually are, despite whether or not she has a public job, her own needs are usually neglected and devalued under stereotyped norms of sacrificing herself for serving others. Such norms for caregivers do not show sufficient respect and concern for the value of caring when it comes to caring for persons who perform caregiving labor. Tronto's two points in the establishment of "care with" give us hope that we can change the devaluation of caregiving labor, leading to a more rewarding outcome for deserving caregivers.

Using these two points, Tronto's vision of caring inclusiveness can help fight against the social hierarchy and reduce the influence of dictatorship or domination of essentialist thinking regarding women or human issues in living a better life. Tronto's challenging insights sound far beyond a debate of *Minben* and *Minzhu*, which addressed issues of inclusion of all people but not just those who prefer to be free from care and able to participate in market competitions. According to Tronto, here we leave aside "the question of those who have been coerced or tricked into such service, whose autonomy and freedom have been compromised."[59] To continue to probe those ignored realities of care laborers crossing home and outside home, Tronto illuminates the complexity of a caring democratic life.

To summarize, the underlined philosophical theme in this chapter is the inseparable relation between social and political systems and the pursuit of women's equality. The combinations of the Confucian concept of *ren* and the feudalist ideal of *Minben* is not the opposite pole of *Minzhu* but a necessary prerequisite for democracy; Mao's view of women's equality in production has merit as a necessary step for women's participation in the public world but his dominant class analysis over women's issues does not provide an open-minded inclusive method for Chinese women to seek their equality. Women as lifelong caregivers not only need the social ideal of equality at the highest abstract level, but also a political environment of democracy in women's concrete situations. What Chinese women should have for their equality is an inclusive, democratic, and antiessentialist approach that states the inseparable relationship between democracy, equality, and their concrete caring experiences. Seeking women's equality requires a democratic social system, a democratic political thought line, and a democratic methodology, but how should we interpret the genuine meaning of foundations of democracy? Feminist challenges of dictatorship, social hierarchy, gender roles in division of labor, and paternalism demand more difficult tasks of unfolding hidden inequality and injustice in a holistic but intersectionality methodology. Although early Confucian thoughts of *ren* in connecting features of ontological oneness could offer provoking ideas of caring democracy, they did bear limitations of *Minben* and social hierarchy that could neglect a devaluation of groups of lower ranks. Nevertheless, the Chinese *Minben*, in particular, emphasizes the inclusiveness of all lives under the heaven's will or the nature's organic course, all of these made a solid foundation of a relational worldview meta-ethics and people's interdependency as the unique truth of human existence. Since the *Minben* thinking model barely analyzes issues of injustice and power imbalance in social relations, it does not seem to help women who are seeking their equal share of caring demands in household work. In order to allow for self-development, we need to further explore contemporary feminist thoughts on gender. Tronto's *Caring Democracy* is valuable in her probing analysis about both care and democracy. According to Wynne Walker Moskop's review of Tronto's *Caring Democracy: Markets, Equality, and Justice*, the main strength of caring democracy is its detailed, penetrating, and expert examination of how the care and democracy deficits are related at multiple levels. "It can be challenging to keep track of the overlapping complex threads of argument about gender and class and freedom and equality that Tronto weaves together."[60] In the next two chapters, I focus on feminist analysis of gender difference and equality and the Confucian Golden Rule of reciprocity.

NOTES

1. Lijun Yuan, *Reconceiving Women's Equality in China: A Critical Examination of Models of Sex Equality* (Lanham, MD: Lexington Books, 2005), chapters 3 and 4.
2. "The Three Kangs as social ethics and the Five Norms as individual virtues are combined together into one moral law, which was established as the root of Chinese culture and civilization." See Yu-lan Feng, *A Short History of Chinese Philosophy* (New York: Macmillan, 1948), 197.
3. Dewey was called the "Second Confucius" during his twenty-six-month visit to China that began on May 1, 1919. But he was condemned as an expression of Western imperialism after the establishment of the People's Republic of China and a purge of Deweyan pragmatism was begun. David Hall and Roger T. Ames, *The Democracy of the Dead: Dewey, Confucius, and the Hope for Democracy in China* (Chicago: Open Court, 1999), 141.
4. The six commonalities are: Ethnocentrism and the importance of narrative; social engagement; self-cultivation; the duty of remonstrance; the importance of tradition; and a democratic vision. Hall and Ames, *The Democracy of the Dead*, 151–58.
5. Hall and Ames, *The Democracy of the Dead*, 151–58.
6. Hall and Ames, *The Democracy of the Dead*, 158–59.
7. New Confucianism is different from neo-Confucianism: the former refers to Confucian scholars after the late nineteenth century, but the latter refers to those Confucians such as Zhu Xi and two Chen in Ming and Song dynasties.
8. Hall and Ames, *The Democracy of the Dead*, 159–60.
9. Hall and Ames, *The Democracy of the Dead*, 170.
10. Hall and Ames, *The Democracy of the Dead*, 174.
11. Qi Liang, *Critiques of Neo-Confucianism* (新儒学批判) (Shanghai: Sanlian Shuku [三联书库], 1995).
12. Qi Liang, *Collections of Writing of Qi Liang* (SiXiangZheWenCong) (Shanghai, China: Xuelin [学林书社], 1998), 437.
13. Liang, *Collections of Writing of Qi Liang*, 43.
14. Liang, *Critiques of Neo-Confucianism*, 438–39.
15. Liang, *Collections of Writing of Qi Liang*, 111.
16. Liang, *Collections of Writing of Qi Liang*, 24.

17. Liang, *Collections of Writing of Qi Liang*, 106–7.

18. Hall and Ames, *The Democracy of the Dead*, 173.

19. Liang, *Collections of Writing of Qi Liang*, 74.

20. Liang, *Critiques of Neo-Confucianism*, 460.

21. Hall and Ames, *The Democracy of the Dead*, 160.

22. Hall and Ames, *The Democracy of the Dead*, 160.

23. Zhang Shiwei (张师伟), "Rendering and Retrofit: People-Oriented Concept in Process of the Sinicization of Modern Democratic Thought (濡染与改造：现代民主思想中国化过程中的民本观念)," *Journal of Culture, History, and Philosophy, Jinan,* 20163 (2016): 5–15 (《文史哲》(济南) 2016年第20163期 第5–15页).

24. Joan C. Tronto, *Caring Democracy: Markets, Equality, and Justice* (New York: New York University Press, 2013), 17.

25. Tronto, *Caring Democracy*, 18.

26. Tronto, *Caring Democracy*, 27.

27. Tronto, *Caring Democracy*, 33.

28. Tronto, *Caring Democracy*, 143.

29. Tronto, *Caring Democracy*, 64.

30. Hall and Ames, *The Democracy of the Dead*, 161.

31. Hall and Ames, *The Democracy of the Dead*, 161.

32. Hall and Ames, *The Democracy of the Dead*, 201.

33. Hall and Ames, *The Democracy of the Dead*, 198.

34. Hall and Ames, *The Democracy of the Dead*, 198.

35. Hall and Ames, *The Democracy of the Dead*, 198.

36. Hall and Ames, *The Democracy of the Dead*, 198.

37. He Qinglian, "Analysis of Social Changes of Women's Status in Contemporary China," *Journal of Dandai Zhongguo Yanjiu* (Modern China Studies) 2 (2001): 77–78.

38. Hall and Ames, *The Democracy of the Dead*, 198.

39. Roger T. Ames, *Confucian Role Ethics: A Vocabulary* (Hong Kong: The Chinese University of Hong Kong), 2011; Daniel A. Bell, "A Comment on Confucian Role Ethics," *Frontiers of Philosophy in China* 7, no. 4 (2012): 604–9, here 607.

40. Li Xiaojiang and Xiaodan Zhan, "Creating a Space for Women: Women's Studies in China in the 1980s," *Signs* 20, no. 1 (1994): 137–51, here 148.

41. Yefu Zheng (郑也夫), *On Prices: A New Perspective from Sociology* (《代价论：一个社会学的新视角》) (Beijing: Sanlian Bookstore, 1995), 74.

42. Li Jingzhi （李静之） et al., *Marxist View of Women* 《马克思主义妇女观》 (Beijing: China People's University Press [中国人民大学出版社], 1992), 177; Jie Tao, Bijun Zheng, and Shirley L. Mow, eds., *Holding Up Half the Sky: Chinese Women Past, Present, and Future* (New York: Feminist Press at the City University of New York, 2004).

43. Zedong Mao, *Selected Works of Mao Tse-tung*, 4 vols. (Beijing: Foreign Language Press, 1967), 1: 46.

44. Zongli Tang and Bing Zuo, *Maoism and Chinese Culture* (Commack, NY: Nova Science, 1996), 190.

45. Mao, *Selected Works*, 2: 308.

46. Tang and Zuo, *Maoism and Chinese Culture*, 166.

47. Mao Zedong, *Quotations from Chairman Mao* (Peking: Foreign Language Press, 1966), 298.

48. Wang Xiaoming, "WTO, a Monster or an Angel for Chinese Women?" in *Women of China English Monthly* 《中国妇女》 英文月刊, December 2000: 25. Sponsored and administrated by All-China Women's Federation, published by ACWF Internet Information and Communication Center (Women's Foreign Language Publications of China).

49. Peiyun Peng, "Women and Economic Development," in *Women of China English Monthly* 《中国妇女》 英文月刊, December 2001: 30.

50. Peng, "Women and Economic Development," 29.

51. Peng, "Women and Economic Development," 29–30.

52. Peng, "Women and Economic Development," 30.

53. Peng, "Women and Economic Development," 30.

54. Yuan, *Reconceiving Women's Equality in China*, 80.

55.   Joan C. Tronto, *Caring Democracy: Markets, Equality, and Justice*. Reviewed by Stephanie Jenkins, *Hypatia Reviews Online* (2014), hypatiareviews.org/review/content/254. Narrated by Miranda Pilipchuk.

56. Tronto, *Caring Democracy*, 29.

57. Zhang, Xianglong, (张祥龙), *Thoughts of Herdger and Chinese Heaven and Dao* (《海德格尔与中国天道：终极视域的开启与交融》) (Beijing: Shenghuo, dushu, xinzhi, Sanlian Shudian [北京：生活 读书 新知 三联书店], 1996), 248–53.

58. Zhang, *Thoughts of Herdger and Chinese Heaven and Dao*, 248–53.

59. Tronto, *Caring Democracy*, 110.

60. Wynne Walker Moskop, "Book Review: *Caring for Democracy: Markets, Equality, and Justice* by Joan C. Tronto," *American Political Thought* 4, no 2 (Spring 2015): 350–54, here 353.

II

Methodological Dimensions

Chapter Three

Feminist Critiques of Gender Inequality and Ethics of Care

Toward Caring Democracy

Since the early 1980s we have seen an increasing belief that women and men are different in post-Mao China, along with a rehabilitation of Confucianism in both mainland China and Chinese Diaspora. At the same time, Western feminisms, in their variety of liberal, socialist, Marxist, and radical feminists, increasingly focus on sex/gender difference and different power assignments. The focus of sex difference in many fields of literature, anthropology, psychology, sociology, philosophy, and politics has deepened discussions in ethical, methodological, and political debates: feminist criticisms of "essentialism" based on *Inessential Women* (Spelman 1988) and the debate continued through 1990s. The idea of sex/gender difference also inspired the ethics of care: A feminine (relational) approach to moral reasoning (Noddings 1984, 2003, 2013). Nevertheless, the original version of care encountered critical assessments from perspectives of feminist political commitment of ending women's subordination (see, e.g., Grimshaw 1986; Jaggar 1995; Tronto 1993). In the critical thinking of care, clarifications of notions of relational self, and a favor of relational approach emerged through broader inquiry of gender justice and care (Robinson 1999). Feminist care ethicists continue to explore relational care in recent decades (e.g., Held 2006; Robinson 2011; Tronto 2013) while a concept of intersectionality became most acceptable.

It is notable that sameness as the ideal of equality has application problems in practice. Considering the real situation at present in different societies, most women have less education and less professional training by social arrangement. In addition, women always have disadvantages in the society in which they live because of their maternity leave during childbirth and rearing children. These factors in ways of intersectionality definitely affect women's free choice for their personal development, even if they have the same opportunities as that of men. If we ignore these factors, we cannot explain why women would lag behind when the society encourages women and men to develop their potentials through the ideal of gender equality. In that case, patriarchal authorities will easily use the result to push people back to the sexual differences. In order to avoid such regression, feminism and society as a whole should raise gender-consciousness relentlessly. Until all human beings realize that there should not be any sex roles assigned by norms to force them to conform their behavior, the idea of equality as sameness will become generally acceptable.

ON SEX DIFFERENCE AND SEX EQUALITY IN FEMINISM

Since the 1970s and 1980s, feminists had reconsidered and explored sex differences and challenged existing inequalities between men and women. Deborah L. Rhode, as the editor and author of the book *Theoretical Perspectives on Sexual Difference*, claims that two different approaches are used in feminist discussion of issues of sex difference: "One strategy has been to deny the extent or essential nature of differences between men and women. A second approach has been to celebrate differences—to embrace characteristics historically associated with women and demand their equal social recognition."[1]

In the first approach of denial, according to Rhode, feminists have explored how data have been constructed, not simply collected, and how cultural influences have been misrepresented as biological imperatives. These feminists do not deny the existence of difference between the sexes, but they can deny its essentiality and identify reasons for its significance that are not biologically determined. The strength of this approach is to expose cultural meanings in the performance of role socialization, sex-based divisions of labor, and devaluation of nonmarket work. The efforts to distinguish cultural and biological factors also have their own limitations as Rhode states: "they risk reinforcing a value structure they seek to challenge."[2] The affirmations of gender sameness may inadvertently universalize or validate norms of the dominant social group, and these norms usually are inattentive to women's interests, experiences, and perspectives. The discussion of sameness seems to take men as the standard of comparison to measure whether women should be like or unlike men at the starting point. In recognition of this difficulty, the second approach of feminists exploring issues of sex differences has sought to challenge not only the significance of these differences, but also the value attached to these differences by society. The strength of the second approach is the insistence that values central to women's experience be valued, which also helps to identify directions necessary for social changes.[3] I will focus on the second approach, looking to feminist thinkers who highlight the importance of care that is taking place in relationships historically linked to women, including such thinkers as Noddings, Jaggar, Grimshaw, Tronto, and Robinson who have made philosophical contributions in the ethics of care.

DIFFERENT MORAL THINKING?

The ethics of care was first articulated in Carol Gilligan's book: *In a Different Voice* (1982). She reported that the moral development of girls and women was significantly different from that of men. Females tended to fear separation from the people close to them and often construed moral dilemmas as conflicts of relationships and responsibilities rather than abstract rights and principles, whereas males tended to see closeness as dangerous and make moral decisions by appeal to abstract rules. Furthermore, women were most likely to act on their feelings of love and compassion for particular individuals, whereas men typically adhered to a morality of justice. Hence, she claimed that studies of moral development based only on a morality of justice did not provide an appropriate standard for measuring women's moral development and should be recognized as male biased.[4]

Some feminists consider *In a Different Voice* as offering a characteristically feminine approach to morality, an approach that seemed to provide a basis for a distinctively feminist ethics. Nevertheless, it is far from clear whether this approach could be reliably deployed to solve so-called women's issues and to advance the feminist goal of ending women's subordination (Jaggar 1995).

Among many proponents of care ethics, the most radical theorist is Nel Noddings (1984). She holds a view of caring as the highest moral ideal or virtue. According to her view, care ethics comes from the natural caring, built up in personal relationships that reach out to others and grows in response to the other. There is no ethical effort required in caring: when we care, we just do what we want and ought to do. We feel "we must do something" in response to the needs of the cared for. Otherwise we are in a pathological state.[5]

Noddings identifies at least three features in her care thinking. First, "since caring is a relation, an ethics built on it is naturally other-regarding."[6] Care ethics focuses on concrete relationship between one-caring and being cared for. Since ethical caring requires an effort to care for other's needs and response, it should not be "tender-minded" but rather tough in demanding that a caregiver "[be] strong, courageous, and capable of joy"[7] in the other's well-being. Second, it seems that care ethics allows and even encourages self-sacrifice, but Noddings stresses that "it does not separate self and other in caring."[8] Since I am defined in the relation, I do not sacrifice myself when I move toward the other as one-caring. When the one-caring feels in conflict, she must seek a way to remain as one-caring. So, "Pursuit of the ethical ideal demands impassioned and realistic commitment."[9] Third, caring "will not allow us to be distracted by visions of universal love, perfect justice, or a world unified under principle."[10] Instead, a caregiver always acts out of feelings, sensitivity, or sentiments for particular others rather than for principles or rules. So, three things are crucial in Noddings's description of caring: other-regarding, relational self, and particular feelings in concrete situations.

Responding to these views, many feminists are skeptical about the ideas of caring. Three questions emerge from an examination of feminist critics on issues of care ethics: (1) Does the idea of other-regarding matter for women's position in the hierarchical societies? (2) If there is no separation between caregiver and being cared for, how can others as being cared-for be benefited? (3) If particular feelings are crucial in care ethics, how can the concept of caring be applied to broad situations beyond family? Feminist theorists have addressed all of these questions.

FEMINIST CRITIQUES OF THE ETHICS OF CARE

Beginning with the first question, some feminist theorists have investigated the ways in which our genders determine the sorts of virtues open or closed to us in a hierarchical gender system. It is a woman's moral luck to be expected by almost every culture to devote herself to the caring of her family even at substantial personal cost to herself (Card 1990). This is exactly the case followed by ethical codes of Confucian *LiJi* that I analyzed earlier in which morality is a matter of performing one's proper role in the society. The proper role for women is at home and that of men is outside the home. Women's role to serve primarily her family (domestic care) is her destined duty. Thus, in Confucian ethics *LiJi* (*The Records of Rites*), a woman's fate is determined under man-made moral laws. She should always have regard for others without self-concern, for supposedly herself should be included in the interests of the family and community. However, the idea of other-regarding as a virtue in care ethics, as some feminists criticized, tends to ignore the distinctive forms of violence within family and community. The suggestion of forgetting the self may make women be silent and accept the historical male control of women's sexual and reproductive capacities and activities, and at worst, it would rationalize this male control rather than challenging the existing social acceptance of it. Thus, as Marilyn Friedman pointed out, the care ethics [the concept of *ren*] "does not (yet) constitute a sufficiently rich or fully liberatory *feminist* ethics."[11]

An ethics that recommends neglecting self will not encourage women to change their position of subordination. Regarding my first question, I would say that whether or not the ethics of care explicitly advocated the suppression of women, its implicit consequences are unfavorable with regard to the position of women.

Second, concerning the relational self, some feminists such as Jean Grimshaw consider two aspects (1986). It is true that an individual is fundamentally a social being, a situated self, relationally and communally defined. On the other hand, the well-being of an individual person can be separated from other persons and the relationships with which he or she is nevertheless deeply intertwined. Our social institutions should respect his or her individual or self regarding needs, rights, or abilities to make decisions.

Joan C. Tronto noted that even care thinking also requires self-awareness and self-knowledge because, as she states, attentiveness requires "a tremendous self-knowledge so that the caretaker does not simply transform the needs of the other into a projection of the self's own needs."[12]

Both Grimshaw and Tronto's discussions are helpful in addressing the second question. A relational self does not mean a self should not separate itself from others, for one must know how others can be benefited by her caring labor. "If I see myself as 'indistinct' from you, or you as not having your own being that is not merged with mine, then I cannot preserve a real sense of your well-being as opposed to mine. Care and understanding require the sort of distance that is needed in order not to see the other as a projection of self as a continuation of other."[13] In other words, care for others, and the understanding of them, are only possible if one can adequately distinguish one's self from others.

The third aspect concerns the particular situation of one-caring. A mother applies "right" or "wrong" most confidently to her own decisions based on her attitudes in concrete and particular conditions. The decisions a mother makes may not depend on any rules but on her feelings for the individual being cared-for. These decisions are typically made in a dyadic situation: a particular relation of caregiver and care receiver. This small-scale particularity has its limitation and weakness to address moral issues in other situations as some feminists realized (Card 1990, 205; Jaggar 1995, 194; Hoagland 1991, 253, 260). Alison Jaggar's article "Caring as a Feminist Practice of Moral Reason," expresses concern about "Care's Focus on the Particular."[14]

Most women as caregivers focus exclusively on the particular. That is not their fault but the limitation of social structures': "the ways in which male-dominant social structures limit the life chances of women and men."[15] Male-dominant societies would be happy to see women put their close attention to the specificity of small-scale situations since those attentions "may obscure perception of the larger social context in which they are embedded."[16] For example, attention to your family's immediate needs for food, shelter, and comfort may distract from moral scrutiny of the social structures that create those needs or leave them unfulfilled. It is so natural and easy for many women to focus their attention on the particular rather than on general features of the society they live in, simply because they spend most of their time and energy at their home.

Care reasoning seems to pay the most attention to particular persons, feelings, and situations. These considerations often limit its views of broader moral issues such as Third World dependency, the globalization of environmental pollution (women mostly are vulnerable in these cases), and most important, the social structures and systems that perpetuate women's subordination. Noddings's version of care ethics has failed to address many broad moral issues beyond the family area. It cannot deal with the problem of justice within the family, either.

Questioning Noddings's (1984) three aspects in her view of caring, feminists suggest that such a narrowly orientated care ethics may not promote women's emancipation but rather may reinforce and even intensify and justify the unequal social arrangement and treatments of different sexes. The puzzle here might not be exposed if we try to derive a philosophical ethics from what is naturally good without critical reflection on how the so-called natural is socially constructed. If care orientation is the most natural and virtuous character for humans to possess, why did so many social norms followers spend their life on the hard work of consolidating this "natural" virtue? Why did they seem to be so afraid of people not committed to this natural difference, and why did they need to count on the notion of heaven to convince women to be virtuous?

As we see, the ethics of care encourages women to do a good job as a caregiver, for it seems a good and natural thing to do. This ethic draws women's attention to focus on women's roles rather than their rights. The very right of women to be treated with equal concern and respect is overlooked from the ideas of care thinking. Thus, the ethics of care cannot meet the feminist political goal—men and women should care and receive care equally. The points made by Grimshaw (1986) and Tronto (1993) seem true: a "feminine" ethics might reinforce the very stereotypes it seeks to overcome because it does not respond to actual gender in all cases. Later on, Tronto developed a new notion of *"care with"* in *Caring Democracy* (2013) to overcome this narrowness.

This early idea of caring has been debated since the middle of the 1980s. Some feminist critics have been revising care ethics during the 1990s. For instance, Tronto has suggested that our vocabulary for discussing caring seems impoverished and narrowed because of the way caring is "privatized." She pointed out the need to "rethink as well how those particular circumstances are socially constructed,"[17] and importantly how the need to rethink appropriate forms of caring raises broad questions about the shape of social and political institutions in society. The charge of the narrowness of care ethics encourages a new direction of rethinking caring, which will relate caring to a broad, global-oriented ethical thinking. For instance, Fiona Robinson developed a revised version of caring in her book *Globalizing Care* (1999).

In the idea of globalizing care, we still need to answer the question "Who cares for whom?" According to Robinson, the answer "is not only a moral but a social and political question, which requires an analysis of the social construction of roles, relationships, communities, and institutions in their different sociopolitical contexts."[18] Such an analysis beyond moral theory and reaching sociopolitical contexts will constantly remind us that all relations are infused with power and within every relationship there exists the potential for exploitation and domination. A new version of caring provided by Robinson is trying to raise *critical feminist approaches* to examining human relations and focusing on the potential for exploitation and coercion. This more sophisticated and feminist version of care ethics is quite different from the traditional Confucian version of care ethics.

THE DEBATE OF INESSENTIAL WOMEN

It seems to me, if feminist theories are going to be trustworthy theories for all women's liberation (also for all marginalized minorities), they need to consider not only the commonality between different groups of women but the differences among women in contexts of race, class, color, and so on. Women of different countries and each individual woman always face problems of her own or her community, but they do have shared common problems that relate to their sexual vulnerability. In today's global market-economic development, women's issues have become of global significance and challenge feminist theories that originated from white middle-class women's experience. Feminist theorists should work out better methods to include other women's experiences and their perceptions on their reality and avoid any kind of bias to exclude other women's voices. By doing so, how can feminists deal with the dilemma of cultural imperialism or relativism, similarity or diversity, sexist or racist bias? Feminist theorists started a serious debate about essentialism and antiessentialism in the 1980s, and it has been a deep epistemological investigation of the notion of inclusiveness and the relationship between women's liberation and other forms of liberations. Challenges to essentialism argue that no essential thinking based on one single perspective or authority could give an appropriate explanation about women's subordination or point out a proper way for women's liberation. If that is the case, does it mean that feminist theories fail to explain the oppression of women by the domination of men under the patriarchal system and to be able to lead women's liberation? What kind of new method for feminists can include different voices among women against gender-based inequality? Let us explore some feminist critiques of essentialism and see what suggestions we can get from a new notion of "intersectionality."

False Generalization

Elizabeth V. Spelman's *Inessential Women* (1988) is well known as a representative work against essentialism in the feminist theoretical field. As Spelman pointed out, essentialists retain two key points: the universalization of their claims, and the authority of dominating theorists. Hence, they must fall into false generalization and exclusion of other voices or differences. Spelman unfolded her arguments against "white solipsism" and "ethnocentrism" through the issues of gender and race. In her view, many feminist theorists like the authors of *The Reproduction of Mothering* (Nancy Chodorow 1978), *Sexual Politics* (Kate Millett 1969), and *Dialectics of Sex* (Shulamith Friestone 1970) have made mistakes of universalizing women's issues. These white middle-class women generalize sexism as the most original one among all oppressing forms through their own group experiences and believe that other women shared the same experience of sexism. Therefore, they derive the conclusion that all women suffer from sexual discrimination in the same way and that they all have shared women-ness in their gender identity. According to this kind of viewpoint, all women have a similar gender position regardless of their race, class, nationality, and so on. These theorists have overlooked the actual reality and particular experiences of specific groups of women, such as African American women. For African American women, who suffer greatly from racism like African American men, their experiences of sexism are not a simple additional oppression of racism and not a shared one with white women. Spelman criticized: "In sum, according to an additive analysis of sexism and racism, all women are oppressed by sexism; some women are further oppressed by racism. Such an analysis distorts black women's experiences of oppression by failing to note important differences between the contexts in which black women and white women experience sexism."[19]

Spelman also addressed that "we are all women" is a view of universalizing women's experiences, which could not explain why different women (white, black, rich, poor, Christian, or Jew) possibly seek different ways to liberate themselves. A universal or unified view of women's liberation may not represent different voices of women in different groups. Similarly, the view of that gender identity is the original identity for all women and exists side by side with other identities (class, race, ethnicity) only reflects the perspective of white middle-class feminists. The universality of sexism claimed by Chodorow in her *Reproduction of Mothering* (1978) focuses on the relationship between white middle-class women and men and ignores relationships between other groups of women and men. But we might inquire whether white middle-class women do have similar experiences of rearing children to poor black women's experiences; whether black women's experiences could serve as evidence for attributes of so-called womanness or the commonality of womanhood. White feminist theorists could not give any satisfactory answer to Spelman's questions.

Susan M. Okin tried to answer the question about shared sexism in her article "Gender Inequality and Cultural Differences" (1994). Against Spelman's charge of white middle-class feminists stressing the commonality of sexism while neglecting the differences of women in different races, Okin claimed: "One can argue that sexism is an identifiable form of oppression, many of whose effects are felt by women regardless of race or class, without at all subscribing to the view that race and class oppression are insignificant. One can still insist, for example, on the significant difference between the relation of a poor black women to a wealthy white man and that of a wealthy white woman to a poor black man."[20]

In order to show that sexual discrimination is identifiable and can be separated from other elements when being analyzed, Okin laid out many instances of gender inequality happening in the Third World countries and she concluded that feminist theory developed under the context of Western culture also can be applicable to women in different cultural circumstances. Jane Flax objected to such a view of women as a homogeneous category: "One cannot assume that 'other' (e.g., nonwhite) women have experiences just like ours."[21] For Flax, Okin has made at least three mistakes in her assumptions about universality for women's oppression. First, her conclusion that "there is collectively shared oppression."[22] Second, her exclusive focus on shared oppression obscures the equally important relations of domination between women. Third, she assumes that First World women as outsiders can locate and speak for the interests of women in the Third World. It is clear that what Okin defended through her generalizations is the superiority of white Western women making decisions for other women.

Exclusion of Other's Voices

If a universally shared sexism were established, there would be no reason why one woman's or group's voice could not represent all others. A unified theory for women's liberation could express all women's wishes and apply to the situations of all women. According to Spelman the privilege of white middle-class women allows them to be the subjects and authorities who describe women's issues and expound the universality of sexism. Their voices and participation have played a dominating role in investigating women's issues, while others' participation has been less important.

According to Spelman's analysis, what feminist essentialists neglected was a realization that gender identity is the one and many. Spelman gave two pictures to explain two ways of sorting people's identities: One is to divide people originally into women and men, and within these two to make many subdivisions like Afro-American, Europe-American, Asian-American, and so on. The other way is to see people in their original situations and within each of them to make the divisions of women and men. Notice that according to the second schema, there are many categories of women, while according to the first sorting there is but one. For the first, what is true of me "as a woman" seems to be what I have in common with all other women in contrast to all other men. For the second, what is true of me "as a woman" would seem to be what I have in common with other women of my ethnic, racial, or class background in contrast to men of the same background. The significance of these pictures is to tell us that it is not right to take any particular group of women's experience as representative of all, but it does not prohibit us from asking what different groups of women have or might come to have in common.[23] Spelman criticized Chodorow's study which implies that we can ignore the cultural differences: "for the same thing that is true of the relationship between men and women of one group will be true of that between men and women of any other group. Mothers always do most of the parenting, and they do it always in the context of sexism."[24] Women in other groups would possibly not accept Chodorow's claim. In Spelman's view, essentialism, in focusing on the features that women have in common, is likely to neglect individual features and differences and thus neglect important aspects of their lives as women. Therefore, feminist theorists who insist on essentialism would be wrong in their generalizations or would miss important feminist issues that may not affect every woman.

I agree with Spelman's argument that theorists cannot universalize the idea from their own position and so are likely to concentrate on issues affecting their own group but not others. When this occurs, feminist theories would face the danger of making unfounded assumptions of shared gender oppression and shared suffering from sexism. But there the question arises: Does antiessentialism lead to the self-defeat of feminism? Is there any way for feminist theorists to address their common interests and aims among the different situations of different women? In other words, we may ask, if we take feminism seriously, as we already have, then what kind of generalization about women's issues would be the best and who will be the best candidates to theorize women's experiences?

As Spelman pointed out, given the heterogeneity of women and women's situations, it may seem as if it is impossible to make any well-founded yet nontrivial statements about all women. But, it "doesn't automatically follow that no generalizations about women are possible."[25] What Spelman wanted to say is that if there is any truth about all women, it cannot be based on a single situation of any group women. She suggests that we keep our theories as a conjunction of different voices as they are. All feminists are equally apprentices and we do not need any master to be an arbiter and determine controversies among us. Allowing differences to coexist seems to be safe to keep away from the accusation of "imperialism."[26] This conclusion appears to be extremely empiricist and subjectivist, especially if the voices disagree with each other, though it sounds better than a universalized view of women from a single perspective.

Okin claims in her article that women's oppression is similar in certain important respects and she believes that sometimes outsiders can speak for the insider's interest and do not necessarily generate a false generalization. Similarly, the person in the situation might accidentally gain a wrong conclusion about her experience. These arguments bring us to the question of similarity and difference among women and under what criterion we are to make judgments. Even if we had no part in the creation of people's identities or categories, if we have learned the ways of our society we have learned which categories we will be expected to fall into and which identities we will be belong to. Perhaps a poor black woman would not agree that she had shared sexism with other white middle-class women even if she had some experience of gender oppression. So Okin is not correct that the question of similarity and difference among women is a simple empirical one. There will always be an element of decision in determining whether women are similar to or different from each other in significant or meaningful ways. It seems that any authority in the position of addressing the commonality of women's oppression would get into the trouble of excluding other's voices and retain the legacy of the privilege and power to satisfy her group's own needs and goals. How can we avoid such privilege and power as dominating opinions and include more voices among less powerful women in order to seek effective and possible ways to reduce and finally eliminate all women's sufferings as women?

The central idea in the debate between essentialism and antiessentialism is: though essentialists do not assert that, for instance, white middle-class women and poor black women share the same experiences of gender oppression, they do think that there exist some similarities and commonalities underlying different appearances of gender discrimination. Here we find some conceptual confusion in their debate: essentialists emphasize that the nature of different women's oppression is similar across class, race, and color, which is the fundamental idea for women's liberation, otherwise we would never enthusiastically engage ourselves into women's issues. Meanwhile, antiessentialists insist that the generalization of different women's experiences must be derived from their different contexts and situations, so there will be no uniformity or commonality among women. Essentialists would claim that there is no essential difference in the nature of sexism among women's different experiences of sex discrimination while antiessentialists would deny this and claim that there is no sameness among women's subordination in different times and spaces of different societies and communities.

In the feudal society of China before the 1950s, landlord class women perhaps had a more miserable history than peasant women because of rich women's environment full of Confucian *li* culture. Sexual oppression is not symmetrical with other forms of oppression and they may be contrary to each other in some cases. It is reasonable for African American women to put racism as the first target they should fight against and put their attention to sexual discrimination secondly. It is possible that poor women weigh class exploitation more than other oppression and regard this as their main concern, and vice versa the rich women may take gender subordination as the main concern in their life and strongly support the feminist idea of ending their subordination. These different needs and interests will remind us that perhaps no single theory can settle women's issues because they are so different in reality, and there is no single criterion for different issues and difficulties in women's different situations. Intersectionality among different oppressions also remind us that any single focus on one oppression is not adequate to analyze women's issues. Since different women face different problems in their particular situations, feminist theories should work out better theories that can explain the complicated connections between gender oppression and other oppressions. In order to do that, we need a deep commitment of inclusion: the more voices included, the more likely to expose implicit injustice. Antiessentialism, as a serious self-criticism, would not lead to self-defeating feminism but rather to a hope for the new development of a type of good social theory that will be more inclusive rather than exclusive, open rather than dogmatic. A continuous discussion of gender essentialism appeared in a book *The Metaphysics of Gender* by Charlotte Witt and she called it "uniessentialism."[27] According to Witt, gender is the "mega social role" and hence it is uniessential to the social individual as a moral agent, which would further explore issues of gender ontology. Nevertheless, the methodology of intersectionality as a feminist tool of analysis for gender becomes significant because of the outstanding work done by Kimberle Crenshaw (1989, 1991). I will continue to explore this intersectionality after the next section.

RELATIONAL SELF AND RELATIONAL APPROACH

In this section, I will examine feminist notions of selfhood and their moral approach to developing different versions of the ethics of care: the early version of 1984 and the new critical version developed in the mid-1990s. I will reflect on the main critical response to the early version of the ethics of care, and then move to the feminist relational approach advanced by Robinson and others. Through these reflections on relational approach, focusing on people's power relationships, it will help to recognize the need for empowerment of women in seeking sex/gender equality.

The ethics of care in the feminist field came from psychology research by Carol Gilligan in her book *In a Different Voice* (1982). She observed that the moral development of girls and women was significantly different from that of men. Hence, she claimed that studies of moral development based only on a morality of justice did not provide an appropriate standard for measuring women's moral development that preferred a sense of care and should be recognized as male biased, as we discussed in the previous section.

We see many feminists wonder whether this female approach could be reliably deployed to solve so-called women's issues and advance the feminist goal of ending women's subordination, and these critiques are concerned with the political impact of women's caring practice rather than mere ethical implication in this experience. Other criticisms of the ethics of care actually celebrate its focus on the particularity but not the universal principles. However, the serious problem of this ethics is its lack of wholesale consideration of the social structure that created a range of fundamental problems specifically for women (Jaggar 1995).

Nel Noddings developed three aspects of care thinking: other-regarding; relational self or inseparable self and others; and particularity in care. These three features met with many critical responses from both feminist and non-feminist ethical theorists. I explained the feminist critiques of the above three aspects early in this chapter. Now I will assess James Rachels's response in the chapter "Feminism and the Ethics of Care," in *The Elements of Moral Philosophy* (1999).

Rachels challenges Gilligan's different voice suggestion by asking a question: Is it true that women and men think differently? The answer remains unclear. But it is reasonable to think that even if women and men do think differently about ethics, the differences cannot be very great. Their differences are sort of difference of emphasis rather than differences in fundamental values. Rachels called this a difference in style and maybe most women are more inclined to adopt a "caring perspective." Most men may be more inclined to think in terms of principles. But the first style is not exclusively female and the second is not exclusively male, because there are women who are devoted to principles and men who care. So the general differences do not apply to every individual. Rachels also evaluates the strength of a feminine care ethics. While it is doing a better job than Kant's theory of duty or Mill's utilitarianism in dealing with family and friends, Rachels also points out that the weak part in this "female perspective" is not being able to deal with issues beyond the family domain. Rachels' criticism of care thinking is partially correct in emphasizing the strength of its special attention to the domain of family and friends; however, whether it is a woman's weakness to omit universal moral law remains a problem. We need to examine the many feminist responses (e.g., Card 1990; Grimshaw 1986; Tronto 1989) that make careful responses to Noddings' three aspects of caring. All of them noticed the limitation of the caring perspective: personal caring cannot reach large domains beyond family and private places since it emphasizes particularity rather than universal care for all. People on the side of care ethics can also criticize the opposite ethical perspective but make similar mistakes like doing a bad job in the family domain, as Rachels's saying: Traditional ethical theory like Kant's theory of duty does not do a good job in providing an explanation of loving relations in families and between friends.

This critical thinking of the ethics of care correctly shows us weaknesses in the early version of care ethics, but it does not rule out the possibility of adopting merit in the care perspective: *a social relational approach* is in a better position to deal with the private domain. The question is how to expand care perspectives into global care. Also, how can we get rid of the risk of that: emphasizing relational self would make women less motivated to pursue their equality and be devalued? Many feminist thinkers such as Minow, Jaggar, and Robinson project a new version of the ethics of care in trying to resolve the problematic issues in care perspective. Tronto (2013) raised an important key in developing care theory in turning a narrow and private concept of care into a public concept.

In her book *Making All the Difference* (1990), Martha Minow explores the "dilemma of difference."[28] She uses examples to explain this term: In bilingual and special education programs, schools struggle to deal with students defined as "different" without stigmatizing them. In both contexts, it is a difficult task of remedying inequality. If schools treated people differently by emphasizing differences, this different treatment would stigmatize or hinder those people on that basis. On the other hand, treating people the same would become insensitive to their differences and likely stigmatize or hinder them on that basis. This dilemma extends to many situations beyond school. For example, women have special needs such as maternity leave in the workplace. Are women merely helped or hurt? Are their biological differences from men accommodated in fulfillment of the vision of equality? Or are negative stereotypes reinforced in violation of commitments to equality? Minow suggests that the dilemma of difference is not just accidental problems in society. These problems grow from the ways in which society assigns people to categories; the assigned categories based on age, race, gender, and so on have been used to determine who gets included and who does not. Minow critically analyzes several unstated assumptions behind the dilemma of difference: difference is intrinsic, not a comparison; norms need not be stated; the observer can see that other perspectives are irrelevant. All these unstated things make the dilemma of difference seem intractable. However, if they were exposed and debated, it would make room for new solutions. The new approaches should reconsider the relationships and patterns of power that influence the negative consequences of difference and explore new possibilities for change. According to Minow, attention to relationships between groups and the power constructed through those relationships leads us to see the importance of the context in which a particular trait of difference comes to matter. The social-relations approach is interested in context and stresses actual social experiences and their meanings to the people involved rather than abstract or formal principles.[29] To Minow, Noddings recommends the similar idea in a feminine approach; an ethic of caring requires a process of "concretization that is the inverse of abstraction":[30] instead of deducing answers from principles superimposed on a situation, moral reasoning should fill out situations with ever more concrete details.

Minow also argues that the feminist challenge to the ethics of care will go further to inquire of differences in power instead of just deepening an interest in "care" or "responsibility." She explains:

> The challenge is to maintain a steady inquiry into the interpersonal and political relationships between the known and the knower; a concern for the relations between wholes and parts; a suspicion of abstractions, which are likely to hide under claims of universality what is in fact the particular point of view and experience of those in power; and a respect for particularity, concreteness, reflection on experience, and dialogue.[31]

Only through relational themes can feminist methodologies frame issues in ways that avoid such constraining assumptions behind the dilemma of difference. Hence, feminists urge recasting issues of difference as problems of dominance or subordination by locating differences within relationships of power differentials and by disclosing social relationships of power within the way difference is named and enforced. The analysis of how difference is named and assigned in relationships or power further questions the implicit of the granted norms; norms based on the male experience become a subject for contest. Rather than assuming that women must adjust to a workplace designed for men, we can advocate that a desirable workplace should be designed for both men and women.[32] Through the above analyses, the idea of an unsituated perspective on issues of difference fails to address the influence of the observer on the observed. Only the relational approach can do the job of disclosing differences and raise the hope of getting out of the dilemma of difference.

Alison M. Jaggar holds another insightful view about the weakness of care ethics. She points out in her article "Caring as Feminist Practice of Moral Reason": it is not that the care ethics is unable to be applied in broader moral issues, but rather as she argues that it has a limit of focusing on the specificity of particular situations, especially the needs of particular individuals. This focus is valuable in encouraging awareness of the moral complexities of situations. However, the weakness of care thinking is that its attention to situations, specificity, and particularity diverts attention away from their general features such as the social institution and the groupings that give these features much of their meaning. Care ethics' emphasis on individual responses to immediate needs encourages so-called social work or band-aid (individual donation of food, clothes, and so on to the poor and homeless) approaches to moral problems. This kind of help actually draws or diverts people's attention from efforts to solve the problems institutionally through social changes. If people focus entirely on individual donations to help the poor, they are not paying attention to the social structure and institutions that created those problems. People always easily conform themselves to social rules and regulations rather than challenge them. That is the point Jaggar made: The conformity reversibly strengthens the existing social institutions by making people insensible to oppressive structures, such as sexism, racism, and class discrimination. She adds: "Significantly improving the lives of the world's women certainly requires the empathy, imagination and responsiveness that distinguish care thinking; but it also requires a kind of moral thinking that focuses not only on meeting immediate needs but on problematizing the structures that create those needs or keep them unfulfilled."[33] This critique is "one of the most penetrating criticisms of care ethics" as Fiona Robinson states in her exploration of care perspective.[34]

Fiona Robinson agrees with Jaggar that the everyday relations give meaning and context to so-called moral problems. However, she adds, "all relations are infused with power, and within every relationship there exists the potential for exploitation and domination." Thus, a critical ethics of care should "advocate *attention to relationships*—among states and nonstate actors in transnational social, political, and economic contexts—as a critical tool for uncovering and remaking the processes leading to the naming of 'difference' and the legitimation of patterns of exclusion." Hence, the relational turn in feminist ethics represents not a denial of or lack of interest in conflict and disunity, but "*a focus on the interpersonal and social contexts in which these and all other human relations occur*."[35] Considering the criticism that relational ideals carry risks for vulnerable people if the underlying patterns of power remain unchanged, Robinson argues that the social-relations approach should appeal to the feminist approach to the international political economy. She believes:

> The perspectives from feminist international political economy complement the epistemology and ontology of an ethics of care; such approaches accept that relationships among real, not abstract, persons must be the starting point of any enquiry, but they also problematize and critique the very structure

within which those relations are located. Ultimately they work towards an emancipatory vision of a more humane world order. [36]

What would this critical ethic of care mean in the context of a global issue, say world poverty? Robinson explains that it would not mean paternalistic care, or one-on-one relations based on charity, because those strategies seem to encourage the reproduction of patterns of inequality and relations of dependence. Nevertheless, its emphasis on critical attention to structures of inequality may not altogether preclude the more personal approach that "may teach us an effective lesson about the nature of moral motivation and responsiveness." [37] Sponsoring a child is a meaningful moral response since it takes care of a concrete rather than a generalized other; the very act of "sponsorship" creates a relationship that is akin to parenting and motivates moral responsiveness.

Furthermore, a critical ethic of care, in order to reduce global poverty, cannot be confined to one-on-one personal relationships. What is required instead is a restructuring of political action in such a way that agents can focus their moral attention and act with the virtues of care: attentiveness, responsiveness, and responsibility. In the context of world poverty, the ethic of care must be a critical approach, which seeks to demonstrate that the existence of "difference" is neither natural nor objective, but that the act of naming difference can be understood only in the context of a relationship. "Viewed in this way, no individual or group can be seen as objectively different and therefore deserving of social exclusion." Such a critical relational ethics of care places moral value on the continuous attention that characterizes stable and caring relations, thereby it also seeks to situate social and personal relations in the wider sociopolitical and structural context of potentially exploitative social relations. From this perspective, the existing patterns of exclusion and domination in global social relations and inequality in power and influence must be examined and challenged. Patterns of local relations, such as familial attachments, gender relations, and social hierarchies would be explored in order to uncover the extent to which they may perpetuate the impoverishment of certain groups within societies. In the case of global poverty, through the analysis of what is the creation of such relations, we would see the structures of the global political economy at least partially be responsible for the case. The perspective of this critical relational approach will force us to rethink the apparently objective processes of capitalism. [38]

INTERSECTIONALITY AS
FEMINIST TOOLS OF ANALYSIS

While feminists criticize essentialist thinking of women's oppression, most of them have turned to positive ways to continue to theorize women's subordination in a different context, that is the rising of notions of intersectionality. In 1989, Crenshaw's landmark article, "Demarginalizing the Intersection of Race and Sex: A Black Feminist Critique of Antidiscrimination Doctrine, Feminist Theory, and Antiracist Politics," introduced the term. She further elaborated the framework in "Mapping the Margins: Intersectionality, Identity Politics, and Violence against Women of Color" (1991).[39] Intersectionality is the opposite of the essentialist way to generalize theoretical and practical issues of social justice. Over the last several decades, inequality in income and wealth has grown exponentially, both within nation-states and across nations on a global scale. "Nearly half of the world's wealth, some USA$110 trillion, is owned by only 1 percent of the world's population. If trends continue, by 2016, 1 percent is expected to own more than the other 99 percent together."[40] According to Collins and Bilge, using intersectionality as an analytic tool can foster a better understanding of growing global inequality. Inequality does not fall equally on everyone. "Rather than seeing people as a homogeneous, undifferentiated mass, intersectionality provides a framework for explaining how social divisions of race, gender, age, and citizenship status, among others, positions people differently in the world, especially in relation to global social inequality."[41] As we see, the concept of intersectionality now grounds feminist theory and research in many disciplines increasingly. To me, antiessentialism and intersectionality similarly emphasize an approach of inclusion through revealing ways of how institutional discriminations happen in complicated situations of marginalization exposed by Crenshaw's example of black women in her landmark essays. I will discuss some criticisms of the term intersectionality and defend the term by responding to the criticism. At the end I ask for possible connections between intersectionality, democracy, and ethics of care.

In "Re-Thinking Intersectionality" (2008), Jennifer C. Nash comments: Intersectionality has become the primary analytic tool for feminist and antiracist scholars theorizing identity and oppression. She focuses four tensions within intersectionality scholarship: the lack of a defined intersectional methodology; the use of black women as quintessential intersectional subjects; the vague definition of intersectionality; and the empirical validity of intersectionality. Despite these criticisms, her project "does not seek to undermine intersectionality"; instead, she "encourages both feminist and antiracist scholars to grapple with intersectionality's theoretical, political, and methodological murkiness to construct a more complex way of theorizing identity and oppression."[42] I believe Nash is correct in summarizing the difficulty of crafting a method that is in demand to provide a clear analysis of the complexity of institutional problems in dealing with injustice to multiply marginalized subjects. More recent articles on intersectionality reiterate the complexity of intersectionality as a work-in-progress, its mobility or transforming feature, so we must know "what intersectionality *is* is to assess what intersectionality *does* as a starting point for thinking about what else the framework might be mobilized to do."[43] To me the term intersectionality continues to remain ambiguous as it is at its incompleteness as a starting point for its inclusion. Next, I try to respond to another critique in a blog "Feminist Current," founded by Meghan Murphy (2013).

A contributing blogger Aphrodite Kocięda makes a claim: "it is pretty accurate"[44] for the most part of intersectionality, the notion has its progressive feature in building up some sort of theory of inclusiveness and multi-dimensionality, which should be highly appreciated by people who are seeking an open strategy approach. Kocięda also criticizes that intersectionality focuses on *how* the excluded group of people are excluded, not *why* the space is inherently exclusionary. To me, this is a great point for encouraging people to fight the framework of space, not within the space; however, the criticism does not sound fair to Trina Grillo's analysis of antiessentialism, which is the idea that came from the analysis of intersectionality. Through a story of "the regular dressing and the other vegetarian dressing,"[45] Grillo tells us why the vegetarian people got marginalized by being labeled non-regular. The tool of intersectionality helps us to realize that a single unified voice can easily exclude others and keep its own as regular, essential, and dominating. The "why" is visible in the invisible way of maintaining regular exclusions as given. Through the metaphor of waiting for our turn at an intersection on the road, we can realize that everyone faces moments where they can behave exclusively toward others, but they also have the option of going forward in such a way that each of us can be inclusive of others, thereby ensuring that, in the practice of intersectionality, we can renounce supremacist domination of each other. There could be great hopes to change the inherent exclusion of an already marginalized group of people rather than reinforcing the supremacist whiteness, maleness, ableism, heteronormativity, and so on. I think that trying to clarify how the group of women is excluded should be the most important *first step* to see the invisible and why, which is more complicated than the scene of waiting for one's own turn at the intersection.

Kocięda made the second point that "intersectionality is incomplete" by which she means that intersectionality relies on the static, fixed oppressive identity. This can be a problem according to her but there is no further explanation of what the problem is. It is not quite clear why the intersectional analysis must be using the static and fixed oppressive identity. Those intersectional research analyses usually focus on marginalized or excluded people's contextual factors, not their fixed identity, because the fixed identity tells us nothing but faulted assumptions about other individuals or groups of people whose subordination is invisible. The meaning of intersectionality can make sense only through contextual demonstrations, not through static or fixed identity. I see the incompleteness of intersectionality is not a weakness but a feature of avoiding exclusiveness and for seeking inclusiveness.

In the third point Kocięda made, intersectionality and simultaneousness are both raised and I will expound on this point in a deeper way. Unfortunately, the author did not see that intersectionality analyses actually go side by side simultaneously in a dynastic and fluid cooperation at the best. Fortunately, the author finally gave a better metaphor to summarize the point: a better analogy would be that the grand trio—race, gender, and class—are different lanes on the same highway, rather than separate roads that sporadically intersect. This metaphor does a great job illustrating how intersectionality embraces the complexity of unfixed identity in any given changeable person, along with their changeable belonging to different categories.

Eleanor Robertson wrote in her "In Defense of Intersectionality—One of Feminism's Most Important Tools":[46] Like the word "feminist" itself, there is disagreement about exactly what it means, but that's par for the course in any developing ideology. So why is it taking so long for mainstream feminists to follow? Why are discussions of race, class, and disability within feminism so often characterized as infighting, or sideshows to the main event? She further pointed out: for some strange reason, marginalized women's experiences with intersectionality and its usefulness are systematically ignored and discredited. I agree with this point and she is right to say that intersectionality is alive and kicking all around us, and not just in exclusive ivory tower gender studies clubs.

In summary, using her words, feminists need to take a long, hard look at why so much of our effort is being expended on making up reasons why we cannot possibly be expected to help the least privileged women among us. We must strengthen the theory of intersectionality as one of the most important tools to clarify problems of marginalization, let all the disadvantaged women's experiences be heard through intersectionality analysis.

Speaking of intersectionality as a social movement as one of the "six important themes from mapping the movements of intersectionality,"[47] the authors see intersectionality situated within Critical Race Theory, but it moves us "to bring the often hidden dynamics forward in order to transform them."[48] Therefore, these contributors provide a conceptual template "that respond to this dynamic view of power and facilitate more productive efforts to transform these structures."[49] To me, this is the most accurate summary of the intersectionality approach and about what it is and what it is doing for social change. I am not sure about the second theme that claims, "there is no a priori place for intersectionality in either its discipline of origin, or more broadly in the academy itself."[50] If there is not a prerequisite for a deeper commitment to common goodness for all, how could we collaborate with others striving for a decent society or a global village?

In a recent article, "A Personal, Professional, and Political Journey as a Feminist Gerontologist" (2017), Nancy R. Hooyman argues for feminist philosophy and its embrace of intersectionality.[51] According to her, we need to collaborate with other marginalized people to address intersecting inequalities to move toward a caring society.[52] Because of the gendered nature of the life course and the resultant inequities experienced by women as givers and recipients of care, gender matters in long-term care. Extending this analysis beyond the private sphere of family care, Hooyman argues that the interconnections between underpaid care by families and between low status caregivers and care recipients must be made visible to ensure gender justice across the life course. Furthermore, in a vision for the future, she aims to integrate her personal and administrative experiences into a broader narrative toward a society in which "caring relationships and interdependence . . . are truly valued by society as a whole."[53] This is similar to the idea emphasized in critical ethics of care and I will enhance it in assessing Held's thoughts on it in chapter 5. Toward the end of the article, Hooyman emphasizes that "Implementing feminist values and an intersectional approach in all of their interactions, they eloquently articulate that as long as caregiving is viewed as a private duty rather than a 'public value,' the economic disadvantage of women who do this work will continue."[54] I see this as echoing Tronto's viewpoint against privatization of care in *Caring Democracy* (2013).

In this chapter, I started to interpret feminist views of sex difference and equality. I examined the merit and weakness of the ethics of caring in its early version; its focus on particularity through women's moral practice brings our attention to the important aspect of moral reasoning, the situated context, and concrete relationships of moral agents. The debates of inessential women in feminist self-criticism methodologically deepen feminist challenges into the core of epistemology, which inspires me to seek for a more democratic conception of women's equality: it must be antiessentialist and inclusive. I also discussed a new version of the ethic of care, a critical relational approach in contrast with the traditional right-based or obligatory approach. This critical ethic of care with the social relational approach has the merit of paying attention to both: the concrete situation of moral agents in power relations with others, and the social structure shaped by the existing norms of the society while it continues to shape, maintain, and strengthen the existent gender norms. Lastly, in analyzing intersectionality and its association with social justice and further connecting to caring democracy, I see a hope of feminist integration of justice and care toward a democratic caring society.

NOTES

1. Deborah L. Rhode, ed., *Theoretical Perspectives on Sexual Difference* (New Haven: Yale University Press, 1990), 3.

2. Rhode, *Theoretical Perspectives,* 4.

3. Rhode, *Theoretical Perspectives,* 5.

4. Carol Gilligan, *In a Different Voice: Psychological Theory and Women's Development* (Cambridge: Harvard University Press, 1982), 31, 160–64, 173–74.

5. Nel Noddings, "Caring," in *Justice and Care: Essential Readings in Feminist Ethics*, ed. Virginia Held (Boulder: Westview Press, 1995), 11–12.

6. Noddings, "Caring," 26.

7. Noddings, "Caring," 26.

8. Noddings, "Caring," 26.

9. Noddings, "Caring," 26.

10. Noddings, "Caring," 27.

11. Marilyn Friedman, *What Are Friends For? Feminist Perspectives on Personal Relationships and Moral Theory* (Ithaca: Cornell University Press, 1993), 151.

12. Joan C. Tronto, "Women and Caring: What Can Feminists Learn about Morality from Caring?" in *Gender/Body/Knowledge: Feminist Reconstructions of Being and Knowing,* ed. Alison M. Jaggar and Susan R. Bordo (New Brunswick: Rutgers University Press, 1989), 178.

13. Jean Grimshaw, *Feminist Philosophers* (Brighton, England: Wheatsheaf Books, 1986), 182–83.

14. Alison M. Jaggar, "Caring as a Feminist Practice of Moral Reason," in *Justice and Care: Essential Readings in Feminist Ethics*, ed. Virginia Held (Boulder: Westview Press, 1995), 193, 195.

15. Jaggar, "Caring as a Feminist Practice of Moral Reason," 193.

16. Jaggar, "Caring as a Feminist Practice of Moral Reason," 195.

17. Tronto, "Women and Caring," 185.

18. Fiona Robinson, *Globalizing Care: Ethics, Feminist Theory, and International Relations* (Boulder: Westview Press, 1999), 33.

19. Elizabeth Spelman, *Inessential Woman: Problems of Exclusion in Feminist Thought* (Boston: Beacon Press, 1988), 125.

20. Susan M. Okin, "Gender Inequality and Cultural Differences," *Political Theory* 22, no. 1 (1994): 7.

21. Jane Flax, "Race/Gender and the Ethics of Difference: A Reply to Okin's 'Gender Inequality and Cultural Differences,'" *Political Theory* 23, no. 3 (August 1995): 501.

22. Flax, "Race/Gender and the Ethics of Difference," 502.

23. Spelman, *Inessential Woman*, 148.

24. Spelman, *Inessential Woman*, 157.

25. Spelman, *Inessential Woman*, 183.

26. Spelman, *Inessential Woman*, 185.

27. Charlotte Witt, *The Metaphysics of Gender* (New York: Oxford University Press, 2011), 6.

28. Martha Minow, *Making All the Difference: Inclusion, Exclusion, and American Law* (Ithaca: Cornell University Press, 1990), 20–21.

29. Minow, *Making All the Difference,* 117.

30. Minow, *Making All the Difference,* 211.

31. Minow, *Making All the Difference,* 217.

32. Minow, *Making All the Difference,* 218.

33. Jaggar, "Caring as a Feminist Practice of Moral Reason," 197.

34. Robinson, *Globalizing Care,* 103.

35. Robinson, *Globalizing Care,* 128–29.

36. Robinson, *Globalizing Care,* 133.

37. Robinson, *Globalizing Care,* 153–54.

38. Robinson, *Globalizing Care,* 154–55.

39. Kimberle Williams Crenshaw, "Mapping the Margins: Intersectionality, Identity Politics, and Violence against Women of Color," *Stanford Law Review* 43 (1991): 1241–99; Crenshaw, "Demarginalizing the Intersection of Race and Sex: A Black Feminist Critique of Anti-Discrimination Doctrine, Feminist Theory, and Anti-racist Politics," *University of Chicago Legal Forum* 140 (1989): 139–67.

40. Patricia Hill Collins and Sirma Bilge, *Intersectionality* (Malden, MA: Polity Press, 2016), 14.

41. Collins and Bilge, *Intersectionality,* 15.

42. Jennifer C. Nash, "Re-Thinking Intersectionality," *Feminist Review* 89 (2008): 1–15.

43. Devon W. Carbado, Kimberle William Crenshaw, Vickie M. Mays, and Barbara Tomlinson, "Intersectionality: Mapping the Movements of a Theory," *Du Bois Review* 10, no. 2 (2013): 303–12.

44. Aphrodite Kocięda, "Marginalization Is Messy: Beyond Intersectionality," *Feminist Current* blog, September 26, 2013.

45. Trina Grillo, "Anti-Essentialism and Intersectionality: Tools to Dismantle the Master's House," in *Theorizing Feminisms,* ed. Elizabeth Hackett and Sally Haslanger (New York: Oxford University Press, 2006), 30–40.

46. Eleanor Robertson, "In Defense of Intersectionality—One of Feminism's Most Important Tools," *Guardian,* December 22, 2013.

47. Carbado et al., "Intersectionality," 304.

48. Carbado et al., "Intersectionality," 312.

49. Carbado et al., "Intersectionality," 312.

50. Carbado et al., "Intersectionality," 305.

51. Nancy R. Hooyman, "A Personal, Professional, and Political Journey as a Feminist Gerontologist," *Generations: The Journal of the Western Gerontological Society* 41, no. 4 (2017): 57–63.

52. Hooyman, "A Personal, Professional, and Political Journey," 60.

53. Hooyman, "A Personal, Professional, and Political Journey," 61.

54. Hooyman, "A Personal, Professional, and Political Journey," 62.

Chapter Four

Notions of Reciprocity

Kongzi, Kant, Beauvoir, and
Critiques of Gender Roles

In this chapter, I will compare the three meanings of notions of reciprocity: they are Kongzi's golden rule, Kant's categorical imperative (CI), and Beauvoir's reciprocal claim. I will trace their implications and influences in Chinese women's status and inferiority and analyze whether the reciprocal claim can help women improve and promote their equality and empowerment under the Confucian idea of social harmony without an oppressive hierarchy, which is compatible with feminist ethics of care. I will explore feminist perceptions on gender roles and issues of reciprocity and how these critiques against patriarchal domination lead to a democratization to promote women's rights in participating in politics.

When I met the female vice president of Peking University, Yue Sulan, she pointed out that there were no women in the current political standing bureau of the Chinese Communist Party, which is known around the world as having a severely low ratio of women's participation at the top leadership rank in China. I was a visiting scholar at the university's Women's Studies Center at the time, December 27, 2009, and I agreed with her that the lack of women representatives in leadership positions shows that women's status in general is going backward rather than making progress. As a woman living through Mao and post-Mao eras, I am deeply concerned with women's status and issues of equality, and I try to explore what could be the cause of women's inferiority. My concern is focusing on a clarification of causes and effects impacting women's subordination through a comparative analysis of three approaches regarding equality or reciprocity issues—Kongzi's Golden

Rule, Kant's CI, and existentialist feminist Beauvoir's reciprocity claim—and their associated issues in gender roles.

CAN CONFUCIANISM HELP IN GENDER EQUALITY?

Hall and Ames answered "yes" in their book, *The Democracy of the Dead.* [1] They argue that the qualitative notion of equality from the Confucius Golden Rule (CGR), the Confucian concept of reciprocity, can provide insights of gender equality. The example they use to support the idea of reciprocity is the father to son relationship: a son's duties will be balanced by his privileges as a parent; similarly one's role as benefactor during his middle years will be paid back when one grows old. However, they have not explained gender relations: the role of being a submissive "wife" would never be balanced across a boundary of being a husband, a superior, in *LiJi* (*The Records of Rites*).

Mary Bockover also answers "yes" in her lecture at Fresno City College on April 4, 2003. She argues that by recasting five basic relationships in the Confucian concept of a person, which are relational, hierarchical, and reciprocal, we can change one of the five (father to son, elder to younger brother, husband to wife, ruler to subject, and benefactor to beneficiary): "husband to wife" into "partner to partner." Therefore, Confucianism does not have to maintain sexism.

My response to the above two arguments is the following: First, in the relationship between a supreme ruler and inferior subject, it was supposed that the ruled must play loyal roles to the ruler in order to be protected. This hierarchy was rigid and inflexible enough to oppress the powerless ruled. Similar situations occurred in husband to wife: women must play their obedience roles appropriately. Most likely, a woman is the benefactor rather than a beneficiary in one's lifetime, caring for her family under a stereotyped division of labor in gender norms. No satisfactory explanation can be found in their argument about how to achieve real equality of the husband and wife if women must be virtuous women through self-cultivation of practicing threefold obedience. Second, Bockover's recasting partnership may not work since the social hierarchy presupposed women as subordinators rather than being equally valued to their husbands.

Hall and Ames reply to these responses and quote, "Hierarchy need not be as rigid and inflexible as it is often thought to be." [2]

Possible responses again can be: Hierarchy could not be as rigid as it is thought in the case of father to son, but not in the case of husband to wife, and ruler to subject. There are more rigid power relations there. According to Hall and Ames, the concept of a person as a specific matrix of roles "will not tolerate any assertion of natural equality." [3] From this natural inequality as a descriptive claim, Confucianism goes to a normative claim implicated in women's obedience, women should be humble and men respectable (*Liji*). A great neo-Confucian Zhu Xi claims: "A wife submits herself to the will of another; her rectitude consists of not following her own will,"[4] which is a devaluation of women, not merely natural inequality.

I continue to argue: a reciprocal relation can work only if it is based on a principle of equal concern and respect, but if the Confucian notion of reciprocity was taken as a kind of psychological reasoning, how could the Confucian role of ethics cope with this concern? The reciprocal is one of the three that constitutes the concept of person. The hierarchical relationship could rule out the partnership because it advocates women's special virtues of subordination as self-cultivation to serve others; we won't have grounds to reach a social ideal of justice for all. In a word, the conflicts between reciprocal and hierarchical relations of persons have not been explained in trying to save Confucianism from sexism.

Sin Yee Chan discusses that how the conception of gender plays out in the context of the Confucian relationship role system and argues that "this conception of gender can neither justify those forms of subordination of women, nor itself be justified on Confucian grounds."[5] She emphasizes the husband-wife relationship "is governed by the principle of distinction,"[6] which is only "a functional distinction."[7] She continues to argue, "While reciprocity cannot entirely eliminate hierarchy, it still ensures that the reciprocating parties have moral duties to each other and enjoy equal status as bearers of moral claims,"[8] and "reciprocity gives women as mothers leverage over males as sons"[9] because they, as mothers, like fathers, have contributed to the care and love of their children, and the children should reciprocate with filial piety to both parents. Therefore, she concludes, though reciprocity in the whole system does not change the fact that female gender as a whole is subordinate to the male gender, "it does help to ameliorate the subordination of women substantially."[10]

To me, Chan rightly points out that the Confucian concept of the gender role system cannot be justified by itself on the Confucian grounds, but her conclusion seems suspicious since she recasts the husband-wife relations with the parents-sons relations. They should not be the same at all if we take Confucian views of gender roles seriously.[11] The problem of distinctive functional roles of gender easily falls into an oppressive hierarchy of gender as gender stereotypes.

Are there any other alternatives to defend on Confucian ethics of *ren* (goodness, benevolence, or humanity) that would go along with a social ideal of gender equality? We need to look at Kongzi's original thoughts of *ren* and *li*, and *zhong* and *shu* (reciprocity) carefully and compare these insights with Kant's CI or a principle of equal concern and respect for the clarification of the issues surrounding women's equality through notions of reciprocity. I argue, in particular, that early Confucians such as Kongzi's and Mengzi's notion of reciprocity is far beyond psychological reasoning; rather, the ontological oneness of *ren* can have hope for balancing personhood of relational, functional, distinctive, and reciprocal as a whole.

CONFUCIAN GOLDEN RULE IN COMPARISON WITH KANT'S CATEGORICAL IMPERATIVE

In the *Analects* 15.24: "Is there one teaching that can serve as a guide for one's entire life?" The master answers, "Is it not 'sympathetic understanding' (*shu*)? Do not impose upon others what you yourself do not desire." Zeng said, "All that the Master teaches amounts to nothing more than dutifulness [*zhong*] tempered by, sympathetic understanding [*shu*]."[12]

Shu is known as a "measuring square," from a short but very important Confucian moral text *Daxue*: "What you would dislike in your superior do not use in employing your inferior; what you would dislike in your inferior do not use in serving your superior; what you would dislike in the one who precedes you, do not use in dealing with the one who comes after you; what you would dislike in the one who comes after you, do not use in dealing with the one who precedes you."[13]

Although David S. Nivison has remarked that CGR does not say, simply, treat another as you would have another treat you,[14] there is little reason to reach for a more complex formulation. Kongzi is only making it plain that, in developing a sympathetic understanding of how we should treat one another, we ought to consider the relational structure that we obtain depending on how others act toward us—either in vertical relations of the superior and inferior, or in horizontal relations of coming before or after.

When applying the square into familiar social, familial, and political relationship, distinctions of precedence and authority are taken for granted. *Zhong* means trying one's best to keep one's words (good faith) and hold oneself to responsibilities generated by one's own personal commitments and promises. *Zhong* means "loyalty" toward superiors or equals but not necessarily to inferiors. Nivison further explains: *shu* means that "you must treat your inferiors not callously and harshly but with decorum and civility"[15] and in accord with the rites. This confirms the *shu* relating to the rites; what is about *zhong* and *ren*? If we read the *Analects* 12.2 and 5.19, we agree with Nivison, "not letting any personal feeling interfere, and qualifying as *zhong* thereby." So, one is "loyal" in the real sense, "one does not follow one's ruler no matter what; one follows the Way—the requirements of public morality of a person in one's role."[16] I think here the meaning of loyalty beyond a level of feeling or favor but rather at the serious sense of duty—duty to follow the way, the heaven's will for people to be identified through under-

standing, also the way of *ren*—is the way of heaven; this is obviously con-
firmed in the Confucian concept of rectification of names in 12.11: "Let the
lord be a true lord, the ministers true ministers, the fathers true fathers, and
the sons true sons." The same issue is addressed in 13.3.[17] In this advice,
Kongzi emphasizes that self-cultivated persons should be fulfilling role-spe-
cific duties. To each of us, in all the five relations of society, personal roles
must relate to social responsibilities. Therefore, *zhong* and *shu* closely relate
to the social responsibility one must follow, and the measuring square is a
social web to understand how we should treat each other in living well to
meet heaven's identity, which is neither an individually based reciprocity,
nor a pure psychological reasoning.

Moreover, what exactly is *ren* about? *Ren* is asked about more than a
hundred times in the *Analects*, and according to Kongzi, it is very hard to
understand. He replies through examples such as in 14.16: "It was Guan
Zhong's strength that allowed Duke Huan, on many occasions, to harmoniously unite the feudal lords without the use of military force. But as for his
Goodness, as for his Goodness."[18] It is obvious that, in the Confucian social
system, *zhong* and *shu* direct persons to play out their roles and accomplish
their duties through self-discipline and self-cultivation so that harmonious
orders will ensue and the society will be prosperous. The notion of reciprocity is based upon a network square, either family or public office, but not on
individualist awards. Are there any constructive insights to compare this
notion of reciprocity with Kantian's principle of reciprocity?

On Nivison's view, the concepts *zhong* and *shu* work together to provide
universalizable laws within a "rich structure of qualification."[19] Kantian CI
would seem to dictate that we tell the truth without exception, even to a
murderer who wants to know where our friend went. By contrast, CGR
operates in a field of tension that allows us to apprehend, on the one hand,
our duty (or *zhong*) to tell the truth, while on the other hand our sense of
compassion (or *shu*) compels us to discern the exceptionally dangerous threat
exemplified, for example, in a murderer's relation to our friend. Yet, according to Kantian CI, one should never tell a lie, no matter what the circumstances are; what matters is that our actions pass the universality test of the
Kantian moral law: to tell the truth. But on Nivison's view, this is *zhong*
without *shu*, and therefore, by the standard of CGR, incomplete. Would you
want your friend to tell the murderer where *you* are?

CGR has different reciprocated expectations with *zhong* and *shu* respect-
fully in the same case: someone else "down there" is to be hurt by my act if I
tell the truth. So the issue is whether I would be willing to accept the hurt
myself; if I would not, I am to hold off. This would be the application with
shu. "Thus, *shu* is a directive for amending or suspending rules, or applying
them flexibly; hence its association with *li*, 'rites,' which are rules that are
flexible and humane."[20] *Zhong*, on the other hand, directs me to notice that,

when hesitating to follow a rule governing my behavior toward someone "up there," it is a rule I would expect all to follow no matter what. "Thus *zhong* is a directive for self-discipline, and for holding rules firm."[21] Through this comparison, we see the flexibility and network-based understanding in the Confucian notion of reciprocity, but how is it relevant to women's status and their self-cultivation? There are only a few advices or descriptions about women in the *Analects*, and this is not a surprise considering, among the legendary three thousand disciples of Confucius or Kongzi, there were no women. As I and other scholars argue, the Confucian conception of gender implies the threefold exclusion of women "from political participation, and thus from the idea of *junzi* and, consequently, from a Confucian education."[22] Although the *Analects* doesn't provide a sufficient view of women, the Confucian conception of gender does appear in one of the world famous Four Books and Five Classics of Chinese civilization, the *LiJi*, which prescribes women's supreme virtues as threefold obedience and outlines four virtues for them to follow.[23] However, from Kongzi's Golden Rule, we do not get a women's oppressed view if we take the *shu* seriously, because a *junzi* as a husband should treat his wife with love and respect as much as he is able based on his sympathetic understanding. In Kant's CI, we may not be as flexible as we could to hold onto those actions based on our sympathy because the universal law of logic would block out any inclinations from situated persons. Kant values the rationality in moral reasoning to do the right thing, and he thinks women are less capable of being rational thinkers of moral issues, so, therefore, he believes women to be morally inferior to men.[24]

According to Tu Weiming, Confucianism seems to offer a sensible start by stressing personal responsibility, communal rituals, and common good of the community. He claims, "[Despite] an apparently rigid hierarchy, Confucianism cherishes at its heart, equality in education and the *Li* (pattern, principle) of change. These two principles, an equal opportunity to learning and an attitude of openness and flexibility, do not counter feminism. Rather, this is where the two philosophies meet and where they are most able to reinforce each other."[25] Tu's view is largely right but it lacks a gender-related specific analysis.

When asked what he set his heart on, Kongzi said in 5.26: "To bring peace to the old, to have trust in my friends, and to cherish the young."[26] Mengzi also advocates that we extend the love to include people in the world. Nothing forced is in this extension of love because the original natures of all men have in them a feeling of mercy, which makes it impossible for them to bear to see the suffering of others.[27] Nevertheless, does this love or care necessarily lead to women's equal concern? It seems not in the norms of social hierarchy. Chinese sociologist Li Yinhe conducted a social investigation about gender issues in Shanxi Province in 2009 and found a social phenomenon that wives in a village were not allowed to eat at the table with their husbands (they were the last persons to eat after making the meals).[28] Without a contextual analysis of how the reciprocity influences women's distinctive role playing, it is not clear that *ren* would take care of all people fairly, especially in women's realities. Nevertheless, the impact of stereotypes regarding women's devaluations may not come directly from Kong/Meng Confucian ethics but from later Confucianism during the Han dynasty and secular ethics of gender through a long history toward today's practice of systematic sexism. Nevertheless, the idealist Confucian role ethics does not offer any challenges against a view of women's inferiority but are tolerant and reinforce women's self-cultivation to accept inequality and injustice, which conflict with the original way of *ren*.

EXISTENTIALIST FEMINIST
BEAUVOIR'S RECIPROCITY CLAIM

The feminist existentialist argument on issues of reciprocity provides an explanation of women's oppressive situations, which differ from concerns of individual equality. Simone de Beauvoir worked out an original form of feminism based on the existentialist philosophy that she and Sartre had developed.[29] Sartre argues that we all have freedom to make ourselves through constantly choosing and acting. Hence, there is no human essence in human but we are free to make who we are, and we must be responsible for what we have chosen. As Alison Stone explains, Sartre holds that one is "fundamentally aware of other people as beings who are free," as *subjects*, by which Sartre means that they are not objects but "authors of their lives." One becomes aware of others as free beings whenever one experiences oneself "being looked at by them."[30] In Sartre's view, every experience of being looked at threatens one's freedom, but as Stone explains, we "each reassert our freedom by determining to view any other person whose look threatens us as a mere object, defined by their body and by fixed properties, and so not really qualified to threaten our own freedom."[31] Beauvoir would sum up this situation as one that "sets up a reciprocal claim."[32]

Beauvoir explains, throughout history women have failed to make these reciprocal claims.[33] Men have followed their tendency to objectify women, but women have not objectified men in turn. Instead, women have internalized and normalized men's view that women are defined by their bodies and their fixed characteristics. So man is the norm and woman is other than the subject: woman as *Otherness*. This notion of woman as *Other* has three parts: first, men had freedom to create their own values (particularly conquering nature) when they hunted, while women tended to their children and domestic care; secondly women accepted men's objectification of women because it pervades Western culture and women had very limited freedom to choose their life; third it is beneficial for women to align with men's view of them, otherwise they would probably be judged to be acting contrary to "women's nature," which would arouse many men's hostility, hence, it benefits women to collude with men's view of them.[34] In Beauvoir's view, women are deceived and seduced into self-deception by men, so it is not completely women's fault but rather they are oppressed.[35]

The lack of reciprocal claim is the root of women's oppression. But why is it that women cannot set up a reciprocal claim to become subjects? Stone uses a philosophical distinction between immanence and transcendence to explain Beauvoir's analysis of gender oppression: oppression as being deceived or tempted into not exercising one's freedom. Stone notices that Sartre views the female body in a negative way because immanence had all along been symbolized as female. If a life of transcendence is the best human life as Sartre confirms, what is symbolically male's (transcendence) is superior to what is symbolically female (immanence), then it seems that women should take on symbolically male traits in order to be free. However, according to Stone, Beauvoir unlike Sartre, does not actually favor a life of sheer transcendence. In *Ethics of Ambiguity* (1947), "all human lives are lives partly of transcendence and partly of immanence."[36] Men have had difficulty recognizing their immanence side, but for Beauvoir, "both sexes should learn to recognize their ambiguity."[37] Rather than valuing transcendence as opposing to immanence, she considers both should be valuable. Rather than wanting women to become symbolically male, "Beauvoir wants both men and women to take on symbolically male (transcendence) and female (immanence) traits."[38] The insight has led Beauvoir to create a distinctive form of feminism: the root of women's subordination is that they have been confined to immanence, but "this can and should be changed,"[39] as Stone emphasized. I think we can further carry on the insight to call that both men and women need to embrace their gender ambiguities. Women should not only be striving to reach a transcendent state, but men should also embrace a state of immanence. By recognizing that these qualities coexist in the same person, we give equal value to all individuals and their various roles in society. What we should change is a matter of redefining and redistributing these symbolic behaviors more fairly, which might be a revolutionary task to eliminate existing sexism in robust stereotypes of norms.

Jack Reynolds also noticed that Beauvoir's notion of freedom is different from Sartre's ontological or absolute freedom on the one hand, but also a more practical freedom "that is freedom to do something or to effect concrete changes in the world."[40] If women lack practical freedom for long enough then they cannot conceive of changing things in the world and this can actually impinge on their ontological freedom. "In other words, if some people are oppressed for long enough their ontological freedom can actually be modified and reduced."[41] That is the case for women in general and, therefore, Beauvoir argues that, when women do not revolt against sexual inequality in part because they have lost a sense of ontological freedom in a historical transformation of patriarchal domination, then women should themselves be held partially responsible for their oppression.

How does the above view shed light on women's status in Confucian society? First, as I see it, the secular Confucian views of women in the *LiJi* have had more than two thousand years to influence people's stereotyped views of women as having inferior social roles, depoliticizing gender-role theory, so that those stereotypes continue to devalue and silence women, suppressing women into not making their reciprocal claim. Even worse, women have internalized the dominant male view, causing women to look down on *themselves*. Second, though Kongzi and Mengzi do not advocate oppressive views of women directly, the secular Confucian ideology did, and continues to do so, without confronting any serious challenges to systemic patriarchal domination. I argue sex/gender equality must go along with a real democratic system (Yuan 2005); thus, unless women's voices are heard with a fair weight of reciprocity claims, there would be no serious discussions of gender justice and equality. Furthermore, gender justice/equality has been integrated in issues of caring democracy that will be involved in political considerations, hence, the depoliticalization of gender roles in reciprocity does not seem to be a sound viewpoint.

BEYOND GENDER-NEUTRAL RECIPROCITY AND ETHICS OF CARE

Under the Confucian idea of social harmony, which might be compatible with feminist ethics of care, its notion of reciprocity can be defended only if it is integrated with gender justice implied in Beauvoir's notion of reciprocal claim as a humanistic approach in analyzing women's realities. How is the notion of reciprocal claim integrated into Confucian notion of reciprocity in order to embrace a deep commitment of equal concern and respect to all people no matter what different functional roles they may play?

The issue of sex/gender equality has become more complicated in the contemporary world. A phenomenon known as the feminization of poverty is evident in China as Chinese women were encouraged to go back home and perform the role of domestic caregiver under the influence of Confucianism. The cultural representations of femininity definitely affect women's political authority as well as their economic ability to compete in job markets. These three elements of politics, economy, and culture combine together to affect women's roles and strengthen the traditional secular views of women as inferior to men.

The defenders of Confucianism interpreted the concept of self as universal among men and women, and reciprocity is a feature of the self. But there is a precondition necessary to actualize the selfhood: the political authority, or using feminist words, "the personal is political." Without political power, women cannot establish the authority to speak up for their own needs and interests. The underrepresentation of women in top decision-making roles illustrates the scale required to achieve sexual equality. Political authorities tend to silence women's voices if they conflict with the authorities' goals. I will argue that the Golden Rule at the heart of Confucianism has a wonderful expression of partnership between men and women but practical implementation could not be achieved because it excludes women's voices in a sense of power-imbalance relations.

How can we project the idealist concept of selfhood and reciprocity in Confucianism while overcoming the exclusion of women in the nonideal Confucian society? I argue that feminist ethics of care can contribute to this project with Held's argument: "One way in which the ethics of care does resemble Confucian ethics is in its rejection of the sharp split between public and private." She continues, "The ethics of care advocates care as a value for society as well as household."[42] Here we can see the two adopt each other in terms of cherishing "the interdependencies of personal, political, economic, and global contexts."[43] Furthermore, Held also notices that "In political and economic contexts, care as benevolence and as motive fails to understand the relations of power that can so easily undermine the value of care."[44] Held's view reminds of the weakness of early Confucian idealist notion of reciprocity: although it does not necessarily lead to an oppressive view of women, it does not offer analysis in a broad vision of how relational selfhood could be relational power in favor of the powerful in the social hierarchal harmony. Since it is taken as a psychological based reciprocity, it has its limitations of its own account in its historical moment. Nevertheless, as Held suggests, "But when we focus on relations, we can come to see how to shape good caring relations so that differences in power will not be pernicious and so that the vulnerable are empowered."[45] Confucianism ultimately summarizes the importance of human virtues into the *ren* (ultimate goodness): the *ren* being ultimately the most important and supreme virtue to follow at all times. If *ren* calls for the liberation and equality of women, then *ren* is still being followed. *Ren* and *shu* (sympathetic understanding or reciprocity) should not be mutually exclusive but harmoniously collaborative. "What makes our world valuable to us is, above all, love that is gladly embraced."[46] *Ren* represents a valuable love that would not allow women to be subordinated.

SEX ROLES AND RECIPROCITY

Women's subordinated situations in the post-Mao era have brought up feminists' attention and enquiry: the traditional view of women's virtues of serving others and the view of different sex roles in the division of labor have influenced women's limited choices to stay home in order to support the husbands' bigger success. Meanwhile, the sex/gender sameness in Mao's time is out of date and the gender gap is increasing. Encountering the rapid changes in women's situations and the decline in women's status, Chinese feminists have been puzzled about how to pursue the social ideal of women's equality.

Chinese feminists realize that the idea of equal opportunity did not help women promote their status if it only meant equal competition in the rapid economic development. The revival of the Confucian view of women's proper roles and new opportunities for women's development put double-role expectations on women and increased their double burdens. The Confucian view of women emphasizes the innate difference of sexes, and so sex roles, which has never been seriously examined during the revolutionary movements in Mao's time.

The real opportunities for women need a material base along with other preconditions for pursuing equal opportunities. What counts as a material base is an issue on which feminists and nonfeminists may hold different views. Male dominant norms would not consider women's needs and interests as they prioritized as their own. In order to assess why the model of equal opportunity did not help women in eliminating their subordination, we need to discuss three related issues briefly: argument against the view of natural sex roles; what a necessary material base for sex equality is from feminist perspectives; and equal opportunity must consider unequal treatment in regards of sex.

Why have people persisted in their belief that there are inherent natural roles for men and women even if they know that sex roles are the product of socialization rather than naturalization? Ferguson gave a convincing answer to this question: "Sex-role ideologies mystify the existing power relations between men and women and economic classes. This mystification justifies the social and economic roles of two dominant groups: men as a caste, on the one hand, and the dominant economic class on the other."[47]

Thus, some feminists advocate the idea of androgyny rather than sex difference. The discussion of androgyny can be summarized as follows: we need a new model of human development; what a good person is like rather than what a woman is like or what a man is like. A good society should enhance a variety of opportunities for a person's free choice and sexual equality by law is the necessary condition for implementing a new model and a neutral standard for a good person and a good society. The first step for

androgyny supporters is to criticize the sex stereotypes by exposing its in-
valid arguments.

Joyce Trebilcot has shown three major ways in which the claims have
been made that natural differences between the sexes prescribe sex roles that
are inevitable, well-being, and efficient. None of them are valid, according to
Trebilcot's arguments. [48]

The advocates of inevitable sex roles held that if there are innate psychological differences between females and males, sex roles are inevitable. The
point is: whatever we decide, there will be sex roles, if we accept the premise
that there are innate differences between the sexes. As Trebilcot states, even
if we accept the premises that the natural and behavioral differences are
inevitable, does it follow that there must be sex roles, that is, the social
institutions must enforce correlations between roles and sex? Surely not!

Why bother to direct women into some roles and men into others if the
pattern occurs regardless of the nature of society? Here, Trebilcot exposes
precisely that this argument fails to show its conclusion that sex roles are
inevitable. Its premises can only entail that there will be roles by nature but
not that certain roles are natural. John S. Mill makes this point very elegantly
in *The Subjection of Women,* as Trebilcot describes: The anxiety of mankind
to interfere in behalf of nature, for fear lest nature should not succeed in
effecting its purpose, is an altogether unnecessary solicitude. [49]

The second argument claims that, because of natural psychological differences between the sexes, the members of each sex are happier in certain roles
than in others, and roles that tend to promote happiness are different for each
sex. In addition, if all roles are equally available to everyone, it is possible for
some individuals to choose against their own well-being, hence, for the sake
of maximizing well-being, there should be sex roles: the society should encourage individuals to make "correct" role choices. Trebilcot pointed out that
the conclusion of this argument needs to add another assumption; that is, the
loss of the potential well-being resulting from society-produced adoption of
unsuitable roles by some individuals is less than the loss that would result
from "mistaken" free choices if there were no sex roles. But how do we know
which system is better than the other? Surely, "we are not now in a position
to compare the two systems with respect to the number of mismatches produced." [50] Hence, the conclusion that overall well-being is greater with sex
roles than without them is entirely unsustainable.

The third argument is concerned with efficiency: in order to save time and
effort for proficiency training, we are better to select the more talented than
the less talented. If there are natural differences between the sexes in capacity
to perform socially valuable tasks, then, efficiency is served if these tasks are
assigned to the sex with the greatest innate ability for them. This conclusion
is too weak when compared with the reasons against sex roles, according to
Trebilcot, because in order to determine whether there should be sex roles,

one would have to weigh efficiency, together with other reasons for such roles, against reasons for holding that there should not be sex roles, yet these reasons "are very couched in terms of individual rights—in terms of liberty, justice, equality of opportunity."[51] Therefore, "Efficiency by itself does not outweigh these moral values."[52] As I understand, efficiency, though it appeals to natural capability of each sex, if it is true, it is also a value that could be based on some prejudices, because the artificial selection is very likely not fair for all candidates regardless of their sex.

All these arguments in support of the view that there should be sex roles are based on a presupposition of natural psychological differences between men and women. It seems to me that this presupposition is not true, because it is just a common presumption made by all male-centered cultures and it is supported by biological determinism. But this presumption is not true because we are not in the position to know whether these sex differences are natural or not.

Contemporary liberal feminists believe that there are certain material preconditions for genuine equality of rights. Poverty is the most obvious factor, which prevents individuals from exercising rights.[53] Liberal feminists consider that equality of opportunity requires equality in children's early education and environment. These thoughts are beyond classic commitment to a formal, sex neutral equality for women, and they are not compatible with the conception of abstract individuals.[54]

Although a material base should be considered as important as one of the necessary premises for people's equal opportunity, it by itself could be irrelevant to the issue of sex equality if it only matters to economic category. Fortunately, feminists realize that what counts as the material base should not be limited only to the economic relationship, and that there are many more relations to be involved in the material base for human activities. Sandra Harding argues for this viewpoint in her article, "What Is the Real Material Base of Patriarchy and Capital?"[55] She criticizes that the Marxist explanation of material base is limited to economic relations analysis and fails to recognize the crucial aspects of social relations of family life and fundamental causes of social conditions. She suggests that the revision in the concept of the material base of capitalism should take seriously the two points drawn from the work of Nancy Chodorow and Jane Flax: First, is that gender and personhood are inseparable because people are distinctively gendered by the process of becoming persons.[56] Second, is that gender is not value-neutral because our division of labor by gender itself produces the repression of infantile experience in both boys and girls.[57]

Socialist feminists proposed a much wider interpretation of what counts as the material base of society. In the socialist feminist view, not only do the human needs for food, shelter, and clothing, but also the needs for children, sexual satisfaction, and emotional nurturance undergo a continuous historical process of transformation. Furthermore, not only are the means to satisfy the needs for familial, sexual, and emotional life produced through human labor; humans can also distribute and exchange the means of fulfilling these needs. Therefore, the system of producing and distributing the means to satisfy those needs is in fact an economic system. In making this point, socialist feminists agree with the radical feminist insightful view, which identifies sexuality and procreation as areas of human activity. Socialist feminists claim that these human practices fall within the domain of political economy.[58]

These feminist perspectives use the conceptual tool of the sexual division of labor to explore relations between women's subordination, the male-defined economic systems, and the sex/gender system. These feminists perceive that the conditions of women's lives are determined not only by the ruling class, but also by men. They see that men of all classes benefit directly though in different ways from women's labor.

The systematic domination of women by men has been so obscure in Marxism that it is not central to Marxist political economy. Hence, Marxist interpretation of the economic base of society is limited and sex blind.

A new conception of the material base of society, from different feminist perspectives, must include the sphere of sexuality and procreation. Without a careful exploration of those special ways of organizing childbearing and childrearing, sexuality, and emotional nurturance, it is impossible to give a more adequate explanation of the pervasiveness and persistence of male dominance.[59]

If we add feminist interpretations of the material base of society to the considerations of women's equal opportunity in China, the shortcomings of this model are obvious: if material base only meant "the economic base" in classic Marxist terminology, the so-called equal opportunities is not fair to women, because it lacks the analysis of the special ways in which only females do the most jobs such as child care and family obligations. Without a thorough exploration of why women always undertake those unpaid jobs and why most cultures instruct women to follow sex roles and sexual division of labor, it would be an inadequate starting point to investigate the issue of equal opportunity. In "Gender Comparison of Employment and Career Development in China" (Wei 2011), Wei's team explored gender difference in roles and its influence on gender equality in the workplace. Although under the state policy of gender equality Chinese women seem to occupy the half sky in the job market in the face of a new socialist market economy and the rate of female employment is continually increasing, Wei noticed that there are problems in women's career development: "the majority of female employment goes to traditionally female jobs such as in health departments, education, hotels, wholesale trade and retail trade. Employed women mainly undertake the duties of nurturing, nursing, assisting, and caring, which are a social extension of their family roles."[60] These new puzzles led Wei's team in the Women's Studies Center of Peking University to work together with Sina Net to launch an online survey on issues regarding gender equality in gender comparison of employment and career development in the workplace in 2009; more than 1,800 responded to the questionnaire with 1,760 valid ones received. In the data and discussion, we see gender gaps in several respects such as professions and duties in ranks, income levels, and chances of promotion. For example, "we see that men have much higher representation among those with higher incomes. 47.3% of men reported earning more than 4000 yuan per month, while only 28.7% of women reported achieving that level, an 18.6 percentage point gap."[61] At the end of the article Wei suggests that "supportive and effective social policies should be developed in order to alleviate women's household duties caused by bearing and fostering children to allow them to work together with men without worries and troubles back at home."[62]

Unfortunately, Chinese feminist dialogues barely propose challenges to the Marxist explanation of the material base as one of the necessary conditions for women's equal opportunity. Nonetheless, Chinese feminists do provide many sociological investigations into women's subordination in the rapid economic changes of the post-Mao era. The investigation of Wei's team on women's confusion over their sex roles and identities shows us that economic opportunity matters with regard to sex. Only women have problems when their double roles (a caretaker at home and a competitor in public career) conflict each other. Men do not have such problems generally, and enjoy their equal opportunity as it appears to be in current state policies. Such a systematically social arrangement limits women's opportunity in their reality.

The model of equal opportunity does not help women if the society encourages double expectations, different gender roles for women, but a single expectation and role for men. It seems that the idea of women's equality became notorious because of women's double burdens—the conflicting domestic responsibility and heavy work in career development—and the perplexing inequality of social arrangement between genders.

The impediment to increase equality falsely led people, especially women, to turn back to the traditional views of women, rather than to a modern view of themselves as self-governing people. This backwardness in women's status, in my view, does not prove the wrongness of the social ideal of equality, but the complication, dilemma, difficulty, and toughness combined in seeking for a far-reaching social ideal of equal concern and respect as well.

I also see great hope coming from discussions of the current situation of Chinese women's inequality: the more perplexed women feel about their lives, the more conscious thinking about their subordination will emerge. The socialist feminist perspective will help Chinese women examine the classic Marxist and Maoist views of women's equality and liberation. The examination should go beyond mere economic aspect and add a critical analysis of gendered society, which is crucial in clarifying issues of women's oppression. Although I doubt that one dominant party ruling state like China would allow women and feminists to make any fundamental challenges to the dominant male-centered ideology that is supported by the existing institutional sexism, I see a great hope in the open-door policy to develop democratic thinking and women's equality. Next, I discuss women's situation in Taiwan to see how women could change their status in political participation with the government support lifting women up to the top leadership positions. In my view, the women in Taiwan strive for women's equality in the twenty-first century, which must be women-centered and empowering for women. From this example, we see that the early Confucian notion of *ren, yi, li, zhi, xin,* and reciprocity could be compatible with the contemporary view of democracy and women's rights and equality.

CONFUCIANISM, DEMOCRATIZATION, AND WOMEN'S RIGHTS IN TAIWAN

In the book, *Confucianism, Democratization, and Human Rights in Taiwan,* Fetzer and Soper discuss issues of women's right and Confucianism. They rightly point out that nothing in early Confucian documents explicitly promote gender equality, instead, what we can draw from reading Confucian documents about women is about gender roles. According to them, Confucian seems to suggest that "women are morally inferior to men"[63] and "at best Confucius promoted a kind of cult of domesticity where women ruled the home and performed the vital, but very traditional, roles of wife and mother."[64] However, as they notice, "a less literal reading that highlight key Confucian values can be meaningfully used to support the rights of women."[65] What they mean by this key value is "an idea actively promoted throughout the document."[66] Reading *Analects* 17.2, Confucius advocates that "men" are by nature "nearly alike."[67] But he constantly insists that people are not born into their distinction but through deliberate learning and virtuous behavior to earn their distinctive positions. Therefore, Fetzer and Soper speak on behalf of Confucius, "the logical implication of his commitment to equality suggests that there is no reason that they could not."[68] According to this sense of equality—what works for men must work for women—men and women might have particular functions to perform in domestic domain, yet those roles are complementary and do not imply women's inferiority to men.

To me, this argument sounds too simple to overcome women's inferiority in the distinct gender roles at home, and it fails to address serious concerns regarding gender performance in the public world. It is a gender-blind argument, perhaps coming out of good intentions to seek equality. However, arguments along these lines did succeed in countering Confucian gender discrimination and inequality in the politics of Taiwan.

Besides the idea of equality discussion, Fetzer and Soper point out another feature in reading Confucius on the status of women, their voice is silence. They state, "The rigid sexism and institutional discrimination against women in East Asian after his death was more a product of the Confucian tradition, and in particular the neo-Confucianism of the Song dynasty, than it was a necessary by-product of what Confucius himself actually taught about the role and status of women (Yao 2000, 183; Chang 2009, 6)."[69] I second this statement: what I explore in chapter 1 on Kongzi and Mengzi is compatible with this statement. I add a suggestion, that there is a hope of eliminating rigid sexism from Confucianism if we return to Kongzi's and Mengzi's original thoughts at the institutional level, but only if society is also infused with a democratizing system. Such democratization would also need to be integrated with a moral agent that is a people-oriented (*Minben*) and relational self— not with an individualistic self that remains isolated and egoist oriented.

The democratization and women's movement had emerged in Taiwan and the Taiwanese women's movement became progressively more active at the same time that the island was democratizing during the 1980s and 1990s. Over the past several decades, the democratization movement has dramatically changed the legal and political landscape for women in Taiwan. After a decade-long effort, in 2002 the government passed the Gender Equality in Employment Act that laid an important foundation for women's rights. The Democratic Progressive Party (DDP) has been particularly active in counting votes on gender issues. "Under DDP president Chen, the number of women in the cabinet increased to one-fourth of the total membership. . . . Annette Lu became Taiwan's first female Vice President in 2000," and now Tsai Ingwen is the top leader there.[70] Women of Taiwan finally entered the highest leadership posts in governing, which would be a dream pursuit for women of mainland China as they have a long way to go. What could be the reasons for women in China to participate less in politics and be silent in regard to promoting women's leadership in governance?

One sure point is that women's movement and gender equality can only be realized through a combination of democratization. *Minzhu* should not be an empty promise but a solid base to support relational but autonomous self that is *Minben*. *Minben* also should make progression toward *Minzhu*, which requires social individual rights to be treated equally as respectful subjects, in particular, rights to freely express one's voice in participation of political issues. *Minzhu* and *Minben* is complementary and compatible, not exclusive to one another. Similarly, early Confucian ideas of *ren*, *yi*, *li*, *zhi*, and *xin* are compatible with democratization.

According to Fetzer and Soper, "Confucian morality forms an even better foundation for human rights than Western thought does."[71] Taking care of people and serving people is the core value of Confucianism, and "there is no real democracy if parties are only fighting for the benefit of their own particular party."[72] They rightly point out the issues of benefiting one's own party is to keep authority and power at the cost of democratization. Early Confucianism focused on both the ruler's and the people's characters being built-up through learning and self-cultivation, developing *ren*-mind through *li* conduct regulations. Such a common-good-based ethics can be a better root to grow for a harmonious and prosperous society. Nevertheless, early Confucian ethics did not pay sufficient care for gender inequality and took social distinctive gender roles as granted.

Contemporary feminist analysis of gender roles and care ethics can provide insights about how to overcome sexist stereotypes in Chinese society and how to reform the traditional view of Confucianism toward women's participation of politics and joining top decision-making leadership, which could be a model for the progression of women's equality in mainland China. What we need to do is the integration of both, early Confucian *ren* ethics and critical feminist care ethics. Next, I will explore metaphysical and epistemic issues in the integration of care and justice from feminist care thinkers Virginia Held and others to clarify meta-ethical issues associated with ethics of care, in a dialogue with further interpretations of Kongzi's Golden Rule reciprocity to deepen the comparison.

NOTES

1. David L. Hall and Roger T. Ames, *The Democracy of the Dead: Dewey, Confucius, and the Hope for Democracy in China* (Chicago: Open Court, 1999).

2. Hall and Ames, *The Democracy of the Dead*, 160.

3. Hall and Ames, *The Democracy of the Dead*, 198.

4. Quoted in Lisa Raphals, *Sharing the Light: Representations of Women and Virtue in Early China* (Albany: State University of New York Press, 1998), 255.

5. Sin Yee Chan, "Gender and Relationship Roles in the Analects and the Mencius," in *Confucian Political Ethics*, ed. Daniel A. Bell (Princeton: Princeton University Press, 2008), 147.

6. Chan, "Gender and Relationship Roles," 156.

7. Chan, "Gender and Relationship Roles," 156.

8. Chan, "Gender and Relationship Roles," 156.

9. Chan, "Gender and Relationship Roles," 157.

10. Chan, "Gender and Relationship Roles," 156–57.

11. See Hong-mei Fu (付红梅), "The Traditional Female Ethics and Ceremony Propriety and Its Modern Value" (中国传统女性伦理与礼仪及其现代价值), *Journal of Studies in Ethics* (伦理学研究双月刊) 26, no. 6 (2006): 100–103.

12. Kongzi, *Analects* 15.24 and 4.15, quoted in *Readings in Classical Chinese Philosophy*, ed. Philip J. Ivanhoe and Bryan W. Van Norden (Indianapolis, IN: Hackett, 2005), 12 and 45–46.

13. Quoted in David S. Nivison, *The Ways of Confucianism: Investigations in Chinese Philosophy* (Chicago: Open Court, 1996), 64.

14. Nivison, *The Ways of Confucianism*, 65.

15. Nivison, *The Ways of Confucianism*, 65.

16. Nivison, *The Ways of Confucianism*, 66.
17. Kongzi, *Analects*, 36–38.
18. *Confucius Analects*, trans. by Edward Slingerland (Indianapolis, IN: Hackett, 2003), 160.
19. Nivison, *The Ways of Confucianism*, 66.
20. Nivison, *The Ways of Confucianism*, 67.
21. Nivison, *The Ways of Confucianism*, 67.
22. Chan, "Gender and Relationship Roles"; Yuan, *Reconceiving Women's Equality in China: A Critical Examination of Models of Sex Equality* (Lanham, MD: Lexington Books, 2005), 6.
23. Jun Li (李军), *Wujing Quanyi: Liji Quanyi* (五经全译: 礼记全译; Interpretations of Five Classics: Interpretations of the Records of Rites), vol. 2 (Chang Chun: Chang Chun Press, 长春: 长春出版社, 1980), 1003.
24. Jennifer Mather Saul, *Feminism: Issues & Arguments* (New York: Oxford University Press, 2003), 201.
25. Tu Weiming, "A Confucian Response to the Feminist Critique," lecture, November 2001, http://tuweiming.com/lecture7.html.
26. D. C. Lau, *Confucius: The Analects* (New York: Penguin Group, 1979), 80.
27. Mengzi (Mencius), "2B6," in *Readings in Classical Chinese Philosophy*, ed. Ivanhoe and Norden, 129.
28. See Li Yinhe (李银河), *Women in Hou Village: Power Relations of Gender in Rural Area* (后村的女人们: 农村性别权利关系) (Huhehaote: Niemenggu University Press, 呼和浩特市: 内蒙古大学出版社, 2009).
29. Lijun Yuan, "Confucian and Feminist Notions of Relational Self and Reciprocity: A Comparative Study," *Journal of East-West Thought* 5, no. 4 (2015): 5–6.
30. Simone de Beauvoir, *The Second Sex* (1949), 17, quoted in Alison Stone, *An Introduction to Feminist Philosophy* (Cambridge, UK: Polity Press, 2007), 194.
31. Stone, *An Introduction to Feminist Philosophy*, 194.
32. Stone, *An Introduction to Feminist Philosophy*, 194.
33. Stone, *An Introduction to Feminist Philosophy*, 194.
34. Stone, *An Introduction to Feminist Philosophy*, 195.
35. Stone, *An Introduction to Feminist Philosophy*, 196.
36. Simone de Beauvoir, *The Ethics of Ambiguity*, trans. Bernard Frechtman (New York: Citadel Press Stone, 1964). Quoted in Stone, *An Introduction to Feminist Philosophy*, 196–97.
37. Stone, *An Introduction to Feminist Philosophy*, 196–97.
38. Stone, *An Introduction to Feminist Philosophy*, 196–97.
39. Stone, *An Introduction to Feminist Philosophy*, 196–97.
40. Jean-Paul Sartre, *Being and Nothingness* (1943), 254–260, quoted in Jack Reynolds, *Understanding Existentialism* (Chesham, UK: Acumen Publishing, 2006), 144.
41. Reynolds, *Understanding Existentialism*, 144.
42. Virginia Held, *The Ethics of Care: Personal, Political, and Global* (Oxford: Oxford University Press, 2006), 21.
43. Held, *The Ethics of Care*, 53.
44. Held, *The Ethics of Care*, 56.
45. Held, *The Ethics of Care*, 56.
46. Richard W. Miller, *Globalizing Justice: The Ethics of Poverty and Power* (Oxford: Oxford University Press, 2010), 260.
47. Ann Ferguson, "Androgyny as an Ideal for Human Development," in *Feminism and Philosophy*, ed. Mary Vetterling-Braggin (Totowa, NJ: Rowman & Littlefield, 1977), 55.
48. Joyce Trebilcot, "Sex Roles," in *"Femininity," "Masculinity," and "Androgyny": A Modern Philosophical Discussion*, ed. Mary Vetterling-Braggin (Totowa, NJ: Littlefiels, Adams, 1982), 44.
49. Trebilcot, "Sex Roles," 44.
50. Trebilcot, "Sex Roles," 46.
51. Trebilcot, "Sex Roles," 47.
52. Trebilcot, "Sex Roles," 47.

53. Alison M. Jaggar, *Feminist Politics and Human Nature* (Totowa, NJ: Rowman & Little-field, 1988), 183.

54. Jaggar, *Feminist Politics and Human Nature*, 194.

55. Sandra Harding, "What Is the Real Material Base of Patriarchy and Capital?" in *Women and Revolution: A Discussion of the Unhappy Marriage of Marxism and Feminism*, ed. Lydia Sargent (Montreal: Black Rose Books, 1981), 135–63.

56. Charlotte Witt also holds this point and enhances it to her gender uniessentialism: see Charlotte Witt, *The Metaphysics of Gender* (New York: Oxford University Press, 2011), 10–11.

57. Harding, "What Is the Real Material Base of Patriarchy and Capital?" 152.

58. Jaggar, *Feminist Politics and Human Nature*, 135.

59. Jaggar, *Feminist Politics and Human Nature*, 138–39.

60. Guoying Wei, "Gender Comparison of Employment and Career Development in China," *Journal of Asian Women* 27, no. 1 (2011): 95–113, here 96.

61. Wei, "Gender Comparison of Employment," 100.

62. Wei, "Gender Comparison of Employment," 111.

63. Joel S. Fetzer and J. Christopher Soper, *Confucianism, Democratization, and Human Rights in Taiwan* (Lanham, MD: Lexington Books, 2014), 28.

64. Fetzer and Soper, *Confucianism*, 28.

65. Fetzer and Soper, *Confucianism*, 28.

66. Fetzer and Soper, *Confucianism*, 28.

67. Fetzer and Soper, *Confucianism*, 29.

68. Fetzer and Soper, *Confucianism*, 29.

69. Fetzer and Soper, *Confucianism*, 29.

70. Fetzer and Soper, *Confucianism*, 30–31.

71. Fetzer and Soper, *Confucianism*, 73.

72. Fetzer and Soper, *Confucianism*, 73.

Chapter Five

Methodology of the Ethics of Care

Integrating Care and Justice

Since the early 1980s, feminist philosophers have started to raise the value of care on the agenda in the study of ethics, investigating issues of valuing care as a balance of justice. In *The Ethics of Care: Personal, Political, and Global*, Virginia Held called her balancing approach as "fairer caring" and "caring justice."[1] These two terms show the essence of her analysis of notions of care and justice: meshing them together as inseparable but emphasizing caring relations as a wider framework into which justice should be fitted. Thus, care should be the priority in a more comprehensive moral theory, while the concerns of justice must not be overlooked.[2] I will explore Held's thoughts and arguments of the ethics of care as a priority in different contexts and how justice and care integrated and why the ethics of care will work out a better way to tackle ethical issues. I also examine Held's thoughts of integrating the two notions with major critiques from reading Engster, *The Heart of Justice* (2007) and Nagel, *The View from Nowhere* (1986). Finally, I will compare feminist care ethics with Confucian reciprocity as the Confucian Golden Rule (CGR) and evaluate methodological dimensions of CGR to highlight its strength of integration, compatible with Held's approach of integration, not polarizing care and justice. I also return to Tronto's public concept of "care with" in *Caring Democracy* and compare it to Kongzi's way of *ren* to reaffirm the inclusive approach in democratic care.

THE ETHICS OF CARE AS A MORAL THEORY

Held characterizes the ethics of care having five features as following: Focuses on compelling moral salience of attending to and meeting the needs of particular others for whom we take responsibility; values emotion rather than rejects it: emotion of sympathy, empathy, sensibility, and responsiveness; respects interdependence and relationships; keeps critical visions of the public/private division and of coercive power; and conceptualizes persons as relational rather than self-sufficient independent individuals in the dominant moral theories.[3]

All these features are devalued in the mainstream of Western ethical theories such as Kantian and Utilitarian ethics. Held points out: "In the dominant moral theories of the ethics of justice, the value of equality, impartiality, fair distribution, and noninterference have priority. . . . In contrast, in the ethics of care, the values of trust, solidarity, mutual concern, and empathetic responsiveness have priority."[4] Held argues that care should be the most deeply fundamental value because "There can be care without justice. . . . There can be no justice without care."[5] Obviously, without care no child would survive and there would be no persons to respect. But, as Held notes, the ethics of care does not itself provide adequate theoretical resources for dealing with issues of justice. To me, this claim seems to invoke possible mistaken views of the ethics of care as a minimum basic moral theory such as in Engster's assessment of care theory that we shall examine later. However, what Held has tried to reject is the way in which the traditional inclination to expand the reach of justice: "in such a way that it is mistakenly imagined to be able to give us a comprehensive morality suitable for all moral questions."[6] Held argues that in a combined integrating approach the ethics of care can expand caring justice to consider how society should be structured and how restricted markets should be.

The ethics of care being feminist ethics differs from traditional moral epistemology such as the Kantian and Utilitarian theories that purport to provide clear answers to questions about what we ought to do. Caring relations is far beyond taking care of or caring about someone or something. These relations include mothering, fathering, workers in hospitals, teachers in their teaching, etc., in situations of tough one-on-one or face-to-face jobs. Caring relations always happen in love's labor or dependency workers' activities. The relation between a caregiver and the cared-for is importantly a relation of trust, belonging to, and sharing enjoyment for common life. What Held is trying to show is that caring relations extend well beyond the caring taking place in families and among friends.

CARE AS VALUE AND PRIORITY

When discussing what is involved in caring, Held includes attentiveness, sensitivity, and responding to needs. On the other side, involvement in justice includes impartiality, equality, and recognizing person's rights. We can see relevance of care to the practices of justice in concrete examples.[7] Held explains that justice and care as values each invokes associated clusters of moral considerations and these considerations are different. A child care center should have as its highest priority the safeguarding and appropriate development of children, including meeting their emotional as well as physical and educational needs. Justice should not be absent: the children should be treated fairly and with respect; violations of justice should not be tolerated. But priority of care rather than exemplifying justice would be the primary aim of the activity. A practice of legislative decisions on funding to localities to improve law enforcement should be its primary aim. Localities where crime is a greater threat should receive more of such funding, so that equality of personal security is more nearly achieved. Care should not be absent in law enforcement: concern for victims of crime, and for victims of police brutality, should be part of what is considered in such efforts. But providing greater justice and equality rather than caring for victims would be the primary aim of such legislative decisions.[8] A question is raised: how to integrate the values of both justice and care?

Explaining two representative justice theories, John Rawls's *A Theory of Justice* as a Kantian approach and utilitarianism, the principle of utility, we see both emphasize impartiality and rationality as opposing partiality and emotional inclinations; in contrast, feminist ethics of care, not only favors caring relations, but also advocates that the concerns of justice must not be overlooked. Thus, Held raises the idea of meshing care and justice. According to Held, justice is badly needed in the family as well as in the state: domestic violence and abuse, welfare programs, child care, health care, and so on infused with the value of care. Care is needed by everyone when they are children, ill, or old. So care should be a central political concern to make sure that care is available to those who need it. Care and justice should not be separated into private and public spheres, but they are different spheres. Because of this difference, Held explains her changing views on these two values: she considered in the past that justice deals with moral minimums, a floor of moral requirement; now she thinks that caring relations should form the wider framework into which justice should be fitted.[9] Although Held points the direction of the two, that care and justice should be integrated, it seems that, with the exception of her view of keeping different priorities in different situations in a matter of care or justice, she did not continue to formulate a substantial argument for how the integration comprehensively plays out in moral, political, and other respects, leaving the puzzles of integrating the seemingly opposite two as a revolutionary epistemological task to later explorations. As I reflect upon the feminist critiques of Held and others against the epistemological mistake that assumes a liberal, binary methodology of "two spheres" in which the private and public are separated, I argue that early Confucian *ren* could be a hope to break the binary with the way of *ren* as a prerequisite in oneness of ontology.

CARE AND EXTENSION OF MARKETS

Held makes convincing arguments about why care should be the priority through a chapter titled "Care and the Extension of Markets" in her book *The Ethics of Care*. According to the market principles, as Held explains, all involved in the market should be aiming to maximize their own economically quantifiable gains. Schools and hospitals need to be run efficiently but earning as much as one can as efficiently as possible easily may not be the primary objective of teachers, doctors, and many others or of the entities organizing their work. The market, on the other hand, values teaching or the practice of medicine or the institutions organizing them only instrumentally for what they produce in economic gain. What might be the moral ground for deciding on the limits or boundaries of the market? According to Held, Kantian theories of a liberal individualist do not give satisfactory grounds for deciding, within the constraints of rights, how wide or how narrow the reach of the market should be. Neither Utilitarian provides adequate grounds for limiting the extension of the market.[10] In Held's view, the ethics of care advocate relationships between persons, rather than individual rights or preferences, personal relationships are a primary focus. Caring relations are seen as being of central value. In ethics of care, understanding values such as those of sensitivity, empathy, responsiveness, and taking responsibility, we could judge more adequately where the boundaries of the market should be.

THE PRIORITY OF CARE OVER AN ACKNOWLEDGMENT OF RIGHTS

Held argues that a caring relation is normatively prior and has priority over an acknowledgment of rights. It makes good sense to say care as primary in the family. Care seems the most basic moral value, as basic as the value of life. There can be no human life or families without the actual practice of care, but, in Held's view, we need to recognize the value of such care properly in order to understand this most basic practice as preconditions for everything else. She argues: "There can be care without justice, but there can be no justice without the care that has value."[11] Hence the moral value of care should be prior to all others but it also has to be compatible with rights. If a parent does care well for a child but fails to recognize the child's rights, the child morally ought to try to resolve the conflicts through compromise within the network of family relations rather than breaking the relation with the parent altogether.[12] In the case of an abusing husband, it is seen as a failure to properly care for the person in the relation. In Held's analysis, the ethics of care do not advocate the actual family relations of patriarchal societies but the morally valuable aspects of human relationships, the caring relations, not an abusing one, because here we emphasize with what we should or ought to do under the ideal situations of human relations beyond patriarchal societies. Feminists have contributed many detailed analyses of what equal rights for women should require, but there should be much more to explore on how to balance rights and keep up substantial relations. All these relations may show more or less power imbalance, and being aware of issues of power over the powerless becomes crucial to maintaining caring relations both at home and beyond.

Held argues in chapter 9 in *The Ethics of Care* that the ethics of care must not lose power to oppose what morality recommends or the power of structures that keep oppression intact. She rightly emphasized that feminists have explored the power to empower others, and the power involved in caring.[13] Held continued to comment on Amy Allen's examination of three conceptions of power as a resource, domination, and empowerment; none of these concepts are satisfactory in Allen's view because they only provide one aspect of the feminist understanding of multifaceted power relations.

There is no doubt that Held agrees that power is a relation, not a possession. Though feminists worry about losing sight of power, especially the power to dominate and constrain progress, Held believes that political life should be geared more toward the values of care and trust in order to transform society. Held makes a claim that there is no "soft-headedness" in care and caregiving since caregivers are most adept in the skills of care that entail dispute settling, peacemaking tactics, establishing rules and enforcing them, and meting out punishments in raising children—all qualities of care that help to diffuse conflicts in the lives of individuals through training and discipline. Transferring these mechanisms to international and global societies can contribute to fund-raising and personnel attraction to control violence and build tolerance as well as promote relatedness with other human beings in the process of understanding and respecting the importance of human rights. This can also lead to corporate power increasing its reach and influence in the values of care without violating liberal rights. One way to constrain corporations from expanding imperialism is to reinstate an assertion of alternative values encased in care, trust, and human solidarity to reach their goals.[14]

In Held's analysis, the ethics of care are capable of examining the social structures of power within which the activities of caring take place. Feminist theories of care ethics have shown us that concern for ongoing relationships, listening and empathy are essential for acceptable uses of power, including democratic power.

ENGSTER'S CRITIQUES OF HELD AND POSSIBLE REPLIES

Daniel Engster discussed Held's thoughts about care and market extension: although he has adopted valuable thoughts of care ethics from main figures of care theorists in tracing the development of care ethics, he challenges Held's viewpoints in the methodology of integrating care and justice. Engster attempts to offer alternative care theory of his own as he claims, "care theory is an incomplete theory of justice"[15] through his book *The Heart of Justice: Care Ethics and Political Theory*. The book has important merits as Tronto states in *Caring Democracy* (2013): Daniel Engster (2007) "derives an admirable set of recommendations from principles that he thinks follow necessarily from the nature of care."[16] And according to Anca Gheaus, there has been a lack of providing "a systematic and fairly comprehensive account of what a caring society and caring politics should look like. Engster's book fills this gap."[17] Engster admits, "No theory of justice can be said to be consistent or complete without integrating the institutional and policy commitments of care theory. Care theory nonetheless does not completely subsume all other theories of justice."[18] These two terms, if they must be integrated, as Engster claims, do not sound as if they can be integrated as equal or equally valuable. Indeed, as Held argues, they have different priorities in different situations. Hence, Engster frankly admits that his own account of care theory offers "a minimal and incomplete theory of justice."[19]

Engster's concerns of care as minimum basic morality is problematic in my view. First, although Engster agrees with many care theorists' views of care and makes his central claim that caring represents a basic morality for the minimally decent treatment of others that we all should follow and suggests that caring is at the heart of any cogent account of human morality and justice, his care theory is different from Held's position. Engster's minimum care morality, compared with Held's pursuit of fairer caring or caring justice, shows that Engster has resisted the integration of justice and care, while Held has pursued it on equal terms. We may ask why Engster argues that the terms cannot be integrated on an equal basis or why justice should have overwhelming weight in relation to a minimal theory of care. Engster rightly realizes as other care theorists do, that an account of caring includes a place for both emotions and reasons: "The emotions of sympathy and compassion are important for motivating and facilitating the delivery of care. Reason, however, can guide and expand these sentiments and perhaps even strengthen and develop them."[20] In this view, although both emotion and reason are equally important and necessary for the development and maintenance of caring persons and a caring society, reason takes the lead to guide and expand while emotion does not. In short, "we live in a web of dependency and caring,"[21] according to Engster, and he extends these insights by arguing that inevitable and pervasive dependence on others can generate a theory of obligation for caring. He carefully sets up five steps of the argument ending with the principle of consistent dependency in the final step:

> *Since all human beings depend upon the care of others for our survival, development, and basic functioning and at least implicitly claim that capable individuals should care for individuals in need when they can do so, we should consistently recognize as morally valid the claims that others make upon us for care when they need it, and should endeavor to provide care to them when we are capable of doing so without significant danger to ourselves.*[22]

By doing so, Engster has limited caring to the lowest level of survival, in the capacity of a starting point, making the role of caring as minimal as possible, so that we can avoid any arbitrary efforts to elevate any higher moral values upon these survival needs. As a result, these higher values are kept free for the choosing, according to an individual's own desire to pursue the aims of their own life. On Engster's account, the practice of care is then subject to a principle of consistent dependency, "similar to the principle of fairness . . . but broader."[23] Consistent dependency "grounds our duty to care for others not in relations of reciprocity but in our common human dependency."[24] This again emphasizes the limitation of caring to what sounds like a liberal noninterference policy: "we must attend and respond to other's needs given their abilities and circumstances instead of projecting onto them our ideas about what we want others to do unto us."[25] Therefore, in his account of care theory, Engster denies the Western Golden Rule of reciprocity and the CGR as well. Engster's account of care theory indicates a "general instability" in Gheaus's "Book Review," "The more we understand it as a minimalistic theory, the easier it will be to uphold it. . . . Such a version of care theory will be less likely to be universally endorsed and will find itself more closely allied with some moral and political theories. . . . It will, at the same time, be more convincing as a theory of justice."[26]

Second, seeing care as minimal help to meet other's survival needs without any higher values in contrast to justice, Engster's evaluation of care shows a similar liberal individualistic approach of valuing individual rationality as the opposite of emotional involvement in morality, and has been far from Held's methodology of equal validation of both care and justice, particularly in the case of economic equality: valuing care labor in a deep commitment under a market competition.

There have been some serious critiques to feminist thinking of impartiality in liberal theorists. Brian Barry in *Justice as Impartiality* claims that justice as second-order impartiality always has priority over considerations of care. Held disagrees with Barry that sometimes the points of view of care and justice provide different moral evaluations and recommendations on the same issues. The issue can be shown in an example of honoring one's father and mother. Can this be partial or impartial? Barry suggests: "To the impartialist the answer would be some form of: because all persons ought always to honor their fathers, ceteris paribus."[27] For the partialist it might be something like: "you probably ought to honor this particular person who is your father because over many years he helped bring you up."[28] Held emphasizes that it would be "particular persons involved and relation between them, rather than the general principle that would be the source of the honoring."[29] To me, these two views emphasize different aspects of the features of honoring. From a care receiver's point of view, a caregiver such as a loving parent deserves a particular kind of honor from the cared-for, endorsement of a principle of caring reversibility. From a general view about honoring as it is, we can synthesize all cases of intimate caring relations as an objective fact of human common sense to honor someone who helps others and establishes an example for all, endorsement of a principle of caring extensibility. I believe both reversibility and extensibility can cover meanings of care and justice, or of partiality and impartiality, but the key here is the integration of care and justice, partiality, and impartiality, thinking of them at the different levels as a whole issue but not separating the two as opposites. These ideas came from the early CGR in the *Analects*, as Bo Mou explained in his article, "A Reexamination of the Structure and Content of Confucius' Version of the Golden Rule" (2004). I explain it later in this chapter.

Another objection is the charge of paternalistic interference from the critique of liberalism. The liberal view overlooks the fact that citizens have all been helpless infants, dependent on others for years for affectionate care according to Held. It fails to address appropriateness, implications, and effects of treating any social relations as if they were between independent, autonomous, and self-interested individuals. So the response to the charge is about the notion of autonomy. Held responds and argues that feminist ethicists in the ethics of care have been shown how autonomy as self-governance is compatible with (not antagonistic to) the ethics of care.[30] Diana Meyers describes autonomy as a set of competencies "repertory of skills through which self-discovery, self-definition, and self-direction are achieved."[31] For relational persons, the point is that as we modify and often distance ourselves from exiting relations, it is for the sake of better and often more caring relations, rather than for the splendid independence, self-sufficiency, and easy isolation of the traditional liberal ideal of the autonomous rational agent. The ethics of care requires us to pay attention to rather than ignore, the material, psychological, and social prerequisites for autonomous choices. These important insights into the key issues of being mutually autonomous persons, while keeping interdependency within networks and relationships in both public and private activities through people's lives, have been overlooked in Engster's critiques of Held's thoughts on the ethics of care and market values. Although admirably having understood Held's first two features in her description of the ethics of care such as attentive, responsive to need, and relational interdependency, Engster does not go far enough to follow up the last two features of a comprehensive theory of care from the feminist political goals of doing ethics of care. These two features as Held described are: *keeps critical visions of the public/private division and of coercive power; conceptualizes persons as relational rather than self-sufficient independent individuals of the dominant moral theories.* Instead of responding to these insights, Engster insists on his minimum care morality in a way that defends the impartiality a market system is supposed to provide. Therefore, Engster also defends individual ability of privatization of care to allow people to openly pursue the best possible option because the constant competition among market systems may provide the same type of care. On the other hand, Held points out that, "Once an educational institution of activity has been taken over by the market anything other than economic gain cannot be its highest priority since corporation's responsibility to its shareholders requires it to try to maximize economic gain."[32] However, Held does note that competition and efficiency should not be removed entirely from our system of public service, but still the market pressure of turning a profit should be lessened substantially. Held states, "It seems better to see education and the market as having different priorities, as ordering their values differently."[33] And she believes that feminist ethics of care help us to see why the resistance of education to takeover by market forces. "This view of how we can appreciate multiple values in human activities while according them different priorities and of recognizing how important it is to order those priorities appropriately seems suitable also for the other activities considered, such as health care, child care, and cultural expression."[34] To me, these wholehearted mindful concerns out of her methodology of integration should be appreciated and further explored, and these will present a new direction of how we should develop *critical features of the ethics of care in a way of rejecting methods of separating concepts of care and justice in concrete issues that are seemingly opposite one another, or one dominating the other.*

Held believes that implementing care-based ethics alongside justice would result in greater economic and social equality among care workers and noncare workers. Engster disagrees and he states, "A caring theory of economic justice is ultimately very different from liberalism. . . . Care theory does not aim to promote individual autonomy, social equality, worker control, or unexploited labor, but instead to assure all individuals access to resources and support necessary to care adequately for themselves and their dependents."[35] We see that this statement denies care as a moral value—as comprehensive morality—but that it is only a materialist-based concern for biological and developmental needs. This comment makes it seem as if it would be difficult to integrate care and liberal justice theories because their focuses are so radically different, a negative implication based upon the root of different understanding of selfhood. On the other side, the main push for care ethics by many feminist proponents has been to start incorporating it into the modern public world alongside justice theory: care is considered to be a large-scale normative theory.[36]

NAGEL AND DEONTOLOGICAL CONSTRAINTS

There have been other ways of exploring the integration of principles of humanity and justice. One of them arises from endeavors to understand Nagel's deontological constraint, which in turn seeks an objectivity of self. In this section, I briefly explain Nagel's original thinking in order to grasp what his problem is in his own way, so that we can have a better vision for understanding the complexity of approaches to reciprocity with both feminist and Confucian ethical insights.

Before we delve into Nagel's idea of the force of deontological constraints, we must understand what deontological theory is. "Deontological moral theories . . . hold that there are principles of right conduct that apply immediately to our actions, requiring or prohibiting certain action in certain circumstances without reference to any further end beyond the action."[37] Nagel presents the paradox of deontology by introducing the difference between agent neutral reasons and agent relative reasons. Agent neutral reasons are in a sense universal to everyone: it is not specific to a certain instance or another. By contrast, agent relative reasons are deontological constraints that are personal goals and values, not reducible to agent neutral reasons through agent autonomy: you have a specific reason to do certain things under certain conditions. Nagel wishes to defend the existence of deontological constraints through agent-relative reasons of autonomy. Nagel's theory of deontology follows closely Kant's universal laws, such as no lying, no harm to the innocent, respecting the rights of others, and so on. Deontology focused around duty and following the rules regardless of the outcomes. Just like Kant's categorical imperative formulation, we follow the universal law of no harm to the innocent child and should not intentionally do the lesser of the two evils. In Nagel's story, there is a car wreck and, to save your friend, you may have to twist the child's arm in a nearby house in order to get the grandmother out of the bathroom with the key to her car to save the injured friend. This would be the deontological constraints, Nagel claims, and they are mandatory. Nagel explains the force of deontological constraint as follows: "The peculiarity of deontological reasons is that although they are agent-relative, they do not express the subjective autonomy of the agent at all. They are demands, not options."[38] These demands contain great force because they are constraints regarding what everyone should not do. When we punish others for doing evil, we are constrained to avoid evil-doing. This constraint demands that we not aim at "our victim's evil" even as we aim at some "particular bad thing" for which the victim of punishment is guilty. However, within that constraint, each individual who undertakes to punish someone "has considerable authority in defining what will count as harming," even within the constraint to avoid doing evil in the process.[39]

The deontological constraints serve as a general guideline on how to behave in relation to others. Nagel believes that agent-relative reasons arise from deontological constraints and since it is not as simple as deciding that agent-neutral reason is the correct moral reasoning, then the nature of this constraint must be further examined. "Deontological constraints add further agent-relative reasons to the system-reasons not to treat others in certain ways. They are not impersonal claims derived from the interests of others, but personal demands governing one's relation with others."[40] All these still leave unsettled the question of justification, according to Nagel, for when you twist the child's arm, you are guided by the aim of rescuing your injured friend, and the good of that aim dominates the evil of the child's pain. In Nagel's analysis, the fact of your trying to produce evil as a subsidiary aim is phenomenologically important, but what we are looking at is why should it be morally important? Nagel claims, "I don't believe there is a decisive answer here."[41] Nevertheless, he continues, when I view my act from outside and think of it as resulting from a choice of the impersonally considered state of the world in which it occurs, this seems rational to him. Why it is rational? Because in thinking of the matter this way, I abstract my will and its choice from my person, and decide directly among states of the world, as if I were taking a multiple choice test. "If the choice is determined by what on balance is impersonally best, then I am guided by good and not by evil."[42] This rational consideration in Nagel's view leads to his idea of the objective self, which regards the world impersonally. But, as Nagel realizes, "each of us is not only an objective self but a particular person with a particular perspective,"[43] so our choices are not merely choices of states of the world, but of action. Every choice is two choices from both an internal and external point of view; a person's choosing a balance of good over evil does not cover up the fact that this is the intrinsic character of one's action. To me, Nagel finally points out the precondition of personal character traits as an important element in connecting a theory of moral justification. He rightly states that the suitability in the investigation of an agent-relative constraint plus something to be said about the point of view of the victim. "There too we encounter problems having to do with the integration of the two standpoints."[44] The problem is deeply rooted in reasons alone dealing in this relation: "The deontological constraint permits a victim always to object to those who aim at his harm, and this relation has the same special character of normative magnification when seen from the personal perspective of the victim that it has when seen from the personal perspective of the agent."[45] Hence, Nagel concludes, "This merely corroborates the importance of the internal perspective in accounting for the content of deontological intuitions. It does not prove the correctness of those intuitions."[46] The puzzle of moral justification remains but Nagel makes a point, "it confirms that a purely impersonal morality requires that general suppression of the personal perspective in moral motivation. . . . When we regard human relations objectively, it does not seem irrational to admit such reasons at the basic level into the perspective of both agents and victims."[47] How can we make moral progress using this account of the force of deontological reasons in applications with special clarity to the constraint against doing harm as a means to your ends? Nagel believes that the key to understanding any of these moral intuitions is the distinction between the internal viewpoint of the agent or victim and an external, objective viewpoint which both agent and victim can also adopt. Then he points out a true philosophical dilemma out of our nature: persons have different points of view on the world, "the complexity of what we are makes a unified answer difficult. . . . A fully agent-neutral morality is not a plausible human goal."[48]

DEEP CARE AND RELATIONAL ONTOLOGY

Stan van Hooft proposed a notion of deep caring in order to integrate the two approaches of the principles of humanity and justice in his article "Caring, Objectivity and Justice: An Integrative View."[49] He argues that a deep form of caring lies behind both approaches and so unites them. I appreciate the points he makes and agree with the idea of integration of the two approaches, and especially support the thesis he raises that a deep and subjective form of caring lies at the base of even our most objective moral reason. Nevertheless, I believe in a further step from the premotivational sets of deep caring to a comprehensive foundation of the ethics of care that goes side by side or mixed with reasons all the time of human lives. I note that Hooft followed up on Engster's strategy, which sees the importance of the element of care in a morally justifiable process, but they both eventually deny the comprehensive theory of the ethics of care by saying that caring only happened as a precondition to morally justifiable reasons and stops there without further functioning so that Hooft states at the end, "Deep caring is both an expression of, and a concern for, justice."[50]

The notion of deep caring Hooft brought up is to solve Nagel's problem of two standpoints, self and others. In his understanding of Nagel's deontological constraints, he focuses on the objectivity of the self, which is undergirding internally between self-alienation and self-acceptance. According to him, the impersonal standpoint delivers a judgment about what would be right or equitable in a given situation but without generating any motivational feeling to move that the person should do anything about it. "Somehow, the personal standpoint must include caring about deliverances of the impersonal standpoint."[51] This claim opens a space in which caring can play a role: an agent must care about the reasons for an action or about the norms to which the agent responds in order to be motivated to perform that action. "To act with rational objectivity requires that caring still be implicitly present as a necessary motivational condition for that action,"[52] and "When I said of Jones that he finally agreed to contribute to Oxfam so as to stop feeling guilty about not having done so earlier, we can see this as an expression of his caring about his own moral status."[53] I would say that something is amiss here that worries Hooft about Nagel's moral agent seeming to be caring about oneself. Is it not more admirable to help others because they are in need, to help them for their own sakes rather than for one's own sake? Hooft realizes that theorists of the ethics of care have written a great deal about this, and this literature talks about being inclined to care about others because of a moral sentiment that Hooft denies. What he resists is to understand caring on sentimentalist terms. What he suggests about deep caring involves "a deeper level of caring"[54] that does not lie near the surface of our motivational sets but moves our motivations forward. He takes the term of "relational ontology" and pictures it as fitted into "a deep and inchoate state of caring that lies below the level of our everyday self-awareness and is, in technical terms, 'preintentional.'"[55] According to his explanation, the deep caring makes no distinction between others and the self. It may alight upon others or it may alight upon one's self, depending on circumstances. Using this deep caring notion to explain why an agent acted in that way focusing upon this agent's self we may help Nagel in dealing with the problem of two standpoints (and this will be similar to another occasion when an agent's reflection may allude to the needs of others for their own sake). In either case, the deep caring can be expressed either as a self-project, as caring for others, or both at once, because it does not discriminate but it does motivate. The deep caring at an inchoate level without specifying the objects of this caring can also make one's subjectivity absent from the above explanation: "My relational ontology ensures that I care for others primordially, and my concern to not be self-alienated ensures that I achieve my existential identity by caring for others in that way. Nagel's objectivity is made possible by a subjectivity that does not establish itself as a subject that then chooses to care about others. Rather, it is a subjectivity that establishes its self by caring for others."[56] This sounds like a total abstraction of a self-other relationship in deep caring, which is moving away from the integration Held proposes. Both Nagel and Hooft emphasize objectivity and objective self in autonomous agents' internally undergirding self-alienation and self-acceptance without a concern for the function of sensitivity of feeling in collaborating with one's moral motivation sets, which is a faulty description of common sense of morality of human life. To me, Hooft raises a great point about deep caring and relates this form to the idea of relational ontology, but he admits deep caring merely at a primordial level, where it cannot even be a matter of going along with reasons in accounting for what I should or should not do when facing moral dilemmas in difficult circumstances. He keeps using the term "I" but denies there could be a subject present, as "there is as yet no ego seeking its own fulfilment."[57] Thus, deep caring becomes a floating abstract form, incapable of any discrimination between self and others that would make it capable of seeing myself objectively—as another—or my seeing others objectively—including myself. If it is merely through objective accounting that moral agents can overcome self-alienation to do what they ought to do, then what exactly is motivating their choosing of what to do? What will register their accounting as they pick up the needs of either self or others in the process of choosing? These matters remain unexplained, because these connections are not being explored through this discussion. His ending words—"Deep caring is both an expression of, and a concern for, justice"[58]—serve as a virtual declaration that immanent caring cannot play as comprehensive a role as transcendent justice in the integration of care and justice.

THE NEED FOR MORE THAN JUSTICE

Annette Baier challenged the assumed supremacy of justice among the moral and social virtues following up a list of philosophers, including Alasdair MacIntyre, Michael Stocker, Lawrence Blum, Michael Slote, in her article "The Need for More Than Justice" (1987). Baier pointed out that the liberal morality for right-holders was surreptitiously supplemented by a different set of demands made on domestic workers, women, and slaves: "rights have usually been for the privileged, talking about laws, and the rights those laws recognize and protect, does not in itself ensure that the group of legislators and rights-holders will not be restricted to some elite."[59] She rightly mentions that the tradition of liberal moral theory has in fact developed so as to include the women it had so long excluded, to include the poor as well as rich, blacks and whites, and so on. Though these theories contained the seeds of the challenge to the patriarchal poison, they are undoubtedly patriarchal. She continues to point out that those values of legalistic moral theory still insist on and reserve for males all the most powerful positions in its hierarchy; "If we are really to transvalue the values of our patriarchal past, we need to rethink all of those assumptions."[60] Baier summarizes three reasons why women are dissatisfied in their pursuit for their own values within the framework of the liberal morality. The first was its dubious record, the second was its inattention to relations of inequality, and the third is its exaggeration of the scope of choice or its inattention to unchosen relations.[61] These reasons have been seen in reading Held's *The Ethics of Care*: "we need an ethics of care, not just care itself. The various aspects and expressions of care and caring relations need to be subjected to moral scrutiny and evaluated, not just observed and described."[62] Traditional explorations of virtue theories could be traced back to ancient Greek times with Aristotle's magnificent works on ethics, but before Aristotelian thinkers, there were the original Chinese Confucian ethics emphasizing the humanity of *ren* as a prerequisite in relational ontology; as benevolence, compassion, and goodness in human nature; and as a universal love of learning to be human beings and a harmonious society in which all people are protected by heaven's will.

THE *REN* AND CONFUCIAN RECIPROCITY

The Golden Rule of Kongzi claims: "Do not impose on others what you yourself do not desire."[63] This is also called *shu* or sympathetic understanding. According to Confucian ethics, human society consists of five relationships: ruler/subject; husband/wife; parent/child; older/younger; and peers/friends/equals: virtues such as *ren*, *yi*, *li*, *zhi*, and *xin* should guide people's behavior so that a great order with hierarchy makes a stable and prosperous society. Harmonious order and each person's obligation to keep great order by playing each social role became commonsense morality and Kongzi's maxim of "已所不欲, 勿施於人"[64] (the Golden Rule in short: "Do not do unto others what you would not desire to do unto yourself") has been embedded in all Chinese cultural beliefs psychologically and morally.

Ames and Hall assess Confucian thoughts of harmonious human relations: "A dynamic field of relationships over time produces a degree of parity in what is perceived as the most vital source of humanity—one's human relations."[65] But this can be challenged as the following: the social hierarchy does not tolerate any equality between the ruler and the ruled. The powerful superior class benefits from this relationship. Here, I think the feminist ethics of care will help through its critical visions of relational power and thoughts of balancing justice and care, the integration of the two. There are important insights with regard to the ideas of dynamic integration in understanding the Confucian principle of reciprocity and Mengzi's thoughts of human nature: both emphasize *ren* as a universal compassion starting from family, extending to the world, and reaching up to a human goal of peace, stability, and joy.

Kongzi (Confucius), as the first master educator, advocates learning the six arts in his teaching, including rites, music, archery, charioteer, calligraphy, and calculation. Teaching six arts actually relates to the political thought of *Minben* (people-oriented), according to a Chinese philosopher You-lan Feng: the differences in teaching between Kongzi and other scholars are in different purposes, "other's teachings aim to spread their own scholarship as a uniqueness, Kongzi's teaching is aiming to cultivate a person into a person of humanity, capable of serving for the state rather than being a unique scholar."[66] Feng also points out that teaching six arts in a way to extend to ordinary people as long as they might pay their tuitions made Kongzi the first master in China to bring the education of the useful six arts down to the common people: "this in fact is a radical revolution"[67] in the enterprise of education for all commoners. Learning six arts and the way of teaching arts are no doubt planting seeds of the modern thought of justice. Feng's comments on Kongzi and Kongzi's Golden Rule are appreciated by David S. Nivison in his book, *The Ways of Confucianism* (1996). Through a rigid examination of different sources regarding specific terminology of *zhong* and *shu* in the Golden Rule of reciprocity, Nivison rightly explicates Feng's understanding of Kongzi's words in different places about the two terms. The first methodology description of *ren* and reciprocity is in the *Analects* 6:30: The term *ren* 仁 (benevolence) means that when you desire getting established for yourself, you help others to get established; and when you desire success for yourself you help others to succeed. The ability to make a comparison from what is near at hand can simply be called the method of benevolence. This is a positive statement about how to apply the rule of *ren* in a program of self-development in general principle. The next is a more explicit statement of the rule in the *Zhongyong* 中庸: "*Zhong* 忠 and *shu* 恕 are not far from the *dao* 道 (way). If you would not be willing to have something done to yourself, then do not do it to others. . . . What you would require of your son, use in serving your father; what you would require of your subordinate, use in serving your prince; what you would require of your younger brother, use in serving your elder brother; what you would require of your friend, first apply in your treatment of your friend."[68] According to Nivison, Feng notes two elements in this statement, the first, two virtuous practices named by Kongzi, *zhong* and *shu*; the second, *shu* being translated into consideration, reciprocity, or even altruism. We see similar dialogues about *zhong* and *shu* in the *Analects* 15:24, with a close paraphrase of this negative formulation; another one is in the *Analects* 4:15, "Our Master's way consists simply of *zhong* and *shu*." All these sources lead to a definition by Kongzi himself that "If *zhong* and *shu* are a pair of concepts that are matched in some way, we sense at once that we will understand each better if we understand them both and see how they are related."[69] So far Nivison agrees with Feng on this definition but he will go to a similar paragraph found in *Daxue* 大学: "What you would dislike in your superior, do not use in employing your inferior; what you would dislike in your inferior, do not use in serving your superior; what you would dislike in the one who precedes you, do not use in dealing with the one who comes after you; what you would dislike in the one who comes after you, do not use in dealing with the one who precedes you."[70] This is called the moral "measuring square," which is readily accepted by the Chinese people who strive to be moral in the Confucian ways. Ironically, as Nivison mentions, Immanuel Kant, who lectured on Chinese philosophy in Konigsberg, dismissed Confucius as having no concept of genuine morality at all: "Their teacher Confucius teaches in his writings nothing outside a moral doctrine designed for the princes,"[71] and "a concept of virtue and morality never entered the heads of the Chinese."[72] Nivison continues to highlight the essence of this golden rule: perhaps the Chinese Golden Rule as always intended—"does not say 'treat another as you would have that other treat you,' but 'treat another as you would have anyone else related to you as you are to that other treat you.'"[73] This clears up that there are at least a trio or multirelationships rather than an interaction between two individuals; the essence of relational ontology is the idea of people's interdependence in relationships, which is emphasized by both feminist ethics of care and Confucian care ethics or benevolence. From here, we have a hope of extending virtues to the four seas in reading Mengzi, but Kongzi's golden rule set up a firm guiding line to develop a universal *ren* morality. We next explore Bo Mou's comprehensive explanation of the Golden Rule.

METHODOLOGICAL DIMENSION OF *ZHONG* AND *SHU*

Bo Mou's article, "A Reexamination of the Structure and Content of Confucius' Version of the Golden Rule,"[74] provided a clear analysis of CGR to help us understand how the three dimensions (methodological dimension, internal starting point, and external starting point) of CGR work together; they are intertwined as "one unified thread" to accomplish *ren* moral demand through self-cultivation progression. Mou articulates what he calls methodological dimension of the CGR of *zhong* and *shu*. The dimension consists of not just the principle of reversibility but also the principle of extensibility, "the latter . . . is distinct from the former in some crucial aspects."[75] These distinctive features are being spelt out through four forms of interpreting the *Analects*: "Do not do unto others what you would not desire to do unto yourself" (15.24), and "Help others to be established the way you wish to be established, and help others to advance the way you wish to advance yourself" (6.30). Mou raises a topic that attracts many scholars to work on: "whether the methodological dimension of CGR consists merely of the principle of reversibility—putting oneself in another's 'shoes'—or also of the principle of extensibility—putting oneself in the moral recipient's, rather than another's shoes."[76] What is interesting and significant, as Mou explains, is how to understand and interpret the methodological dimension of the CGR as presented in the text of 15.24 and 6.30. Through Mou's clarification of different interpretations from James Legge, Wing-tsit Chan, and D. C. Lau, four forms of English translations, labeled (a), (b), (c), and (d), are indicated and examined. We see the most near to Confucius' original is the text 15.24, the one that is "subject to two different interpretations, (b) as the negative version of the principle of reversibility and (c) as the negative version of extensibility."[77] As Mou continues to clarify, if the negative version of the methodological dimension of the CGR covers both (b) and (c), then it would capture not only the negative version of the principle of reversibility, as its Western counterpart does, but also the negative version of the principle of extensibility, which the Western counterpart of the CGR does not seem to cover. "In this way, the negative version of the methodological dimension of the CGR would have a richer implication than its Western counterpart in this regard."[78] This would be the difference in the connection between CGR and its Western counterpart. I find this clarification is, in particular, significant to the comparative study of early Confucian *ren* and feminist ethics of care with regard to the issue of extensive compassion of care as a comprehensive moral value integrating with justice morality if applying it in women's particular experience in the division of labor. This difference could open up further explorations about how to understand notions of empathy and sympathy, and the way of their connection with one another.

It seems to Mou that while the methodological dimension of one Western counterpart (the Christian version) consists of one principle in its two forms, the positive and negative versions of the principle of reversibility, the methodological dimension of the CGR consists of two principles with their four forms, namely the positive and negative version of the extensibility as well as the positive and negative version of the principle of reversibility. Here, Mou sees a crucial difference in each case: the methodological dimension of the Western counterpart of the CGR focuses on the case in which the moral agent in the imagined situation is the moral recipient in the current situation, while the moral recipient in the imagined situation is the moral agent in the current situation; in addition, "the methodological dimension of the CGR also takes care of the case in which the moral agent in the how-to-treat-others moral situation is both the moral agent and the moral recipient in the imagined or retrospective how-oneself-is-treated situation"[79] In this case, the moral agent has to make efforts to establish herself or himself through self-cultivation, then extends the way to others. The significance of the principle of extensibility presents itself twofold, according to Mou. First it would provide a *distinct* moral reference to regulate how to treat others, which is different itself from what the principle of reversibility. For example, when we determine to make one's efforts (to help those in need) to establish oneself to become a good person; one might take one's own desire in this connection as one's guide to establish one's child to become a good person—say educating one's child to help those in need. Second, the principle of extensibility would provide a more fundamental moral guide to regulate how to treat others than the principle of reversibility does, to the following extend. As indicated by the text in 6.30, both principles of reversibility and extensibility claim to take care of the situations in which one considers the ways one desires either others (in the case of reversibility) or oneself (in the case of extensibility) to *establish* (*li* 立) or advance (*da* 达). One's moral cultivation is essentially a kind of moral *self*-cultivation that fundamentally involves how one "reflectively desires *oneself* to treat others without involving too much how one desires others to treat oneself."[80] To this extent, how the moral agent would be morally *self*-cultivated contributes to how to treat others. This is the unique, more fundamental moral reference to regulate how to treat others under the principle of extensibility. Thus, it directly points to and is intrinsically connected with the moral self-cultivation, which, in Mou's view, is one central concern in Confucian moral thought. I fully agree with Mou's analysis in the above.

In further analysis, Mou brought up another important question, "the way of putting *ren* into practice."[81] Although it is clear in the context of 6.30 that a moral agent who is ready to apply the methods of reversibility and extensibility is considered to have already possessed a certain degree of moral sensibility of *ren* as her internal starting point for appropriately applying these methods, what is not clear is how to put the initial moral sensibility of *ren* into practice to treat others morally by following the methods of reversibility and extensibility. In other words, can the initial sensibility of *ren* go together with the procedure of applying the two methods toward a person of *ren* or achieve a moral sensibility at a higher level? Mou explains that the way of humanity in *shu* has two levels of meaning: first Mou notices that initial moral sensibility here does not necessarily mean something like a moral sprout or beginning in Mengzi's sense (Mencius 2A: 6, 6A: 6–7, 6A: 14); "it might result either from a certain degree of moral conscience in human nature or from cultivating one's virtue in response to the advocacy of some moral ideal that is not necessarily connected with the principle of reversibility or from both."[82] Second, it also means the way forward or realizing, *ren* as the result or consequence of putting the initial moral sensibility into practice. "This dual meaning reflects a dialectical relation between the two aspects of *shu* in the CGR."[83] Thus, *Shu*, as both "the internal starting point" and the methodological practice of reversibility and extensibility, depends deeply upon the assumption that reaching higher levels of moral sensibility requires that one's own self-cultivation of *ren* is already underway. To answer the question of how one would desire oneself or others to treat oneself morally so as to become *junzi*, Mou states, "the internal starting point in this step should be something more fundamental than interpersonal love or care,"[84] which is addressed in the text 13.19 of the *Analects*. The text reads, "Be respectful in dwelling by oneself, be serious in handling one's responsibilities, and be loyal in dealing with others. Even if living among barbarians, one may never cast away these principles."[85] Mou comments, there is one important point worth noting here: "Be respectful in dwelling by oneself."[86] This "does not even concern one's attitude toward others but rather one's attitude toward oneself."[87] And Mou continues to support the following point made by Shu-hsien Liu: "*Jen* in this sense cannot be interpreted as merely interpersonal love or benevolence. . . . *Jen* implies a profound reverence for one's own life as well as a concern for others lives . . . its meaning is for wider than mere benevolence or even altruism, rather, it is the root of them."[88] I think this point would be compatible with Held's considerations of altruism and other related issues, and with Tronto's idea of "caring responsibility" in *Caring Democracy*. Both may learn from one another.

TRONTO'S CONCEPT OF "CARE WITH" IN *CARING DEMOCRACY*

In the development of feminist ethics of care, Held argues that care involves emotion as well as reason, leading to her project of integrating care and justice as a moral methodological inquiry. Tronto points out in *Caring Democracy*: "Held's definition presumes that care duties are focused on particular others. This is useful . . . but it leaves out a way to discuss self-care or public forms of care."[89] Tronto makes the case for conceiving of care as a public value and as a set of public practices, at the same time recognizing that care is highly personal and, in this regard, "private." Thus, she claims in the larger case that "without a more public conception of care it is impossible to maintain democratic society."[90] Another important dimension of the context of particular kinds of caring is about power differentials, as Tronto examines: care is always a dyad between one more powerful caregiver and a weaker care receiver in particular cases; in broader "service" cases of care, the more powerful actors provide the care work for less powerful or more vulnerable recipients. The difference is in who appears to be in command.[91] What is distinctive about democratic caring is that it presumes that we are equal as democratic citizens in "being care *receivers*."[92] Though these needs vary not only from individual to individual at one moment in time, but for each individual and for groups within the society over time. The quality of being *needy* is shared by all humans. To Tronto, this does make sense to think of "an equal capacity to voice needs."[93] Then the task of democratic politics needs to be much more fully focused upon care responsibilities: their nature, allocation, and fulfillment. According to Tronto, a feminist democratic ethics of care (FDEC) differs from more familiar accounts of justice such as those described by John Rawls, or even from other feminist and nonfeminist accounts of an ethics of care such as those offered by Eva Kittay and Daniel Engster. The FDEC begins by envisioning a series of caring practices nested within one another. The goal of such practices is to ensure that all of the members of the society can live as well as possible by making the society as democratic as possible. This is the essence of her concept of "caring with." Thus, *"democratic politics should center upon assigning responsibilities for care, and for ensuring that democratic citizens are as capable as possible of participating in this assignment of responsibilities."* [94] The FDEC in Fisher/Tronto's term, must add the fifth quality of care, aligning with the four phases of care of *attentiveness, responsibility, competence*, and *responsiveness*: "Care with. This final phase of care requires that caring needs and the ways in which they are met need to be consistent with democratic commitments to justice, equality, and freedom for all." [95] Through Tronto's explanation of why association of care with democracy, we have seen the two need one another for solving problems of inclusion: care needs democracy to be complete and we need more than a concept of care; democracy as the theoretical framework for allocating care responsibilities, needs care to take inclusion seriously. Tronto analyzes, "The democratic process itself is no guarantee that members of a political community will arrive at the correct decision, but including all in allocating responsibilities might make it less likely that some potential changes are hidden behind the claim of necessity, or that paternalistic or parochial ideas will prevail without challenge." [96] Including care as a public concern upsets the distinction between public and private life, but including care in public life forces a reconsideration of how to think about gender, race, class, and the treatment of "others." It will require thinking more broadly about caring responsibilities: people who have been given a pass (the protection pass and the production pass discussion in her chapter 3) have exercised privileged irresponsibility will need to step up and assume greater roles in direct and intimate caring. [97] To me, Tronto redefines basic terms of democratic life as the following: freedom as an absence of domination rather than as making autonomous rational choices; equality as a condition of equal voice rather than individual right for equal opportunity; justice as an ongoing process of assigning and reassigning caring and other responsibilities in a framework of nondominated inclusion rather than being the opposite of care. When we think of the role of caring democratic citizens: "One of the challenges of an expressive-collaborative morality is to include the views of everyone in setting the agreements of what moral principles should hold." [98] The scope of discussion should be wide enough to ensure that all are engaged in caring with others.

Tronto also highlights how caring involves breaking hierarchies: the problem with caring dyads. Think of some cases of supposedly dyadic care such as the doctor/patient relationship, the mother/child relationship, or a student/teacher relationship: according to Tronto, despite our attachment to the dyadic relationship as a model of care, "it is hardly ever an accurate description."[99] We may notice that doctors do not provide health care alone; they are involved in a complex set of social relationships of care. An important part of democratic caring concerns the breaking down of hierarchical relationships: one starting point for doing so is to undermine the logic of care as dyadic. "Care rarely happens between two people only. And to create opportunities to 'triangulate' care also creates opportunities to break up a relentless hierarchy of power."[100]

How can we justify that democratic caring is better caring and preferable for people? Being the kind of political arrangement, democracy at its best permits humans to care for one another, for other animals and things in the world, and for the world itself. If people care about living in a planet where everything on it can be well cared for, then they should favor democracy because democratic care is better care. Also, care benefits were being done by more people; solidarity as a social value creates the conditions for caring among people and for greater responsiveness to democratic values; democratic caring flattens hierarchy and improves the quality of caring; crews were able to work within a more flattened hierarchy to resolve problems more effectively. My question is: what should Confucians learn from the feminist democratic ethics of care? The two share a core value of relational ontology about human nature, emphasizing people's interdependency and caring responsibilities for others in pursuing a common good, but they are quite different in respect to politics. Under the Chinese turbulent Warring States before the feudalist transformation, Confucian *ren* remains an open-minded and inclusive approach, aligning with *li* hierarchy for a harmonious social order and solidarity. The feminist democratic ethics of care under today's democratic polity in the United States would not tolerate the idea of hierarchy that is not compatible with all other values of democracy. But what should the FDEC learn from CGR of reciprocity? As Nivison's analysis in the *The Way of Confucianism* shows, Kongzi's conversations with students in the *Analects* require that we consult "trio or multiple" relationships in the measuring square of *shu* in figuring out how to treat others; thus one cannot sustain any sharp separation between private and public relationships.

To sum up the discussion in this chapter on different thoughts of integrating care, justice, and democracy, we have seen the Confucian way of humanity in the CGR consistently pursue identifying human sensitivity with heaven's way: learning the six arts to enjoy the meanings of life, living in different social roles to keep order in a harmonious world, and goodness as core value to guide human relational ontology, which would always be associated with objectivity since no one could be isolated but interdependent with family, clan, and communities. The Confucian way is not far from Nagel's objective self and capable of getting rid of Nagel's problem in deontological constraints: our very identity is bound up with others and we achieve and develop our selfhood by being responsible for them and responsive to them. Here the Confucian way of *ren* in reinforcing initial moral sensibility of *ren* and achieving such a moral sensibility at a higher level in treating both oneself and others, which is compatible with feminist ethics of care. Both can learn from each other but the key in each is about caring as a guiding principle to do a comprehensive moral work and caring responsibility is not separable but infused with considerations of justice. Infused into one another, care and justice as emotional and reasoning roles play together and share equal values in moral decision making and in moral practice as well.

In the next chapter, I will compare Mengzi's thoughts of innate human nature and benevolence as extensive virtue with Humean and feminist ideas of virtue, a trio comparison of moral epistemology.

NOTES

1. Virginia Held, *The Ethics of Care: Personal, Political, and Global* (Oxford: Oxford University Press, 2006), 71.
2. Held, *The Ethics of Care*, 66.
3. Held, *The Ethics of Care*, 11–13.
4. Held, *The Ethics of Care*, 15.
5. Held, *The Ethics of Care*, 15.
6. Held, *The Ethics of Care*, 17.
7. Held, *The Ethics of Care*, 39–40.
8. Held, *The Ethics of Care*, 41.
9. Held, *The Ethics of Care*, 71.
10. Held, *The Ethics of Care*, 117–19.
11. Held, *The Ethics of Care*, 134.
12. Held, *The Ethics of Care*, 135.
13. Held, *The Ethics of Care*, 150.
14. Held, *The Ethics of Care*, 151.
15. Daniel Engster, *The Heart of Justice: Care Ethics and Political Theory* (Oxford: Oxford University Press, 2007), 5 and 126.
16. Joan C. Tronto, *Caring Democracy: Markets, Equality, and Justice* (New York: New York University Press, 2013), 11.
17. Anca Gheaus, "Book Review: *The Heart of Justice: Care Ethics and Political Theory*, by Daniel Engster," *European Journal of Philosophy* 18, no. 4 (2010): 619–23.
18. Engster, *The Heart of Justice*, 5.
19. Engster, *The Heart of Justice*, 5.
20. Engster, *The Heart of Justice*, 39.
21. Engster, *The Heart of Justice*, 43–44.
22. Engster, *The Heart of Justice*, 49; emphasis added.
23. Engster, *The Heart of Justice*, 49.
24. Engster, *The Heart of Justice*, 50.
25. Engster, *The Heart of Justice*, 50.
26. Gheaus, "Book Review," 622–23.
27. Held, *The Ethics of Care*, 79.
28. Held, *The Ethics of Care*, 79.
29. Held, *The Ethics of Care*, 79–80.

30. Held, *The Ethics of Care*, 81, 84.

31. Diana Tietjens Meyers, "Intersectional Identity and the Authentic Self: Opposites Attract!" in *Relational Autonomy*, ed. Natalie Stoljar and Catriona Mackenzie (Oxford: Oxford University Press, 2000), 174–75; Held, *The Ethics of Care*, 48.

32. Held, *The Ethics of Care*, 115.

33. Held, *The Ethics of Care*, 122–24.

34. Held, *The Ethics of Care*, 122–24.

35. Engster, *The Heart of Justice*, 152.

36. See Held, *The Ethics of Care*; Fiona Robinson, *The Ethics of Care: A Feminist Approach of Human Security* (Philadelphia: Temple University Press, 2011); Tronto, *Caring Democracy*, 2013; Stephanie Collins, *The Core of Care Ethics* (London: Palgrave, 2015).

37. Oliver A. Johnson and Andrews Reath, eds., *Ethics: Selections from Classical and Contemporary Writers* (Boston: Wadsworth Cengage Learning, 2012), 420.

38. Thomas Nagel, "The View from Nowhere," in *Ethics*, ed. Johnson and Reath, 427.

39. Nagel, "The View from Nowhere," 428.

40. Nagel, "The View from Nowhere," 422.

41. Nagel, "The View from Nowhere," 422.

42. Nagel, "The View from Nowhere," 428.

43. Nagel, "The View from Nowhere," 428.

44. Nagel, "The View from Nowhere," 429.

45. Nagel, "The View from Nowhere," 430.

46. Nagel, "The View from Nowhere," 430.

47. Nagel, "The View from Nowhere," 431.

48. Nagel, "The View from Nowhere," 431.

49. Stan van Hooft, "Caring, Objectivity and Justice: An Integrative View," *Nursing Ethics* 18, no. 2 (2011): 149–60, sagepub.co.uk/journalsPermissions.nav 10.1177/0969733010388927.

50. Hooft, "Caring, Objectivity and Justice," 159.

51. Hooft, "Caring, Objectivity and Justice," 156.

52. Hooft, "Caring, Objectivity and Justice," 156.

53. Hooft, "Caring, Objectivity and Justice," 156.

54. Hooft, "Caring, Objectivity and Justice," 156.

55. Hooft, "Caring, Objectivity and Justice," 157.

56. Hooft, "Caring, Objectivity and Justice," 157.

57. Hooft, "Caring, Objectivity and Justice," 157.

58. Hooft, "Caring, Objectivity and Justice," 158–59.

59. Annette Baier, "The Need for More Than Justice," in *Science, Morality and Feminist Theory*, ed. Marsha Haren and Kai Nelson (Calgary, Alberta: University of Calgary Press, 1987); repr. in *Ethics*, ed. Johnson and Reath, 534–46.

60. Baier, "The Need for More Than Justice," 542.

61. Baier, "The Need for More Than Justice," 543.

62. Held, *The Ethics of Care*, 11.

63. Kongzi, *The Analects*, 15.24.

64. Kongzi, *The Analects*, 15.24.

65. David L. Hall and Roger T. Ames, *The Democracy of the Dead: Dewey, Confucius, and the Hope for Democracy in China* (Chicago: Open Court, 1999), 198.

66. Youlan Feng (冯友兰), *History of Chinese Philosophy*, 2 vols. (中国哲学史 上下二册), 16th ed. (Shanghai, China: Huadong Normal University Press [上海，中国，华东师范大学出版社], 2016), 1:35.

67. Feng, *History of Chinese Philosophy*, Vol. 1: 35.

68. David S. Nivison, *The Ways of Confucianism* (Chicago: Open Court Publishing, 1996), 63; *Zhongyong*, ch. 13, in James Legge, *Confucius: Confucian Analects, The Great Learning and The Doctrine of Mean* (New York: Dover Publications, 1971), 394.

69. Nivison, *The Ways of Confucianism*, 64.

70. Nivison, *The Ways of Confucianism*, 64; *Daxue* Commentary, ch. 10, in Legge, *Confucius*, 373–74.

71. Nivison, *The Ways of Confucianism*, 65; quoted in Ching, "Chinese Ethics and Kant," *Philosophy East and West* 28, no. 2 (April 1978): 161–72, here 169.

72. Nivison, *The Ways of Confucianism*, 65.

73. Nivison, *The Ways of Confucianism*, 65.

74. Bo Mou, "A Reexamination of the Structure and Content of Confucius' Version of the Golden Rule," *Philosophy East and West* 54, no. 2 (April 2004): 218–48.

75. Mou, "A Reexamination," 218.

76. Mou, "A Reexamination," 221.

77. Mou, "A Reexamination," 224.

78. Mou, "A Reexamination," 224.

79. Mou, "A Reexamination," 227–28.

80. Mou, "A Reexamination," 228.

81. Mou, "A Reexamination," 234.

82. Mou, "A Reexamination," 234.

83. Mou, "A Reexamination," 234.

84. Mou, "A Reexamination," 235.

85. Mou, "A Reexamination," 235.

86. Mou, "A Reexamination," 235.

87. Mou, "A Reexamination," 235.

88. Mou, "A Reexamination," 235–36.

89. Tronto, *Caring Democracy*, 20.

90. Tronto, *Caring Democracy*, 18.

91. Tronto, *Caring Democracy*, 22.

92. Tronto, *Caring Democracy*, 29.

93. Tronto, *Caring Democracy*, 30.

94. Tronto, *Caring Democracy*, 30.

95. Tronto, *Caring Democracy*, 23.

96. Tronto, *Caring Democracy*, 63–64.

97. Tronto, *Caring Democracy*, 143–45.

98. Tronto, *Caring Democracy*, 63.

99. Tronto, *Caring Democracy*, 152.

100. Tronto, *Caring Democracy*, 152–53.

III

Meta-Ethical Matters

Chapter Six

Hume's Sympathy, Mengzi's Empathy, Feminist Interpretations

Extensive Virtue

In this chapter, I will develop a comparative study of Hume, Mengzi, and feminist care ethics, comparing their thoughts along two lines. The first line of comparison will examine Hume and Mengzi on the notion of extensive virtue in normative thinking of morality. For the second line, I will develop a comparative feminist interpretation of Hume and Mengzi. In examining Hume's notion of extensive virtue in his normative thinking of morality, I will do so through a discussion of feminist critiques of Hume's principle of sympathy, which indicates a starting point that a need of integration of sympathy and empathy. This brings up Mengzi's thought of human nature and "four sprouts" theory to see the significance of empathy and feminism in a corrected notion of extensive virtue toward a normative ethics for a gender equal/just society. Through the comparison of the trio regarding extensive virtue in ontological broad senses, we can see clearly gendered experiences matter in interpreting the ethical dilemma of whether political power imbalance plays significant roles in deciding women and men's ethical choice.

Hume's "sympathy" and Mengzi's "four sprouts" provide thoughts that an instinctual virtuous motive can give rise to some sort of general or normal moral obligations. Nevertheless, how could "ought" be derived from "is"? Both Hume and Mengzi are positive about the extension of virtues from instinctual natural feelings toward general and genuine benevolence or care. What kind of relationship is there between "is" and "ought?" Hume points out the importance of the "impartial" or "disinterested" character of moral judgment while his theory is based firmly on natural feeling and sentiment.

Hume's principle of sympathy, together with his problem of is-ought, has been offering important elements for understanding why a binary distinction of reason and emotion be assumed in dominating theories of moral philosophy, and feminist critiques of Hume's sympathy and extensive virtues try to clarify Hume's weakness of circularity in holding up this distinction.

Mengzi's theory of human nature could be a quite adequate formula to be understood to mean merely that it is human nature to become benevolent and dutiful as it is the nature of water to tend downward. A problem arises when Confucians come to think of nature as a metaphysical concept on the same level as heaven and the way and to ask whether it is good in itself. Being paradoxical as it may seem, Mengzi's theory of human nature remains as interesting and important as Hume's principle of sympathy and the problem of is-ought. At this point, I believe that they both raise a big issue of "two roots or one" that remains open.

A feminist reinterpretation of Hume's notion of sympathy can open up the possibility of a less conservative Hume, giving space to the more dynamic and democratic aspects of his thought. Hume's notion of sympathy, especially in his imagination of the androgynes, is a promising starting point for an answer to the problem of inequality. These inspiring thoughts encourage further exploration of comparisons of the trio: Mengzi, Hume, and feminist moral epistemology. I argue to consider a further viewpoint of Mengzi associated with feminist care ethics as a promising starting point.

HUME'S PRINCIPLE OF "SYMPATHY"

Hume states in Book I of *Treatise* that all ideas borrowed from impressions and these two kinds of perceptions differ only in the degrees of force and vivacity. It is that different degrees of force and vivacity can distinguish the two perceptions. Hume also finds the double relationship in these two perceptions.[1] He compares two properties of the passions, their object (self) and their sensation (pleasure or pain) to the two supposed properties of the causes, their relation to self and their tendency to produce a pain or pleasure, independent of the passion. He finds that the cause, which excites passion, related to the object (self), which nature has attributed to the passion; the sensation, which the cause separately produces, also related to the sensation of the passion. In all these circumstances, sympathy found to be exactly correspondent to the operations of our understanding, and sympathy is the most important principle among all considerations about Hume's theory of moral judgment. Since sympathy has great influence on both our direct passions and indirect passions, it produces our sentiment of morals in all the artificial virtues (justice, promise, etc.) and natural sentiment for another virtue (beneficence, charity, generosity, moderation, etc.). All these natural and artificial virtues have the tendency to the good of society, and moral distinctions arise mainly from the tendency of qualities and characters to the interest of society and it is our concern for that interest that makes us approve or disapprove of them. Thus, it is the extensive sympathy, on which our sentiments of virtue depend, that produces our approbation for four qualities or characters: naturally fitting to be useful to others or to the person himself, or agreeable to others, or to the person himself. To me, Hume does believe in the possibility of producing normative moral judgments from natural feelings of moral goodness, though perhaps he could not give quite adequate explanation about this relationship.[2] Nevertheless, he does point out the importance of the "impartial" or "disinterested" character of moral judgment while his theory was based firmly on natural feeling and sentiment. Nevertheless, how could "ought" be derived from "is"? If we regard that "a new obligation supposes new sentiment to arise,"[3] this new one is neither the natural nor moral obligation, but something connected with both, which can be a new motive arising from our sympathy. Therefore, Hume is positive about the extension of virtues from instinctual natural feelings toward general and genuine benevolence or care.

MENGZI'S HUMAN GOODNESS AND METHOD OF EXTENSION

Mengzi argues that there are incipient virtuous inclinations in one's nature (*Mengzi*, 6A6), and he frequently describes these inclinations through a metaphor of "sprouts," and emphasizes that ethical cultivation must tend these virtuous sprouts (*Mengzi*, 2A6, 2A2, 6A7–8).[4] According to Mengzi, the four sprouts represent the four beginnings of *ren*, *yi*, *li*, and *zhi* in human nature. The heart of compassion is the sprout of benevolence; the heart of disdain is the sprout of righteousness; the heart of deference is the sprout of propriety; and the heart of approval and disapproval is the sprout of wisdom. The four sprouts match up the four cardinal virtues in Confucian teaching. These virtues, if not hindered by external conditions, develop naturally from within, just as a tree grows by itself from the seed, or a flower from the bud. In a study on Mengzi's thoughts of extension of moral feelings, McRae (2011) emphasizes a classic point that the ancient Chinese philosophers do not make clear the conceptual distinction between reason and emotion, and they don't think there is any reason to conceive of mind and body as a different kind.[5] The notion of "heart/mind" or *xin* (心) indicates that a person's *xin* has desire (*yu*) and emotion (*qing*) and can take pleasure in or feel displeasure at certain things. Xin can also deliberate about a situation or direct attention to and ponder about certain things and keep those things in mind. In a word, the notion of *xin* can help us understand how Mengzi could formulate his method of extending moral feelings or sympathy toward others or all people in the four seas. Through a comparison between Mengzi's and Mohist scholar Yi Zhi's thoughts of extending moral feelings, McRae emphasizes the most important one of the three criticisms of Yi Zhi from Mengzi: an issue of "two roots or one."[6] Mengzi's view emphasizes compassion and only compassion can be cultivated into the virtue of benevolence. Nevertheless, how could an affection allow itself into a compassion? It seems to me that there is a lack of explanation through this transition. How could one's affective feelings grow into compassions that drive one into the performance of their obligation to do the right thing and care for others at a far distance? Mengzi definitely draws our attention back to our moral feelings we start with; and the notion of *xin* cannot be separable with whatever our feeling capacities move us to do next in performing our obligations. Hume distinguishes between "natural" virtues, such as kindness and compassion, and "artificial" virtues, such as justice. Mengzi does not formulate any such distinction, but he is aware that what looks or feels benevolent may not be genuinely benevolent. Within the concept of heaven there is consequently a tension between factual and normative requirements, the way of heaven must somehow be both how things do happen, and how they ought to happen. Yet a problem arises when later Confucians come to think of nature as a metaphysical concept on the same level as heaven and the way and to ask whether it is good in itself. The word "goodness" is normally applied to actions and agents who in accord with heaven and the way, not to heaven and the way themselves. Thus, it becomes doubtful whether nature can be good in itself any more than the nature of water is as entity that tends downward. Being paradoxical as it may seem, Mengzi's theory of human nature remains as interesting and important as Hume's principle of sympathy and the problem of is-ought. At this point, I believe that the problem of "two roots or one" remains open, but both Hume and Mengzi have provided us with insightful, relevant elements for further explorations of human sympathy.

FEMINIST INTERPRETATION OF
EXTENSIVE VIRTUE IN HUME

Feminist approaches of epistemology are distinguished by their interest in exploring the ways in which the reason/emotion dichotomy is symbolically gendered—as well as associated symbolically with racial and class divisions. One of the epistemological approaches in feminism is feminist naturalism and the naturalistic element of it expressed in its "concern for empirical adequacy in general, but its feminist aspect lies in the special focus of that concern."[7] According to Jaggar, since feminist philosophy resists to the devaluation of women and the feminine, feminist naturalism seeks moral understandings that reveal rather than obscure empirical inequalities related to gender. This concern tends to make feminist philosophers distrustful of approaches to ethics that are exclusively rationalist.

While she realizes people's interdependencies as a crucial moral value, Held notices that, "In political and economic contexts, care as benevolence and as motive fails to understand the relations of power that can so easily undermine the value of care."[8] Held suggests, "But when we focus on relations, we can come to see how to shape good caring relations so that differences in power will not be pernicious and so that the vulnerable are empowered."[9] Feminist perspectives of evaluating extensive virtue in care ethics have been trying to empower the powerless through awareness of domination and subordination in relationships in order to resist injustice and inequality in the name of gender distinctions. My exploration of feminist interpretations of Hume follows the above line of feminist arguments for clarity of Hume's insights and weakness in reviewing his views of extensive virtue.

Sociability and Individualism

Baier has developed a great point in interpreting Hume's "The Reflective Women's Epistemologist?" In reading Hume's taking passions to be intrinsically reflective, cases of a "return upon the soul,"[10] desires for a repetition of a past pleasure and "lively" wish for the pleasure's continuation. Such desires for repetition of pleasure as reflection are surely reflection-tested pleasures: they are not merely good at the time but good in retrospect, desire that generates at a later date. To a question that "Why should we regard what we collectively, with as much information as we can get, prefer to prefer as our values?" a fair answer seems to be (in reading Hume): "What else could they be?"[11] It seems that we have no other choice than to discover our own values by collective reflection, starting from our less reflective desires, preferences, and loves. This shows an empiricist naturalized version of our cognitive process, which is compatible with the lines of feminist naturalistic concern, as I take it to help the feminist agenda and goals of opening up to multiperspective voices of the less authoritarian or marginalized. To see this more clearly, we turn to another feminist interpretation of Hume's notion of sympathy.

As Hume's researchers have known that Hume grounds political society and our allegiance to it in the importance to human happiness of relationships and society with his argument that the sympathy humans naturally feel for one another is "a vital part of our political allegiance"[12] and this shows a similar viewpoint to some feminist theorists according to Hirschmann. She points out that there is a tension in Hume's theory between human sociability and individualism, which could lead to different directions deriving from it. A feminist recuperation of Humean sympathy, in her exploration of it, can help resolve the tension, and thereby open up a more democratic potential in Hume.

Through a survey of feminist ethics of care, notions of empathy, "cofeeling," and "connected knowing,"[13] we see knowledge comes from experience, and the only way we can hope to understand another person's idea is to try to share the experience that has led the person to form the idea. Empathy as "feeling with" as merging the self with the other, rather than imposing the self on the other. By contrast, "separate knowing" is an "adversarial form" from premises of separation between knower and known; "Its concept of objectivity, with its rule-governed-ness and mastery over the known disjoins knowing and feeling."[14] All maternal dimensions of women's caring labor such as child rearing, cleaning, and cooking establish the ground for a feminist-standpoint epistemological framework. Some critiques may worry about women's tendency to overidentify with the other and lose the self, so-called pathology of the feminine model; but these perceptions are often part of cultural definitions and expectations of women's "empathy" in Hirschmann's analysis. "On this view, the 'feminine' exaggeration of connection is no more pathological than the 'masculine' exaggeration of separation between individuals, an exaggeration that similarly has come to be seen as normal in political philosophies of abstract individualism."[15] Knowing from experience allows one to not simply project their experience onto the other, but rather hear the other's account in a more profound way. The profound way, according to feminists, is not the way that experiences are merely similar but more profound and requires that one set aside her/his own mental stance and imagine having the different stance adopted by the another person; this is what Sandra Harding describes "reinventing ourselves as other."[16] This keen feeling of sharing (empathy) is the key to attending or responding to the other's needs.

Comparing Hume's notion of sympathy with feminist notion of empathy, Hirschmann points out Hume's weakness in two accounts. First, Hume has made a disjunction between feeling and action through ambiguous discussions of sympathy. Second, Hume lacks a developmental conception because of his static notion of self. But feminist theorists, as Hirschmann points out, are excited to include "an understanding of how male and females tend to develop their supposed orientation toward separateness or connectedness—through socially constructed social relations of reproduction and divisions of labor, as well as socialization norms of femininity and masculinity."[17] In the first account, Hume suggests that sympathy engenders the other's actual feeling in me so that "there is no difference in principle between the thought of pain and real pain."[18] At the same time, "his account of sympathy is quite individualistic"[19] in spite of the fact that sympathy is social, connects us with the whole world, and is an important principle for seeking the common good of morality. As Hirschmann explains, for Hume, "benevolence and sympathy are often at odds; while sympathy can result in benevolent action, it does not have to."[20] Sympathy may create a predisposition toward particular kinds of action, "approval" and "disapproval," but it does not itself produce action. Thus, Hume does not make a firm connection between feeling and action, which seems to conflict with feminist understanding of empathy that profoundly connecting oneself with the other and this related self is "dynamic, fluid, and responsive."[21]

Hume argues that because people are inadequate alone as isolated individuals, they cannot get what they want; Hume thus locates individuals in societies and describes them as "inescapably social."[22] Since the passions governed by the imagination, and since contiguous interests, being more immediate, impress themselves more vividly on the imagination, the passion will give preference to contiguous interests over remote ones. Yet, in the situations of interest that no longer guarantee allegiance, Hume claims this is where sympathy takes on its central political role, as Hirschmann states, for sympathy facilitates our adoption of "the general point of view,"[23] which is necessary to understanding the remote interests. Summarizing the importance of sympathy to political obligation, "Sympathy enables us to feel for others, to extend the feelings we have about our personal experience to those others, and thence to approve of justice and disapprove of injustice."[24]

According to Hirschmann, Hume's consideration of sympathy contains an odd mixture of strong individualism and strong sociability, a self-referential psychology undercuts his strong sense of social ontology, and a society as a whole where the law should be obeyed; on the other side, fear of sanction and self-interest can undercut strong sociability. As long as my sympathetic feelings stay locked inside me, public interest may not motivate me to do things that "sympathy ought to approve."[25]

Hume's Flawed Circularity?

Hirschmann also makes a final point regarding social obligations derived from a principle of sympathy: in the situation that government may not be serving the public interest and yet people may still feel obligated out of a habit of obedience, a conservative Hume "implies that in such cases, people can be mistaken in feeling obligated and in feeling sympathetic approval."[26] It seems that Hume owes us a clear explanation on his theory of society with its notion of "corrected" sympathy, "but his moral epistemology may make that impossible."[27] Hume did not go far enough to consider what exactly could be the feeling that starts from our actual feelings and extends into social feelings we ought to feel: he is simply denying that we can have a new kind of feeling to bridge the two. Thus, Hume's notion of sympathy in forging the social link is "flawed by a certain circularity"[28] Hirschmann proposes a feminist rereading of Hume in order to address his inadequacies and move on in a democratic direction in accord with Hume's incomplete line of thinking of the complicated link between natural feelings and social feelings with a firm approval or disapproval.

Hirschmann suggests that a rereading of Hume's approach to sympathy draws our recognition to his inconsistency and tension as a conservative individualist, encouraging a new view of Hume as a constructive and creative thinker of connected knowing, especially through his underdeveloped account of the way that shared experience leads toward substantial sameness in sociality. Since Hume cannot "overcome his individualist tendencies and forge the social link,"[29] how can he provide a basis for the full circle that is traveled when individual sympathy for political relations comes around to "corrected sympathy?"[30] It should be based on some objective "judgment" about what we ought to feel obligations to, but it would be impossible because approval is based on our feelings; this seems a circularity of sentimental criterion for moral judgment.

A feminist rereading must start to examine why Hume seems to be stuck in such a flawed circularity. "The feminist perspective of connectedness produces a conception of sympathy not as a natural emotion . . . but rather as a social dynamic that develops in and through relationships."[31] A feminist perspective of human connectedness and obligations need to be considered in a "different light from what Hume suggests. . . . The centrality of sympathy to human community need not lead to a conservative enshrinement of the status quo; on the contrary, it requires a communal effort to improve the social and political situation for all."[32] According to Hirschmann, feminist literature on empathy can help us to understand that the experience of gender and inequality in social relations begins with an account of sympathy that is inconspicuous in Hume unless and until "a different voice" from women is—as it *ought* to be—presented and heard.

The Wholeness of the Mind

Continuing with Baier's suggestion that Hume can be seen as "the reflective women's epistemologist,"[33] Lloyd offers a vision of Hume as "a source of insight into how unities of intellect, imagination, and emotion can be integrated into philosophical practice."[34] Her view of Hume as a whole will be particularly important for understanding Hume's contribution to feminist practical ethics in which sympathy, imagination, and intellect can integrate into the wholeness of the mind out of dialectic thinking through one's contextual circumstances. Instead of a detail-argumentation of Hume's general line of the wholeness of the mind, Lloyd briefly explains Hume's reading of a cluster of classic figures such as the "Epicurean," the "Stoic," the "Platonist," and the "Skeptic." By bringing these four types together, according to Lloyd, Hume has imbued each persona with his own spirit, a distinctively

Humean skeptic as the final words, "which resist the idea that anything can really be the final word."[35] This is what Hume left for us, no final words.

Is there a real Humean feminist philosopher? Lloyd prefers to find in Hume a mind well aware of its own "maleness," a limited position from which he spoke and wrote, "a perspective from which he engages generously with what is different from himself."[36] Although Hume limited himself into his maleness, a feminist consideration for gender equality could help to draw much more valuable elements from rereading Hume's thoughts of sympathy. Hough points out that Hume and Nietzsche comparatively hold some similar views of women's nature, but their views are differing in regard to essentialist versus antiessentialist accounts of female nature.[37]

According to Hough, Hume claims that female behavior is constantly sensitive and passive, and this passivity is "natural" in our interpretation of a fact of nature that we get: "Nature is mute on the question of how culture and education providing an account of it."[38] In Hough's interpretation of Hume, a question of whether Humean female "nature" determined by "nature" or "nurture" is not particularly useful. In Hough's analysis of a comparison between Nietzsche and Hume, both of them acknowledge that women can comport themselves as men do. Both argue that feminine manners are the result of socialization, not a female "nature"; the real difference between them is what each will count as a "truth" about human nature. We find Hume's claim that "we can never free ourselves from the bonds of necessity."[39] In Hough's analysis, Hume describes that female/male creatures as blessed by the gods and these "Androgynes" are utterly happy: each individual was in himself both husband and wife. "This union, no doubt, was very entire, and the parts very well adjusted together, since there resulted a perfect harmony between the male and female."[40]

Sympathy has played essential roles in such imagination about closeness in a perfect harmony. Sympathy is essentially as a precondition to exercise any imagination in double relations of impressions and ideas through extensions of cofeelings and collected knowing, but sympathy is not the solid emotion of morality; it requires more than itself to reach a corrected sympathy or extension of self. "Our sympathy for others imparts virtue to justice,"[41] thus, "the point of individual acts of justice cannot be seen except by reference to a rule or convention."[42] In reading Hume, although self-interest is the original motive to a general view of justice; sympathy with public interest is the source of the moral approbation associated with that virtue. So, "Sympathy is the quality that makes morality more than an exercise in prudence or rule following."[43] Since sympathy can mislead us when people close to us are involved, we should be seeking for the help of virtue which would correct our decision making when a wrong is done and we feel "unease" at the wrongness of actions. Sympathy therefore matters the most when we examine any unjust treatment of women.

Empathy and Sympathy

Some feminists have been considering the important roles of empathy and sympathy in moral epistemology. Oxley claims: "my own theory of empathetic deliberation is methodologically feminist in that it emphasizes empathy for the purposes of seeing situations from the perspective of others, in order to respond in a morally justified way."[44] Empathy can help us overcome the problem of "difference," the systematic unjust social exclusion of minority or powerless social groups, and the exclusion of their points of view. Oxley also argues that the cognitively advanced kinds of empathy she emphasized involve both the rational ability to fit others' beliefs and feelings into our own worldview, and the emotional ability to feel another's emotions in an effective way. Empathy, therefore, "includes elements of both rationality and emotion," and they are both important to moral deliberation and action. To me, this emphasis upon a hopeful integration of reason and emotion is certainly right. Hume's limited experience prevents him from considering the division of labor among different genders, and his individualistic tendency of sympathy could not fit well in the mothering experience.

Feminist ethics always emphasizes people's interdependence and caring relationships as necessary in a better society as a whole. As the social beings we are, the basis of our empathy and social sympathy starts with a social network at the moment of birth, so that being moral is not being alone or isolated; thus, overcoming the disconnected self is and should be a focus of morality as a starting point.

Feminist interpretation of Hume clarifies Hume's weakness in his analysis of abstraction insisting on individualistic ways of understanding "is" versus "should," and his failure of a circularity in a proof for a sentimentalist moral epistemology. The wholeness of the world and human relationship, which confronting feminist challenge of gender role differences and uneven powers in gender, race, class, and variety of relations, needs to be explored further.

FEMINIST INTERPRETATIONS OF
EXTENSIVE VIRTUE IN MENGZI

How do feminists interpret Mengzi's four sprouts in terms of a course of extensive virtue? Reading Mengzi and his unique contribution to Kongzi's thoughts of benevolence, we must admit that he should be the first to articulate one of the three major cornerstones as the foundation of Confucian cannons, "恻隐之心 (Sympathy)," along with the other two—"敬畏之心 (Respect Heaven)" and "己所不欲，勿施於人 (Golden Rule)."

McRae carefully used moral feelings (instead of emotions) to interpret Mengzi's method of extension. According to her, feeling is a broader concept that encompasses not only emotions but also feeling of respect, awe, and wonder, as well as intuition and sensations.[45] McRae is right with her intention in using moral feelings to a good grasp of the full scope of extension. In a comparison between Mengzi and Yi Zhi (a Mohist scholar), their different ideas of extending moral feelings, McRae emphasizes that the most important criticism of Yi Zhi from Mengzi is an issue of "two roots or one."[46] McRae points out that the differences between Yi Zhi and Mengzi is that Mengzi actually sees the feelings as primary and doctrine as merely a way to allow such feelings to mature into their corresponding virtues (in King Xuan's case in *Mengzi* 1A7). McRae states: To use Mengzi's analogy, if the moral feelings are sprouts, then we might think of reflection on philosophical doctrine as analogous to weeding. The weeding helps the sprouts to grow unimpeded by removing obstacles, but it cannot change the nature of the sprout.[47]

Here we can see that Mengzi's view emphasizes compassion and only compassion can be cultivated into the virtue of benevolence, "the object which is all people."[48] We understand that according to Mengzi, affection for one's parents needs to be transforming into a compassion through extending toward others' parents. Nevertheless, how could an affection allow itself into a compassion? It seems to me that there is a lack of explanation through this transformation. How could one's affective feelings grow into compassions that drive one into performance of one's obligation of doing the right thing and caring others in a far distance? Nivison would claim that Mengzi cannot take a stern Kantian line and say, "If it's your duty, do it! Forget about how you feel!"[49] Instead, Mengzi draws our attention back to the moral feelings we start with and the notion that *xin* (heart) cannot be separable with whatever our feeling capacities move us to do next in performing our obligations. Throughout a long debate on issues regarding "two roots or one," Nivison gave us a sort of answer about Mengzi's position: Mengzi would hold, he thinks, "that my judgment that I ought to do something is not, in itself, a feeling moved toward doing it, still less a feeling moved in the right way."[50] Therefore, I do not think that Mengzi attempts to clarify the problem of moral motivation (whether it is from a pure sense of duty or natural inclinations) but clearly, Mengzi emphasizes our feeling capacities as what we start with.

McRae continues to interpret two main features of Mengzi's extension: first is that extension is a rational process, the other is that extension must be sensitive to the particular feelings we start with. By these features and a details-interpretation of them, McRae argues that Mengzi's method of extension is a gradual process for sustaining itself through time, which is compatible with human psychological tendencies. Here I see a lack of further explanation of the extension so that we need to explore other interpretations of Mengzi such as David Wong (2015) in the following.

Hume distinguishes between "natural" virtues, such as kindness and compassion, and "artificial" virtues, such as justice. Mengzi does not formulate any such distinction, but he is aware that what looks or feels benevolent may not be genuinely benevolent. He gave an example in *Mengzi* 4B2. A high official on occasion lends his carriage to help people ford local rivers; but he could have built footbridges. Through this and other examples, Mengzi has shown that if a ruler extends his kindness through action, it will be sufficient for him to care for all within the Four Seas. To me, the core of Mengzi's extension is his emphasis on "doing what you feel the right to do," which is clearly laid out in 7A15 and 7B31. Mengzi says: "People all have things that they will not bear. To extend this reaction to that which they will bear is benevolence. People all have things they will not do. To extend this reaction to that which they will do is righteousness. If people can fill out the heart that does not desire to harm others, their benevolence will be inexhaustible."

This is Mengzi's exercising of Kongzi's Golden Rule of sympathetic understanding (*zhong* and *shu*) among human community. Using his straightforward words, "Treating one's parents as parents is benevolence. Respecting one's elders is righteousness. There is nothing else to do but extend these to the world" (7A15). Here we see a similar feminist point in reading Held's view of ethics of care advocating care as a value for society as well as the household, though she does not go further for a detailed analysis of extensive virtues. David Wong provides a detailed analysis of Mengzi's rich thoughts on extensive virtues in chapter 2 of *The Philosophical Challenge from China* (2015). Wong emphasizes a notion of *qi* (气) from Mencius: Mencius notices that the heart-mind is the commander of the *qi*. It forms aims (志) and when aims are focused or concentrated (*yi*), the *qi* follows and manifests as movement of the body so that it, in turn, can move the heart-mind's aims. That is, "the energy-stuff of *qi* can gather so as to influence the heart-mind in the aims or directions it takes. Thus, the conception of the person as constituted by *qi* underlies not only the feeling component but also the motivational component."[51] This inspires a thought of dialectical transmission of one's natural feelings toward more complicated relatedness of expanding feelings as compassion, as Wong explains, "The inborn motivational directionality in the sprout of compassion lies in concern for the suffering other."[52]

Mengzi discusses the decree of heaven in addition of his theory of human nature: to him, heaven is responsible both for the way things are and the way they ought to be, for the fact to which we must be reconciled and the standards by which we judge them. Within the concept of heaven there is consequently a tension between factual and normative requirements, the way of heaven must somehow be both how things do happen, and how they ought to happen. Mengzi's theory of human nature could be a quite adequate formula to be understood to mean merely that it is man's nature to become benevolent, and dutiful, as it is the nature of water to tend downward. Yet a problem arises when later Confucians come to think of nature as a metaphysical concept on the same level as heaven and the way and to ask whether it is good in itself. The word "goodness" is normally applied to actions and agents who are in accord with heaven and the way, not to heaven and the way themselves. Thus, it becomes doubtful whether nature can be good in itself any more than the nature of water is an entity that tends downward. As I understand Mengzi's thoughts on this puzzle, the answer is "Following the will of Heaven"[53] and try our best through cultivating virtues to reach "our Heaven-endowed nature."[54] This sounds like a contrast to Hume's "no final words"[55] but is left to us as a myth.

According to Zhen-gang Li (李振纲), the Chinese philosophical concept, the "Unity of Heaven and Humanity," has set up a profound commitment for the relationship between Heaven, Earth, all things in nature, and human society. Heaven as the supreme authority for keeping inherent goodness in nature's display on all things including humans, plants, and all animals in a harmonious order of the world in the original pursuit for life-preserving values. Nature, as the origin of all things alive in the world, has the "inherent goodness"[56] without doubt and as the origin of all values as well. Being aware of this origin and continuously approaching the "Unity of Heaven and Humanity" requires Confucians' hearty reflections, respectful comprehensions, and conversational discussions to better grasp this supreme source of all the world's spiritual and material wholeness. Mengzi's view of human nature and his view of "one root" definitely is associated with the concept of "Unity of Heaven and Humanity." Therefore, Mengzi is not similar to Hume's sentimentalist view of humanity and not to Hume's idealist view of Androgyne in patriarchal society either.

Three prerequisites of extension of virtue seem to be crucial in Mengzi's method of extension: social environment, education, and individual efforts. A benevolent ruler of a sage king is necessary for a well-ordered society seeking common good for all people; learning to be a moral person is necessary for the young following teacher's examples; and all individuals must correct their names in playing each role to keep up the harmony and peaceful relationships for a prosperous society. Among all cannon virtues, such as *ren*, *yi*, *li*, *zhi*, and *xin*, filial piety to parents and loyalty to the state and others are the primary roots, but they're the oneness of being and should be in the "Unity of Heaven and Humanity" (6A3 or 15, reflective xin [heart]). We extend family loyalty to the far reaches of the world through an analogy of sympathetic understanding to all under the heaven. This line of extension sounds mystical and beyond human control and grip.

A Daoist point of view will help clarify the puzzle—mythical guarding force of dynamic and dialectical transformation of harmony of the opposite. This myth is dominating over the universe, and *dao*, or nature, perhaps will always be beyond our understanding of the ways things are and the ways things should be. Therefore, perhaps the two or one root debates are only existing in human minds but not the original root of the nature that displays herself as the wholesomeness of all varieties of the world, including human-kind as a part of the whole. The nature or way is oneness for all connected without a doubt.

The identity of heaven and humanity plays an important role in people's extension of their virtues in Mengzi, which was usually ignored by Mengzi scholars due to Mengzi never explaining or formulating a comprehensive theory of heaven and humanity but only providing scattered points made through the book of *Mencius*. Nevertheless, we can try to connect him with other scholars' discussions of heaven and humanity to reveal and highlight his position so that we understand his contribution to the significance of helping today's thoughts of anti-anthropocentricism in ecofeminism about how human beings should treat other animals and plants in a diversifying ecological world as a whole.[57] In a tumultuous world of the Warring State period, Mengzi saw people's suffering through violence, greediness, and evil in their constant fighting against each other and between states, and his urgent task in following Kongzi's idea of bringing peace and stability back to the people became so crucial to continuing the authentic Confucian world-view of *ren/care* with compassion.

The extensive virtue of *ren* speculated by Mengzi can go together with feminist ethics of care as I observed; Held argues: "The ethics of care advo-cates care as a value for society as well as household."[58] The two should adopt each other in terms of extending the value of care at home to the broader community and global world since both will cherish "the interdependencies of personal, political, economic, and global contexts."[59] Further-more, feminist critical ethics of care also can help the Confucian idealist concept of *ren* overcome the exclusion of women in the nonideal Confucian society. Held points out that "In political and economic contexts, care as benevolence and as motive fails to understand the relations of power that can so easily undermine the value of care."[60] This reminds us to see the weakness of the early Confucian idealist notion of reciprocity: I emphasize that even it does not necessarily lead to an oppressive view of women—it does not offer a broad vision of how relational selfhood could be relational power in favor of the powerful in the social hierarchical harmony. Since it seemed to be a psychological-based reciprocity, it has limitations of its own account in its historical moment. Nevertheless, as Held suggests, "But when we focus on relations, we can come to see how to shape good caring relations so that differences in power will not be pernicious and so that the vulnerable are empowered."[61] Early Confucianism ultimately summarizes the importance of human virtues into the *ren* (benevolence or goodness): the *ren* being ultimately the most important and supreme virtue to follow at all times. If *ren* calls for the liberation and equality of women, then *ren* is still to be followed.

If *ren* is the roots and *shu* is the ways (sympathetic understanding or reciprocity) they should not be mutually exclusive but harmoniously collaborative. The contemporary Confucian *ren* should reach out to integrate with the feminist goal of deleting gender inequality in order to embrace a profound feeling of justice in deep care.

Why should feminists place an emphasis on the important roles of empathy and sympathy in moral epistemology? Many answers may be given here but one is from Oxley: "my own theory of empathetic deliberation is methodologically feminist in that it emphasizes empathy for the purposes of seeing situations from the perspective of others, in order to respond in a morally justified way."[62] So, empathy helps us to overcome the problem of "difference" as the systematic and unjust social exclusion of minority or other powerless social groups and the exclusion of their points of view. Oxley also argues that the cognitively advanced kinds of empathy she emphasized involve both the rational ability to fit others' beliefs and feelings into our own worldview, and the emotional ability to feel another's emotions in an effective way. Therefore, "Empathy includes elements of both rationality and emotion"[63] and they both are important to moral deliberation and action. To me, this emphasis upon both sounds like a good step toward challenging Hume's skeptical stance on the difficulty of developing disinterested social sympathy from individual interests. But with Mengzi no challenge is called for. One root nurtures four sprouts. People's hearts cannot flourish if they will not act to prevent harm from happening, and this is called benevolence, which, if nourished, assists the gradual process of learning the four virtues. In respect to their weakness, Hume's maleness prevents him from considering the division of labor between sexes, and his individualistic tendency of sympathy could not work well for mothering experiences. Mengzi's maleness also prevents him from seriously thinking of the differences in gender roles and uneven relational powers in family, community, and state.

Feminist care ethics emphasize people's interdependence and caring relationship as necessary in a better society as a whole. As the social beings we are, the base of our empathy and social sympathy starts with a social network at the moment of birth, so that being moral is not being alone or isolated, but instead overcoming self (the *Analects*) should be a focus of morality from the start. Aristotle's *Nicomachean Ethics* articulates the notion of true self-love as other-regarding, noble, and spiritual, which is compatible with a feminist starting point, as Sherman states: in thinking about self-empathy, it is useful to turn to Aristotle's remarks about self-love (or self-friendship) in *Nicomachean Ethics* (Aristotle, 1984, NE IX.8), "there is room for a good kind of self-love, he insists, that is, the capacity of a self to listen to reason with equanimity. He associates this kind of self-love with nobility and the sacrifice characteristic of reason's excellence."[64] When we have self-empathy as Sherman argues, one as both a subject and object, can evaluate self through a perspective of the other, and Aristotle's idea of finding the right way to befriend oneself is useful here. The best kind of character friendship is an area for character critique and moral growth,[65] which, like all friendships, requires positive feelings toward one's object and feelings of goodwill. Aristotle's idea of self-love evaluation can be a companion to Mengzi's idea that people all have things that they will not bear, though Mengzi does not reason like Aristotle. Instead, he uses a narrative story to illustrate his idea similar to Aristotle.

CONCLUSION

Feminist interpretations of Hume and Mengzi clarify Hume's weakness in the "maleness" of his time, insisting on an individualistic way of understanding "is" versus "should" and a failure of a circularity in proof for sentimentalist moral epistemology. Mengzi's extensive virtue methodology does not commit a fault circularity since he made heaven's will as an objective moral resource to rely upon. The notion of unity of heaven and humanity provides a holistic approach to understanding how a moral person should act in accordance with nature's supreme force—the wholeness of the world and human relationship, which confronts the feminist challenge of gender role differences and uneven powers in gender, race, class, and a variety of relations. Heaven's will as a supreme, respectful authority could lead to the dominating interpretations that all things happened as they should happen, and it would be unlikely the powerless turn over the dominating interpretation of heaven's will by powerful authority such as Dong's *yin-yang* doctrine in Han and in *LiJi*. Mengzi's moral extension method lacks serious responses to such concerns. But feminist critical ethics of care can take strength from both lines of empathy and sympathy as integrated capacity without a separation of a binary of reason and emotion, so that we begin from a fresh starting point: natural tough caring with justice is capable of extending caring practice and value into a global scale.

NOTES

1. David Hume, A *Treatise of Human Nature*, ed. L. A. Selby-Bigge, 2nd ed. (New York: Oxford University Press, 1978), Book I: 1–273.
2. Hume, *Treatise*, Book III: 455–621.
3. Hume, *Treatise*, Book III: 455–621.
4. *Mengzi*, in Philip J. Ivanhoe and Bryan W. Van Norden, eds., *Readings in Classical Chinese Philosophy*, 2nd ed. (Indianapolis: Hackett, 2005), 115–59.
5. Emily McRae, "The Cultivation of Moral Feelings and Mengzi's Method of Extension," *Philosophy East & West* 61, no. 4 (2011): 587–608.
6. David Nivison, *The Ways of Confucianism: Investigation in Chinese Philosophy* (Chicago: Open Court, 1996), 133–48.

7. Alison M. Jaggar, "Ethics Naturalized: Feminism's Contribution to Moral Epistemology," *Mataphilosophy* (2000): 452–68, doi: 10.1111/1467–9973.00163.

8. Virginia Held, *The Ethics of Care: Personal, Political, and Global* (New York: Oxford University Press, 2006), 56.

9. Held, *The Ethics of Care*, 56.

10. Annette C. Baier, "Hume: The Reflective Women's Epistemologist?" in *Feminist Interpretations of David Hume*, ed. Anne Jaap Jacobson (University Park: Pennsylvania State University Press, 2000), 26–27.

11. Baier, "Hume: The Reflective Women's Epistemologist?" 27.

12. Nancy Hirschmann, "Sympathy, Empathy, and Obligation: A Feminist Rereading," in *Feminist Interpretations of David Hume*, ed. Jacobson, 175.

13. Hirschmann, "Sympathy, Empathy, and Obligation," 177–78; Sandra Harding, *Whose Science? Whose Knowledge? Thinking from Women's Lives* (Ithaca: Cornell University Press, 1991), 268.

14. Hirschmann, "Sympathy, Empathy, and Obligation," 177–78.

15. Hirschmann, "Sympathy, Empathy, and Obligation," 177–78.

16. Hirschmann, "Sympathy, Empathy, and Obligation," 177–78.

17. Hirschmann, "Sympathy, Empathy, and Obligation," 181.

18. Hirschmann, "Sympathy, Empathy, and Obligation," 177–78.

19. Hirschmann, "Sympathy, Empathy, and Obligation," 179.

20. Hirschmann, "Sympathy, Empathy, and Obligation," 179.

21. Hirschmann, "Sympathy, Empathy, and Obligation," 181.

22. Hirschmann, "Sympathy, Empathy, and Obligation," 182.

23. Hirschmann, "Sympathy, Empathy, and Obligation," 182

24. Hirschmann, "Sympathy, Empathy, and Obligation," 183 (Hume, THN 581).

25. Hirschmann, "Sympathy, Empathy, and Obligation," 184.

26. Hirschmann, "Sympathy, Empathy, and Obligation," 188.

27. Hirschmann, "Sympathy, Empathy, and Obligation," 188.

28. Hirschmann, "Sympathy, Empathy, and Obligation," 188–89.

29. Hirschmann, "Sympathy, Empathy, and Obligation," 189.

30. Hirschmann, "Sympathy, Empathy, and Obligation," 189.

31. Hirschmann, "Sympathy, Empathy, and Obligation," 189.

32. Hirschmann, "Sympathy, Empathy, and Obligation," 190.

33. Genevieve Lloyd, "Hume on the Passion for Truth," in *Feminist Interpretations of David Hume*, ed. Jacobson, 56.

34. Lloyd, "Hume on the Passion for Truth," 56.

35. Lloyd, "Hume on the Passion for Truth," 56.

36. Lloyd, "Hume on the Passion for Truth," 57.

37. Sheridan Hough, "Humean Androgynes and the Nature of 'Nature,'" in *Feminist Interpretations of David Hume*, ed. Jacobson, 226–36.

38. Hough, "Humean Androgynes and the Nature of 'Nature,'" 220.

39. Hough "Humean Androgynes and the Nature of 'Nature,'" 231 (Hume, *Treatise*, 408).

40. Hume essays 555 cited from Hough, "Humean Androgynes and the Nature of 'Nature,'" 231.

41. Hough, "Humean Androgynes and the Nature of 'Nature,'" 234.

42. Hough, "Humean Androgynes and the Nature of 'Nature,'" 234.

43. Hough, "Humean Androgynes and the Nature of 'Nature,'" 234.

44. Julinna C. Oxley, *The Moral Dimensions of Empathy: Limits and Applications in Ethical Theory and Practice* (New York: Palgrave Macmillan, 2011), 158.

45. McRae, "The Cultivation of Moral Feelings and Mengzi's Method of Extension," 588.

46. Originally discussed by Nivison, *The Ways of Confucianism*, 133–48.

47. McRae, "The Cultivation of Moral Feelings," 591.

48. McRae, "The Cultivation of Moral Feelings," 591.

49. Nivison, *The Ways of Confucianism*, 135.

50. Nivison, *The Ways of Confucianism*, 148.

51. David Wong, "Growing Virtue: The Theory and Science of Developing Compassion from a Mencian Perspective," in *The Philosophical Challenge from China*, ed. Brian Bruya (Cambridge: MIT Press, 2015), 27.

52. Wong, "Growing Virtue," 27.

53. Bryan Van Norden, "Menicus," *The Stanford Encyclopedia of Philosophy* (Spring 2017 Edition), ed. Edward N. Zalta. https://plato/stanford.edu/archives/spr2017/entries/mencius/.

54. "Mencius," *Stanford Encyclopedia of Philosophy.*

55. Lloyd, "Hume on the Passion for Truth," 56.

56. Li Zhen-gang (李振纲), "Interpretation of Four Levels in the Philosophy of Identity of Heaven and Humanity," (解读 "天人合一" 哲学的四重内涵) *Journal of Zhongshan University, Social Sciences* (中山大学学报社会科学版) 46, no. 5 (2006): 49–54.

57. Franklin Perkins, *Heaven and Earth Are Not Humane: The Problem of Evil in Classical Chinese Philosophy* (Bloomington: Indiana University Press, 2014), 143–50.

58. Held, *The Ethics of Care*, 53.

59. Held, *The Ethics of Care*, 53.

60. Held, *The Ethics of Care*, 56.

61. Held, *The Ethics of Care*, 56.

62. Julinna C. Oxley, *The Moral Dimensions of Empathy: Limits and Applications in Ethical Theory and Practice* (New York: Palgrave Macmillan, 2011), 158.

63. Oxley, *The Moral Dimensions of Empathy*, 158.

64. Nancy Sherman, "Recovering Lost Goodness: Shame, Guilt, and Self-Empathy," *Psychoanalytic Psychology* 31, no. 2 (2014): 217–35, here 229.

65. Aristotle, *Nicomachean Ethics*, in *The Complete Works of Aristotle: The Revised Oxford Translation*, ed. J. Barnes (Princeton: Princeton University Press, 1984); N. Sherman, *Making a Necessity of Virtue: Aristotle and Kant on Virtue* (New York: Cambridge University Press, 1995), 187–239.

Chapter Seven

China's Population Policy

Aging, Gender, and Sustainability

China is about to undergo a stunning demographic transformation, a rapidly aging population. Despite the influence of the aging process on women's lives, very few works analyze the interconnectedness of gender and aging. This chapter analyzes the interrelationship between China's aging population, gender inequality, and elderly women's poverty. Since gender issues in aging have been ignored, idealistic models put forward to promote the well-being of the elderly fail to address the specific needs of aging women. Traditional attitudes in China toward caring for the elderly have met serious challenges as a result of China's economic reform, one-child policy, and social acceptance of individualistic development and competitive lifestyles. I argue that a fruitful way for dealing with the "graying" population of China is not to abandon her traditions but to call upon a Confucian notion of reciprocity that provides guidelines for the respect and care for the elderly through a joint effort of family, community, and government support. When properly revised and infused with gender consciousness, the Confucian tradition points the way to attending specifically to the needs of disadvantaged elderly women.

While Confucianism emphasizes how humans can live together and create a just society with a benevolent government, it, like Daoism, reminds us of the importance of harmony with nature. I will argue that the needs of elderly Chinese will be well-served not just by interweaving gender consciousness into the tradition of Confucianism, but also by emphasizing an ecological consciousness; cooperation with nature will foster limited growth within a steady state economy and sustainable development that will help all elderly, both women and men, in the long run. I also explore more details on

Mengzi's notions of *ren* governance and the importance of the common people in terms of their dignity to call on the responsibilities of the state and government on eldercare.

ONE-CHILD POLICY AND ITS PROBLEMS

When the post-Mao regime took power in 1978, Deng's new policies focused on strengthening China's economy. He saw overpopulation as a roadblock to economic development. The one-child policy was introduced to ensure that China, which has historically been prone to floods and famine, could feed all her people. At the end of 1970s, China was home to a quarter of the world's people, who were occupying just 7 percent of the world's arable land. The baby boomers of the 1950s and 1960s were entering their reproductive years. The government saw strict population control as essential to economic reform and to an improvement in living standards. So the policy started in 1979 and was enforced as the national law of "one-child" for one family. "After more than 30 years of different endeavors, the effort to modify Chinese population trends has achieved remarkable success that has been recognized all around the world."[1] China's population is expected to increase and "the total population in China will peak at 1.486 billion by 2034, and then slightly decline to 1.44 billion by 2050."[2] The director of China's National Population Control and Family Planning Committee declared that the one-child policy reduced about 0.4 billion births at the end of 2005 and stressed that China would not change the policy in the future.[3] The reduction in fertility reduced the severity of problems that come with overpopulation, like epidemics, slums, overwhelmed social services (health, education, law enforcement, and more), and strain on the ecosystem from abuse of fertile land and production of high volumes of waste. Despite all of these achievements resulting from the implementation of "one child," a number of problems were created through this policy. Although the one-child policy phased out at the end of 2015, a new policy in early 2016 allowed all Chinese families to have two children. According to state media reports citing China's National Health and Family Planning Commission, it seemed that Chinese families adjusted to the one-child policy during several decades and did not want to have more children for many reasons such as finances and medical and education costs.

Among these problems, two severe issues include the imbalance of sex ratios at birth and the rapidly aging population.[4] Sociologists say that 30 million more Chinese men will be unable to marry by 2020 because there are not enough female counterparts for the men; the inability to find suitable spouses could trigger aggressive behavior among frustrated bachelors, including kidnapping and trafficking in women. These consequences could be a real threat to China's stability in the future.

"Although the one-child policy has been blamed for the high male sex ratio, it is probably just one contributory factor. There was a sex-ratio imbalance in China in the 1930s and 1940s, mostly resulting from infanticide of girls."[5] It is likely that, even in the absence of the policy, sex-selective abortion has continued. "The solution will come only with a change in attitudes toward female offspring."[6] The influence of traditional ideologies such as widespread remnants of Confucianism have definitely played an important role in preferring sons over daughters. People's mentality of "more sons, more happiness" has been shaped through and deeply rooted in Chinese culture. Chinese feminists need to provide a critical analysis of the traditional bias against women and to clarify that the problem is a matter of ideology that devalues women and girls.[7]

What are feminist thoughts concerning Chinese aging and women? Do gender issues matter in regard to aging? I will describe how gender inequalities have made elderly women's lives harder than that of their male partners and will propose how the state policy should change toward a more sustainable and equitable approach to improve the quality of the lives of aging women in China.

China will rapidly age because of the one-child policy that prompted a steady slide in total fertility rates to a level estimated at about 1.5 today.[8] When the People's Republic of China was born in 1949, life expectancy was only forty-five for women and forty-two for men. Now it is rising steadfastly along with a rapidly growing economy and an improving standard of living. "By 2050 life expectancy could be as high as 81 for women and 76 for men. The combination of low fertility and longer life spans will create the phenomenon of an aging China."[9] The burden of aging is a spur to Chinese leaders to pursue policies that will better prepare the country for meeting the cost of caring for its huge elderly population.

HOW CAN TRADITIONAL VIRTUE OF FILIAL PIETY MEET THE NEED OF THE ELDERLY?

Before economic reform, as a socialist society, China was steeped in its unique cultural tradition of filial piety and strongly endowed attitudes of promoting the well-being of the elderly. A definite goal for the elderly is so-called Five Haves, that is Lao You Suo Yang (the elderly have appropriate material and financial support), Lao You Suo Yi (appropriate medical care), Lao You Suo Xue (educational opportunity), Lao You Suo Wei (accomplishment), and Lao You Suo Le (entertainment/enjoyment).[10] Although the "Five Haves" sound very idealistic for ordinary people who had low earnings and small pensions after retirement, they have become endorsed in the system as a practice for young generations to care for their elderly parents.

The central value of the Chinese familism is Xiao (filial piety). Xiao or the sense of filial piety was instilled among children to foster the desirable attitudes toward their parents and other family members of older generations. "As the family was the basis of the social structure in traditional China, the idea of Xiao played a vital role in maintaining support of old persons and helped fashion a respectful societal attitude towards the elderly."[11]

Traditional Chinese society was a feudalistic one characterized by its sociopolitical hierarchy. To maintain social hierarchy a set of cardinal principles regulating social relations were needed and observed as "San Gang Wu Chang," which dictated the positions of subjects submissive to the king, sons to parents, and wives to husbands. "Xiao as an idea differentiating the family status of parents and sons thus became a major means to uphold the social hierarchy in the traditional Chinese society."[12] Such a feudal society was marked not only by its social hierarchy but also by strong mutual obligations and common interests. A harmonious and happy family relationship was an ideal shared among family members. Family went before individuals, and different roles and mutual obligations of family members to each other were essential and maintained from generation to generation. The reciprocal nature of the Chinese intergenerational caring relationship was not just exemplified in supportive activities through life but also was manifested by efforts of both the younger and older on a daily basis of exchange and cooperation to satisfy the common interests of the family.[13]

All in all, "the equation 'community care = family care' seems to be a claim historically relevant to China."[14] According to Chen's analysis, since women were prescribed the lowest status in the family and society, Xiao did have a side effect in balancing the threefold subordination requirements for the mother; hence, "it is perfectly permissible to say that elderly men benefitted more under Xiao, than women, because women did not enjoy the same social status and privileges as men during that time."[15] However, Chen continues to point out that the requirement of Xiao eventually led to the promotion of female well-being in relation to their grownup sons. "When women entered older ages Xiao was a major means to guarantee their living with support mostly from their sons"[16] and the reason for this, according to Chen, is that grown-up sons "were considered as the mainstay of the family and the society."[17] To me this argument sounds like begging: the mainstay roles of the sons were actually prescribed by the society, and their responsibility of providing Xiao for their mothers was assumed. In the realities of a family with young and old generations, the wife is most likely doing the household chores and providing emotional support for families. Socially assigned roles and different obligations to women should not be the cause of their bearing less responsibility compared to that of men to their elderly mothers. Furthermore, in reality, everyday-based caring practices most likely were accomplished by women—daughters or daughters-in-laws—but those providing the caring work were not considered as equally valuable as sons.

Lau's article "Changing Family-Related Values in Communist China" points out further issues of gender inequality. When the earnings of men and women are compared, observable inequality prevails. Husbands earn much more than their wives do and have higher positions at work. In Lau's report, the present Chinese pension scheme includes a monthly pension of 70 percent to 80 percent of the basic salary. This scheme is restricted mainly to those living in the city, and working as officials, educators, scientists, and so on. As a result, "a large number of Chinese citizens still do not receive any pensions."[18] "The old people who have only a meager pension or even none at all will have no choice but to rely upon the family as the most important source of support."[19] Very fortunately, the tradition of filial piety is still prevalent for those old in need. Nevertheless, under the current market economy, new lifestyles and burgeoning consumerism have accelerated young people toward developing individualistic attitudes, replacing both the traditional and the new social values introduced by the Cultural Revolution. "The ideal of total devotion to the family or the state is being replaced by individualism. A survey in Beijing also finds that '80% of those aged 15 to 25 wanted to set up financially independent families and maintain some physical distance from the parents.'"[20]

Other scholars also demonstrate challenges to the "family care only" system. Milligan cites a 2007 commentary in the *Beijing Review* that predicts the family-based system of support for older people will come to an end in the next twenty years.[21] The migration of working age adults from rural to urban areas leaves behind the many elderly Chinese who remain in their rural homes. As Milligan states, "Whilst urban populations doubled from 16 percent to 32 percent between 1960 and 2000, three-quarters of all elderly people in China still live in rural areas."[22]

Cheung has specifically addressed gender issues in the aging population, and, in particular, has analyzed the differential implications of aging for men and women. Women live longer than men but are more likely to be widowed or single and are more likely to be economically dependent. "Their lifetime earnings are substantially lower than those of men. They do not receive the benefits of pension schemes or provident funds, which are tied to paid employment."[23] She argues for the life-cycle approach to the gender and aging analysis across Asian countries, a gender mainstreaming method endorsed by the All-China Women Federation, Women Research Institution.[24]

ANALYSIS OF POSSIBLE STRATEGY/POLICY FOR
A TRANSITION TO A SUSTAINABLE MODEL
OF CARING FOR THE ELDERLY

Sustainability is characterized by Guo and Marinova as "meeting the needs of current and future generations through an integration of environmental protection, social advancement and economic prosperity."[25] They point out that sustainability is a new concept and is not China's priority at present. It seems that China has emphasized economic growth at the expense of environmental protection and social advancement. The response of Chinese leaders, of course, would be that her most important focus has rightly been economic growth so that people could rid themselves of poverty and have a "warm and full stomach," in Deng's terms. But can China maintain economic growth and preserve her arable land, water, and other limited natural resources and at the same time support social advancement, health care, and the quality of life for her population? In a team report of "Ten Big Challenges Confronting Population and Development in China"[26] they point out that China is confronting the most serious environmental problems relating to water and soil erosion, land desertification, and grassland destruction. Polluted water and air, noise, and garbage in the city and the abuse of chemical substances "have obviously imposed severe threats to food security and people's health in China."[27] What will be better strategies for China to employ in order to promote sustainable growth of the economy and meet expanding domestic demands that will come from an increasingly large aging population?

Guo and Marinova do mention that China's aging will result in an increased demand for home-based care for the disabled, frail, and elderly, and will lead to more pressure on the environment to meet the demand. Although they rightly state, "Future economic prosperity and growth are not certain if there are risks to the natural environment,"[28] they seem to see the polarization only as a dilemma. They offer no suggestions for a possible solution, and do not see how China's traditional values of harmony with nature and filial piety and reciprocity might provide a key to crafting a solution.

According to Wang and Shanahan, both Daoism and Confucianism convey insightful ecological themes. The principle concern in Daoism is for harmony with the Dao, the nameless way that is the source of all existence. In Confucianism, the stress is on how humans can live together and create a just society with a benevolent government. For both the Daoists and the Confucians, harmony with nature is important. The Daoists emphasize the primacy of unmediated closeness to nature to encourage simplicity and spontaneity in individuals and in human relations. The Confucians, especially the neo-Confucians, stress harmonizing with the changing patterns in nature so as to adapt human action and human society appropriately to nature's deeper rhythms.[29]

Daoism advocates that yielding is a form of strength. Its calls for non-interfering action with enormous implications for our interactions with nature—namely that humans cannot arrogantly or blindly force nature into our mold. To cooperate with nature in a Daoist manner requires a better understanding of and appreciation for nature's processes. While an extreme Daoist position might advocate complete noninterference with nature, a more moderate Daoist approach would call for interaction with nature in a far less exploitive manner than China engages in at present. Such cooperation with nature would sanction the use of appropriate or intermediate technology when necessary and would favor the use of organic fertilizers and natural farming methods. In terms of economic policy, it would foster limited growth within a steady state economy that could support sustainable, rather than exploitive development. Clearly, a Daoist ecological position is one with significant potential in the contemporary world. And this ecological position offers us insight into the aging population as well: aging is a part of a natural cycle. To ignore the special needs of aging men and women is to "fight" or "ignore" nature, quite contrary to Daoist thought. To recognize the fact of aging is to fully acknowledge that humans are part of—not removed from—the natural ecological cycles.

In *Dao De Jing*, Laozi states, "There is no greater calamity than not knowing what is enough,"[30] which implies that in issues of aging we go along with the path of the nature. Someone may raise a challenge to Laozi that it sounds too easy to give up life. Laozi would reply in chapter 50, don't give up easily but be good at holding on to life. Reading the two chapters (46 and 50) together, clearly, the *dao* asks us to follow the law of nature—the mystic of life—and knowing that is enough to bring people serenity. The *dao* put human life as a part of the natural ecological cycles as a whole so people could have peace of mind when their time comes.

An aspect of human life often obscured by an emphasis on individualism is our interdependence with the rest of nature and with other human beings. As the feminist philosopher Eva Kittay points out in *Love's Labor*, we are all some mother's child; we are all equal in the sense that we inevitably depend on other humans for our own well-being.[31] Kittay is right when she argues that care should be a moral value of considerable importance. But I would add that a person's place in the lifecycle affects how and on whom the person will be dependent. There is a difference between a parent-child relationship, a husband-wife relationship, and an adult child-aging parent relationship—and how caring is best expressed will be shaped by the differences in these relationships.

In traditional Confucianism women were to be obedient to their parents and husbands and thus more likely to be the benefactor than the beneficiary in their caring relationships. Confucianism, though, must be understood as a living, dynamic theory—not a fossilized code—and should be modified to meet better the needs of both women and men. Attention to gender consciousness leads us to call for a Confucian ethics that extends its moral sense to encompass gender equality. In order to care for all, Confucianism must delete its call for the "threefold obedience of women"[32] and commit fully to gender justice. Properly revised, Confucianism's family-oriented ethical thought is compatible with a feminist ethics of care and serves well as a general guide for dealing with public life. At their best, both Confucianism and the ethics of care properly emphasize contextual- and connection-based reciprocity.

In denying individual exchange reciprocation, Kittay raises a notion of reciprocity-in-connection:

> Significantly, the reciprocation is based not on the care her mother gave her daughter and which she now expects her daughter to return. That would turn the mother's care for her daughter into a sort of advance payment for later care—a maneuver typical of exchange reciprocity. The daughter instead invokes a set of nested obligations. The fulfillment of those obligations is now her responsibility and hers uniquely.[33]

This set of nested obligations demands human relationships to extend from family to community and society, from today's generations to future generations. Today's generations should look after their young and old, and future descendants as a whole.

The post-Mao government has kept Mao's commitment for women's equality and tried to focus on community construction and service through a call of taking humanity as a *Root* principle which serves everyone, including women. The city of Beijing has built 107 residential community centers and almost 3,000 service stops since 1998.[34] Wenmei Cai, professor of Peking University, argues that old-aged people should be taken care of at home through the community service and not to be sent to a senior center.[35] According to Cai, living at home is the best way for old people to enjoy the rest of their life, and actually, it is desirable for the old through the investigations of their choices. For example, the Hepingli residential community realizes old people's needs and interests and organizes various forms of activity to energize their lives such as calligraphy and drawing groups, singing and dancing groups, sports and games associations, and so on. With regular meetings retired and elderly people get together in order to communicate with each other and to share their common interests. The goals of community are to take care of the two important stages of life: birth and old age. Laid-off and unemployed women get service jobs and are able to practice public care in their own resident community. This benefits both family and society in general. Shumin Li states that everyone is going to be old and need help, so helping the old is to help one's self.[36] For today's old and tomorrow's self we must care for everyone and take care as the most important value in a good life.

The Women Studies Center of Peking University conducted a survey of elder women's lives in the western suburb of Beijing in 2008:[37] most of them are lower income or poor women. According to the survey of 304 women ranging in age from 60 to over 80 and few over 90, one-third of them were living with their children or relatives, less than two-thirds were living near family members with close contacts, and one-sixth of them were living with three generations of family. All of them except one expressed their will of living with family rather than being alone. The purpose of the survey is to make suggestions regarding laws that protect elder women's rights and interests. Thus, the survey laid out many questions about those women's everyday activities and about their economic status, health care, medical situations, and so on.

When a recognition of the natural rhythm of aging and the interdependency of humans is combined with the Confucian social values of filial piety and reciprocity, we have the keys to better strategies for China's future as it promotes sustainable economic growth and meets the demands of an aging population. In my view, the state should carry on the traditional values of the harmonious relationship between the young and the old and increase the pensions of the elderly. Since there have been increased gaps between genders, and most elderly women have no pension in the countryside, the state should put the neediest elderly women as the priority in aging relief policies. The state also needs to develop further social programs in the local community that imitate the diversity of nature itself; both individuals and companies should be looked to for financial support for social programs, and volunteers from neighborhoods should be solicited to watch out for and help the elderly who live alone. Since the problem of 4/2/1[38] will increase rapidly in the next two decades, older people will be living alone more often than before and the demands of intensive care will be increasing immensely as well as the pressure on the environmental costs. The government should consider more sustainable options that will allow the elderly to stay at home or be housed in the local community rather than in more expensive and centralized senior centers that would be yet another drain on energy reserves. Although public services should be available for those having special needs, "people in the community helping people" should be the guiding principle for care of the elderly—and it is precisely in this principle that we find a deep recognition of human interdependency.

CARING FOR ELDERLY WOMEN IN
THE CRISIS OF CHINA'S AGING

Elderly women are more likely than men to be widowed and to live alone. "The proportion of old men and women living alone is 8 percent and 10.2 percent, respectively."[39] Also, older women are more likely to be economically dependent because of their past unpaid household labor and lower-paid jobs.[40] Therefore, "the disadvantages of women in marital life and living arrangements are substantially more serious than those of men at old ages."[41] Older women are less likely than older men to get remarried due to their economic status, educational level, and other factors.[42] Elderly women's care, especially for those living in the countryside, should be the priority in the government policy dealing with an aging population.

According to Leung, women are entitled to five years of early retirement in high-risk professions. But, women are also compelled to retire earlier than men and, so, have a shorter career life span. The retirement age is sixty for men and fifty-five for women. Why are women required to leave their jobs five years earlier than men? Theoretically this policy protects women, "but the protection can be seen as paternalistic and restrictive, and in concrete terms might be seen as inhibiting women from attaining equal working conditions and wages to men"[43] Leung emphasizes that so-called harmony between men and women is superficial, based as it is on the absolute dominance by the male of the female. "There cannot be real harmony until men and women can live with dignity and respect as equals."[44]

We should not ignore these social causes of women's economic dependence. The government should consider providing for the needs of the poor elderly women with special funds while supporting the traditions of family care for the elderly. For those elderly who live alone or have needs beyond those provided for by the family, the state and local communities should take up the responsibility for their everyday care. The retirement age of women in professional fields should be made equal to that of men. The causes of the gender gap in China's current pension system has been examined in a recent article, "Reform of Pension System Design Based on the Gender Equality Perspective" by Junfu Hao and Xinyu Li (2017). They analyzed main reasons for the gender gap in pensions, including "the gender gap for the employment rate and unemployment rate, gender wage gap, gender gap in workers engaged in informal employment, gender gap in statutory retirement age and gender gap in life expectancy."[45] According to them, the current inequitable design of the pension mechanism not only fails to compensate for the gender inequality, but also exacerbates the gender inequality of pension benefits. So they claim: "It is necessary and urgent to reform the mechanism design of the pension system based on the gender equality. The main reform includes: to expand the coverage of contributory pension scheme; to implement gender equalization of the statutory retirement age; to use 'unisex life table' actuarial hypothesis; to provide care credits for women; to establish the derived pension rights; to establish noncontributory pension scheme."[46] All these suggestions should be put into action immediately.

A CONFUCIAN SOCIOETHICAL VISION OF ELDERCARE

Jing-Bao Nie's research focuses on Confucian ethical sources for eldercare in recent years. His article, "The Benevolent Polity: A Confucian Socio-Ethical Vision of Eldercare" highlights Mengzi's particular thoughts on issues of why and how we should respect and take good care of the elderly. According to Nie, a legendary founding King Shun (舜), revered in China as the embodiment of filial piety and humane polity, excellence in caring for the elderly one millennium later was a salient feature of King Wen's rule, exemplifying the fundamental Confucian political ideal of benevolent polity. Over subsequent centuries, the notion of *jinglao yanglao* (敬老養老, respecting and caring for the elderly) evolved to become a core value of the Confucian belief system and social order, and became a characteristic norm of Chinese civilization. However, this core value of taking good care of the elderly faces numerous challenges in China today. More than 200 million people over the age of sixty are now living in China, nearly 15 percent of the total Chinese population.[47]

As Nie states, eldercare is primarily a moral undertaking, "no society can develop adequate levels of care for all its older people without a sound ethical vision."[48] Nie argues that it is vital to revive Chinese cultural traditions such as classical Confucianism to address eldercare in today's China. Nie demonstrates two notions from Mengzi's political and moral thoughts to highlight the value of elderly care: one is benevolent governance (仁政); the other is importance of people (民貴). Mengzi often refers to the example of King Wen, whose primary sociopolitical concern was to care for the abandoned and destitute: "There were the old and wifeless, or widowers [*guan*]; the old and husband-less, or widows [*gua*]; the old and childless, or solitaries [*du*]; the young and fatherless, or orphans [gu]—these four classes are the most destitute of the people, and have none to whom they can tell their wants."[49] King Wen, "in the institution of his government with its benevolent action, made them the first object of his polity, as it is said in the Book of Poetry, 'The rich may get through life well; but alas for the miserable and solitary!'"[50] Nie explains that this is Mengzi's response to a question of *renzheng* (仁政) or *wangzheng* (王政, royal government or kingly governance). A basic standard to judge if a ruler's governance conforms to the principles of *renzheng* is whether, as Mengzi states, "all widowers, widows, orphans and the childless have been provided with adequate support and

care"[51] (鰥寡孤獨, 皆有所養, *guan gua gu du, jieyou suoyang*). Nie emphasizes, that realizing the political and social ideals of Meng Zi, King Wen's
governance improved his people's lives by providing employment and good
education, lowering taxes and imposts, valuing the voice of the people, and
eschewing draconian laws and harsh punishments."[52] All these infused into
Mengzi's advice to rulers he served. The book of *Mengzi* shows compelling-
ly, in Nie's highlighting, that the central theme of classical Confucian moral
and political thought is *the responsibilities of rulers or the government to the
people including the elderly*, rather than the other way around.

Mengzi is probably best known, as Nie rightly argues, for another notion
of importance and value of the common people (民貴論, *mingui lun*).
Among the three categories—the people, the kingdom, and the ruler—Mengzi assigned the first place to the people, and gave the ruler last place: "The
people are the most important element in a nation; the spirits of the land and
grain are the next; the sovereign is the lightest."[53] Mengzi believes that "the
people are the masters and the ruler is their servant, and that the people are
the essence and the state merely the function."[54] This being the case, "the
government had the absolute duty of nourishing the people and maintaining
peace and stability in the country, while the people did not have any duty of
obedience to the government. If the government should fail in its responsibilities, then the people need not be loyal to it."[55] What would be the individual
duties for elderly care? Filial piety as a primary virtue has nowhere else been
emphasized to the degree it has in classic Confucian Xiaojing (孝经): xiao is
defined as the foundation of morality in both family and society, "the pattern
of heaven, the standard of the earth, the norm of conduct or the people."[56]
"Thus from the Son of Heaven to the common people, unless filial piety is
pursued from beginning to end, calamities will surely result."[57] According to
Nie, the Confucian definition of filial piety, "not merely providing one's
parents with the means of subsistence, but caring for them in a genuinely
respectful way, and extending the concept to the wider society far beyond
one's own family,"[58] means that "eldercare is a matter of respecting and
honoring the human dignity of the elderly."[59] Reading *Mengzi*, this fundamental dignity is more valuable even than life itself for people of every social
stratum. Mengzi analyzed this profound dignity by saying "there are things
one desires more than life and there are also things one hates more than
death. It is not the case that only the worthy person has this heart. All humans
have it. The worthy person simply never loses it."[60] Therefore, Nie makes
the point that Mengzi is not so concerned with the responsibilities of individuals, but rather the obligations of the ruler and the governing authorities to
the common people, including the elderly. Thus national "law on the Protection of the Rights and Interests of the Elderly" promulgated in 1996, and
revised in 2009 and 2012. But the moral justification of this law came out of
the classic Confucian filial piety and notions of *ren* governing and *Minben*

(people-oriented) or *Mingui* (the importance of the common people). The Confucian socioethical vision of eldercare, in Nie's view, is centered on the responsibilities of the state and government to the elderly, respect for the rights and dignity of the elderly, and the primacy of *ren* morality. I agree with such a viewpoint, though more detailed analyses about whether there are gender issues in dealing with today's graying population remains open to critique.

China must secure the current population control and stabilize the present low fertility level. Learning the positive elements of Confucian and Daoist traditions is necessary in order to secure a harmonious and green society—even if it means a slowed economy and readjustment to meet healthy and sound standards for development. The Chinese government started to limit the number of private car purchases (one car for one family) in Beijing since 2011 in order to reduce air pollution. This is just one important step in trying to make economic development fall into harmony with the natural environment.

To conclude: China can move toward a sustainable and equitable development through a joint effort of family, community, and the state. To confront aging, the family, community, and state must work together to meet all older people's needs, but the government must take major responsibility for eldercare, especially for those disadvantaged elderly women who do not have pensions yet. These tasks can be accomplished with the help of a Confucian framework of filial piety based on nonindividualistic, contextualized reciprocity but only when this framework is properly infused with both gender and ecological consciousness.

NOTES

1. Gong Chen, Guangzong Mu, Xinming Song, and Xiaoying Zheng, "Ten Big Challenges Confronting Population and Development in China," *Asian Population Studies* 4, no. 1 (2008): 97–105.

2. Chen et al., "Ten Big Challenges."

3. The one-child policy changed into the two-children policy by the Chinese government in 2015.

4. Chen et al., "Ten Big Challenges."

5. Therese Hesketh, Lu Li, and Wei Xing Zhu, "The Effect of China's One-Child Family Policy after 25 Years," *England Journal of Medicine* 353 (2005): 1171–76.

6. Hesketh et al., "The Effect of China's One-Child Family Policy."

7. Yanguang Wang, "The Causes of China's Abnormal Sex Ratio and Improved Approaches," paper presented at the XXII World Congress of Philosophy: Rethinking Philosophy Today, Seoul, July 31, 2008.

8. Yun Zhou, "Fertility Control and Women in China," paper presented at the Women and Gender Research Collaborative Symposium, LBJ Student Center, Texas State University-San Marcos, March, 4, 2011.

9. Robert Stowe England, *Aging China: The Demographic Challenge to China's Economic Prospects* (Westport, CT: Praeger, 2005).

10. Cang-ping Wu, "Family Planning and Population Aging: General Law and the Reality in China," *Chinese Elderly*, no. 5 (1986) (in Chinese), cited in Sheying Chen, *Social Policy of the Economic State and Community Care in Chinese Culture* (Avebury: Ashgate, 1996), 57.

11. Chen, *Social Policy*, 59.

12. Chen, *Social Policy*, 60.

13. Chen, *Social Policy*, 61.

14. Chen, *Social Policy*, 62–63.

15. Chen, *Social Policy*, 62–63.

16. Chen, *Social Policy*, 63.

17. Chen, *Social Policy*, 63.

18. Stephen Shek-lam Lau, "Changing Family-Related Values in Communist China," in *Aging Gender and Family in Singapore, Hong Kong and China*, ed. Kenneth Wing-kin Law (Taipei, Taiwan R.O.C: Program for Southeast Asian Area Studies, Academia Sinica, 2001), 187–207.

19. Lau, "Changing Family-Related Values in Communist China," 187–207.

20. Lau, "Changing Family-Related Values in Communist China," 203.

21. Christine Milligan, *There's No Place Like Home: Place and Care in An Ageing Society* (Burlington, VT: Ashgate, 2009), 50.

22. Milligan, *There's No Place Like Home*, 50.

23. Fanny M. Cheung, "Ageing Population and Gender Issues," in *New Challenges for Development and Modernization*, ed. Yue-man Yeung (Hong Kong: Chinese University Press, 2002), 211.

24. See Bohong Liu, Shuo Guo, and Rui Hao, *Research Report on the Retirement Age* (Geneva, Switzerland: Publications Bureau, International Labour Organization, 2011), 69–77.

25. Xiumei Guo and Dora Marinova, "Population Ageing and Sustainability in China: Comparisons with Australia," 2006, http://http://www.cfses.com/06confchina/documents/Final-Papers/Paper-Guoxiumei-Population-Ageing-and-Sustainability.pdf.

26. Chen et al., "Ten Big Challenges."

27. Chen et al., "Ten Big Challenges."

28. Guo and Marinova, "Population Ageing and Sustainability in China."

29. Timothy Shanahan and Robin Wang, *Reason and Insight: Western and Eastern Perspectives on the Pursuit of Moral Wisdom*, 2nd ed. (Belmont, CA: Wadsworth, 2003), 485.

30. Lao-tzu (Laozi), chapter 46, in *Tao Te Ching* (*Dao De Jing*), trans. Stephen Addiss and Stanley Lombardo (Indianapolis: Hackett, 1993).

31. Eva Feder Kittay, *Love's Labor: Essays on Women, Equality, and Dependency* (New York: Routledge, 1999), 23.

32. Shanahan and Wang, *Reason and Insight*, 485.

33. Eva Feder Kittay, *Love's Labor*, 67.

34. Zhongliang Ma and Lingzhen Yin (马仲良, 尹玲珍主编), eds., *Women's Work and Community Construction* (妇女工作与社区建设) (Beijing: China Personal Press [中国人事出版社], 2003), 124.

35. Ma and Yin, *Women's Work and Community Construction*, 127.

36. Ma and Yin, *Women's Work and Community Construction*, 136–37.

37. I received email attachment of the draft of the survey from the deputy director of the Women Studies Center, Professor Wei, September 2008 (in Chinese).

38. Sun Xi, "4-2-1s Hemmed-in between Two Generations," http://www.womenofchina.cn/Issues/Marriage-Family/223429.jsp.

39. Y. Zeng and L. George, "Family Dynamics of 63 Million (in 1990) to More Than 330 Million (in 2050) Elders in China," *Demographic Research* 2, no. 5 (2000), www.demographic-research.org/Volumes/Vol2/5/ doi: 10.4054/DemRes.2000.2.5.

40. Shawn Meghan Burn, *Women across Cultures: A Global Perspective* (New York: McGraw-Hill, 2011), 90–119.

41. Zeng and George, "Family Dynamics."

42. Zhenzhen Zheng (郑真真), "Finding Issues through Phenomenon: Population and Gender Studies" (透过现象看本质: 人口学与性别研究), in *Gender Issues: Multidisciplinary Perspectives* (他们眼中的性别问题：妇女/性别研究的多学科视野), ed. Tan Lin and Meng

Xianfan (谭琳，孟宪范主编) (Beijing: Social Sciences Academic Press [社会科学文献出版社], 2007), 83.

43. Alicia S. M. Leung, "Feminism in Transition: Chinese Culture, Ideology and the Development of the Women's Movement in China," *Asia Pacific Journal of Management* 20 (2003): 359–74, here 367.

44. Leung, "Feminism in Transition," 372.

45. Junfu Hao (郝君富) and Xinyu Li (李心愉), "Reform of Pension System Design Based on the Gender Equality Perspective" (基于性别公平视角的养老金制度设计改革), *Journal of Renmin University of China* 3 (2017): 118–127.

46. Hao and Li, "Reform of Pension System Design," 127.

47. Jing-Bao Nie, "The Benevolent Polity: A Confucian Socio-Ethical Vision of Eldercare," *Asian Bioethics Review* 7, no. 3 (September 2015): 260–75.

48. Nie, "The Benevolent Polity," 260.

49. Nie, "The Benevolent Polity," 263; *Mengzi*, bk. I, pt. II, ch. 5; James Legge, *The Works of Mencius* (New York: Dover Publications, 1970), 162, with minor modifications by Nie.

50. Nie, "The Benevolent Polity," 263.

51. Nie, "The Benevolent Polity," 264.

52. Nie, "The Benevolent Polity," 264.

53. Nie, "The Benevolent Polity," 266, *Mengzi*, bk. VII, pt. II, ch. 14; Legge, *The Works of Mencius*, 483.

54. Nie, "The Benevolent Polity," 266.

55. Nie, "The Benevolent Polity," 266.

56. Nie, "The Benevolent Polity," 267.

57. Nie, "The Benevolent Polity," 267.

58. Nie, "The Benevolent Polity," 268.

59. Nie, "The Benevolent Polity," 268.

60. *Mengzi* 6A10, cited in Philip J. Ivanhoe and Bryan W. Van Norden, *Readings in Classical Chinese Philosophy*, 2nd ed. (Indianapolis: Hackett, 2005), 150.

Bibliography

Allen, Amy. *The Power of Feminist Theory: Domination, Resistance, Solidarity*. Boulder, CO: Westview Press, 1999.

Ames, Roger T. *Confucian Role Ethics: A Vocabulary*. Hong Kong: Chinese University Press, 2011.

Angle, Stephen C., and Michael Slote, eds. *Virtue Ethics and Confucianism*. New York: Routledge, 2013.

Aristotle. "Nicomachean Ethics." In *The Complete Works of Aristotle: The Revised Oxford Translation*, edited by J. Barnes. Princeton, NJ: Princeton University Press, 1984.

Baier, Annette C. "Hume: The Reflective Women's Epistemologist?" In *Feminist Interpretations of David Hume*, edited by Anne Jaap Jacobson, 19–38. University Park: Pennsylvania State University Press, 2000.

———. "The Need for More Than Justice." In *Science, Morality and Feminist Theory*, edited by Marsha Haren and Kai Nelson. Calgary, Alberta: University of Calgary Press, 1987.

Bell, Daniel A. "A Comment on Confucian Role Ethics." *Frontiers of Philosophy in China* 7, no. 4 (2012): 604–9.

———., ed. *Confucian Political Ethics*. Princeton: Princeton University Press, 2008.

Burn, Shawn Meghan. *Women Across Cultures: A Global Perspective*. New York: McGraw-Hill, 2011.

Carbado, Devon W., Kimberle William Crenshaw, Vickie M. Mays, and Barbara Tomlinson. "Intersectionality: Mapping the Movements of a Theory." *Du Bois Review* 10, no. 2 (2013): 303–12.

Card, Claudia. "Gender and Moral Luck." In *Identity, Character, and Morality: Essays in Moral Psychology*, edited by Owen Flanagan and Amelie Oksengerg Rorty. Cambridge: Massachusetts Institute of Technology Press, 1990.

Chan, Sin Yee. "Gender and Relationship Roles in the Analects and the Mencius." In *Confucian Political Ethics*, edited by Daniel A. Bell. Princeton: Princeton University Press, 2008.

Chang, Doris T. *Women's Movements in Twentieth-Century Taiyuan*. Urbana: University of Illinois Press, 2009.

Chen, Gong, Guangzong Mu, Xinming Song, and Xiaoying Zheng. "Ten Big Challenges Confronting Population and Development in China." *Asian Population Studies* 4, no. 1 (2008): 97–105.

Chen, Sheying. *Social Policy of the Economic State and Community Care in Chinese Culture*. Avebury: Ashgate, 1996.

Cheung, Fanny M. "Ageing Population and Gender Issues." In *New Challenges for Development and Modernization*, edited by Yue-man Yeung. Hong Kong: Chinese University Press, 2002.

Chodorow, Nancy. *The Reproduction of Mothering*. Berkeley: University of California Press, 1978.

Collins, Patricia Hill, and Sirma Bilge. *Intersectionality*. Malden, MA: Polity Press, 2016.

Collins, Stephanie. *The Core of Care Ethics*. London: Palgrave Macmillan, 2015.

Confucius. *Analects*. Translated by Edward Slingerland. Indianapolis: Hackett, 2003.

Crenshaw, Kimberle Williams. "Mapping the Margins: Intersectionality, Identity Politics, and Violence against Women of Color." *Stanford Law Review* 43 (1991): 1241–99.

———. "Demarginalizing the Intersection of Race and Sex: A Black Feminist Critique of Anti-discrimination Doctrine, Feminist Theory, and Anti-racist Politics." *University of Chicago Legal Forum* 140 (1989): 139–67.

De Beauvoir, Simone. *The Ethics of Ambiguity*. Translated by Bernard Frechtman (New York: Citadel Press Stone, 1964). Quoted in Alison Stone. *An Introduction to Feminist Philosophy*. Cambridge, UK: Polity Press, 2007.

———.*The Second Sex* (1949). Translated by H. M. Parshley, copyright 1952 and renewed 1980 by Alfred A. Knopt, a division of Random House, Inc. Introduction of *The Second Sex* in *Theorizing Feminisms: A Reader*. Edited by Elizabeth Hackett and Sally Haslanger. New York: Oxford University Press, 2006.

Engels, Friedrich. *The Origin of the Family, Private Property, and the State*. New York: Pathfinder Press, 1972.

England, Robert Stowe, *Aging China: The Demographic Challenge to China's Economic Prospects*. Westport, CT: Praeger Publishers, 2005.

Engster, Daniel. *The Heart of Justice: Care Ethics and Political Theory*. Oxford: Oxford University Press, 2007.

Feng, You-lan (冯友兰). *History of Chinese Philosophy* (中国哲学史 上下二册). 2 vols. 16th ed. Shanghai, China: Huadong Normal University Press (上海，中国，华东师范大学出版社), 2016.

———. *A Short History of Chinese Philosophy*. New York: Macmillan, 1948.

Ferguson, Ann. "Androgyny as an Ideal for Human Development." In *Feminism and Philosophy*, edited by Mary Vetterling-Braggin. Totowa, NJ: Rowman & Littlefield, 1977.

Fetzer, Joel S., and J. Christopher Soper. *Confucianism, Democratization, and Human Rights in Taiwan*. Lanham, MD: Lexington Books, 2014.

Fincher, Leta Hong. *Leftover Women: The Resurgence of Gender Inequality in China*. London: Zed Books, 2014.

Flax, Jane. "Race/Gender and the Ethics of Difference: A Reply to Okin's 'Gender Inequality and Cultural Differences.'" *Political Theory* 23, no. 3 (1995): 500–510.

Friedman, Marilyn. *What Are Friends For? Feminist Perspectives on Personal Relationships and Moral Theory*. Ithaca: Cornell University Press, 1993.

Fu, Hong-mei (付红梅). "The Traditional Female Ethics and Ceremony Propriety and Its Modern Value" (中国传统女性伦理与礼仪及其现代价值). *Journal of Studies in Ethics* (伦理学研究双月刊) 26, no. 6 (2006): 100–103.

Gheaus, Anca. "Book Review: *The Heart of Justice: Care Ethics and Political Theory*, by Daniel Engster." *European Journal of Philosophy* 18, no. 4 (2010): 619–23.

Gilligan, Carol. *In a Different Voice: Psychological Theory and Women's Development*. Cambridge, MA: Harvard University Press, 1982.

Goldin, Paul Rakita. *The Culture of Sex in Ancient China*. Honolulu: University of Hawai'i Press, 2002.

Grillo, Trina. "Anti-Essentialism and Intersectionality: Tools to Dismantle the Master's House." In *Theorizing Feminisms*, edited by Elizabeth Hackett and Sally Haslanger, 30–40. New York: Oxford University Press, 2006.

Grimshaw, Jean. *Feminist Philosophers*. Brighton, England: Wheatsheaf Books, 1986.

Groenhout, Ruth. "Virtue and Feminist Ethics of Care." In *Virtues and Their Vices*, edited by Kevin Timpe and Craig A. Boyd, 482–501. Oxford: Oxford University Press, 2014.

Guo, Xiumei, and Dora Marinova. "Population Ageing and Sustainability in China: Comparisons with Australia." 2006. www.cfses.com/06confchina/documents/Final-Papers/Paper-Guoxiumei-Population-Ageing-and-Sustainability.pdf.

Hall, David L., and Roger T. Ames. *The Democracy of the Dead: Dewey, Confucius, and the Hope for Democracy in China*. Chicago: Open Court, 1999.

Hao, Junfu (郝君富), and Xinyu Li (李心愉). "Reform of Pension System Design Based on the Gender Equality Perspective" (基于性别公平视角的养老金制度设计改革). *Journal of Renmin University of China* 3 (2017): 118–27.

Hao, Yan. *China's Growing Middle Class in an Increasingly Stratified Society*. EAL Background Brief No. 307, October 26, 2006.

Harding, Sandra. *Whose Science? Whose Knowledge? Thinking from Women's Lives*. Ithaca: Cornell University Press, 1991.

———. "What Is the Real Material Base of Patriarchy and Capital?" In *Women and Revolution: A Discussion of the Unhappy Marriage of Marxism and Feminism*, edited by Lydia Sargent, 135–63. Montreal: Black Rose Books, 1981.

He, Qinglian. "Analysis of Social Changes of Women's Status in Contemporary China" (当代中国妇女状况的社会变化分析) 《当代中国研究》). *Modern China Studies* 2 (2001).

Heilbrun, Carolyn G. *Toward a Recognition of Androgyny*. New York: Alfred A. Knopf, 1973.

Held, Virginia. *The Ethics of Care: Personal, Political, and Global*. Oxford: Oxford University Press, 2006.

———, ed. *Justice and Care: Essential Readings in Feminist Ethics*. Boulder, CO: Westview Press, 1995.

Hesketh, Therese, Li Lu, and Zhu Wei Xing. "The Effect of China's One-Child Family Policy after 25 Years." *England Journal of Medicine* 353 (2005): 1171–76.

Hirschmann, Nancy. "Sympathy, Empathy, and Obligation: A Feminist Rereading." In *Feminist Interpretations of David Hume*, edited by Anne Jaap Jacobson, 174–93. University Park: Pennsylvania State University Press, 2000.

Hoagland, Sarah Lucia. "Some Thoughts about 'Caring.'" In *Feminist Ethics*, edited by Claudia Card. Lawrence: University Press of Kansas, 1991.

Hooyman, Nancy R. "A Personal, Professional, and Political Journey as a Feminist Gerontologist." *Generations: The Journal of the Western Gerontological Society* 41, no. 4 (2017): 57–63.

Hough, Sheridan. "Humean Androgynes and the Nature of 'Nature.'" In *Feminist Interpretations of David Hume*, edited by Anne Jaap Jacobson, 218–38. University Park: Pennsylvania State University Press, 2000.

Hu, Shi. *Collections of Writings of Hu Shi, Series 6: On Issues of Chastity*. Hong Kong: Hong Kong Yuanliu Press, 1986.

Hume, David. *A Treatise of Human Nature*, edited by L. A. Selby-Bigge. 2nd ed. New York: Oxford University Press, 1978.

Ivanhoe, Philip J., and Bryan W. Van Norden. *Reading in Classical Chinese Philosophy*. 2nd ed. Indianapolis: Hackett, 2005.

Jacka, Tamara. *Rural Women in Urban China*. Armonk, NY: M.E. Sharpe, 2006.

Jaggar, Alison M. "Ethics Naturalized: Feminism's Contribution to Moral Epistemology." *Metaphilosophy* 35, no. 5 (2000): 452–68.

———. "Caring as a Feminist Practice of Moral Reason." In *Justice and Care: Essential Readings in Feminist Ethics*, edited by Virginia Held, 179–202. Boulder, CO: Westview Press, 1995.

———. *Feminist Politics and Human Nature*. Totowa, NJ: Roman & Littlefield, 1988.

———. "On Sexual Equality." *Ethics* 84, no. 4 (1974): 275–91.

Jenkins, Stephanie. "Joan C. Tronto, *Caring Democracy: Markets, Equality, and Justice*." Narrated by Miranda Pilipchuk. *Hypatia Reviews Online*. hypatiareviews.org/review/contents/254.

Jiang, Xiaoyuan (江晓原). *Chinese People under Tensions of Sexuality* (性张力下的中国). Shanghai (上海): Shanghai People's Press (上海人民出版社), 1995 《会稽刻石》 (Huiji Stone-inscription).

Johnson, Oliver A., and Andrews Reath, eds. *Ethics: Selections from Classical and Contemporary Writers*. Boston: Wadsworth Cengage Learning, 2012.

Kittay, Eva Feder. *Love's Labor: Essays on Women, Equality, and Dependency*. New York: Routledge, 1999.

―――. "The Moral Harm of Migrant Carework: Realizing a Global Right to Care." In *Gender and Global Justice*, edited by Alison M. Jaggar, 62–84. Malden, MA: Polity Press, 2014.

Kocięda, Aphrodite. "Marginalization Is Messy: Beyond Intersectionality." *Feminist Current* (blog). September 26, 2013, https://www.feministcurrent.com.

Lao-tzu (Laozi). *Tao Te Ching (Dao De Jing)*. Translated by Stephen Addiss and Stanley Lombardo. Indianapolis: Hackett, 1993.

Lau, D. C. *Confucius: The Analects*. New York: Penguin Group, 1979.

Lau, Stephen Shek-lam. "Changing Family-Related Values in Communist China." In *Aging Gender and Family in Singapore, Hong Kong and China*, edited by Kenneth Wing-kin Law, 187–207. Taipei, Taiwan R.O.C: Program for Southeast Asian Area Studies, Academia Sinica, 2001.

Law, Kenneth Wing-kin, ed. *Aging Gender and Family in Singapore, Hong Kong and China*. Taipei, Taiwan R.O.C: Program for Southeast Asian Area Studies, Academia Sinica, 2001.

Legge, James. *Confucius: Confucian Analects, The Great Learning and The Doctrine of Mean*. New York: Dover Publications, 1971.

―――. *The Works of Mencius*. New York: Dover Publications, 1970.

Leung, Alicia S. M. "Feminism in Transition: Chinese Culture, Ideology and the Development of the Women's Movement in China." *Asia Pacific Journal of Management* 20 (2003): 359–74.

Li, Jingzhi (李静之), et al. *Marxist View of Women*《马克思主义妇女观》. Beijing: Renmin University of China Press (中国人民大学出版社), 1992.

Li, Jun (李军). *Wujing Quanyi: Liji Quanyi* (五经全译：礼记全译; *Interpretations of Five Classics: Interpretations of the Records of Rites*), vol. 2. Chang Chun: Chang Chun Press (长春：长春出版社), 1980.

Li, Xiaojiang, and Xiaodan Zhan, "Creating a Space for Women: Women's Studies in China in the 1980s." *Signs* 20, no. 1 (1994): 137–51.

Li, Yinhe (李银河). *Women in Hou Village: Power Relations of Gender in Rural Area* (后村的女人们: 农村性别权利关系). Huhehaote: Inner Mongolia University Press (呼和浩特市: 内蒙古大学出版社), 2009.

Li, Yufu (李育富). "Research on Female Ethics of Zhou Yi" (《周易》女性伦理析论). *Chongqing: Journal of Chongqing University of Sciences and Technology; Social Sciences*, no. 5 (2015): 94–100 (《重庆理工大学学报：社会科学版》2015年第20155期 第94–100页).

Li, Zehou (李泽厚). *Grand Viewpoints Remarks in Boulder Study Room* (波斋新说). Hong Kong: Cosmos Books (香港天地图书有限公司), 1999.

Li, Zhen-gang (李振纲). "Interpretation of Four Levels in the Philosophy of Identity of Heaven and Humanity" (解读"天人合一"哲学的四重内涵). *Journal of Zhongshan University* (中山大学学报社会科学版) 4, no. 5 (2006): 49–54.

Liu, Bohong. "Seeking Development Alternatives in Meeting Challenges of Global Economic Crisis." 2010. apwww.isiswomen.org/index.php?option=com…view.

Liu, Bohong, Ling Li, and Chunyu Yang. "Gender Equality in China's Economic Transformation." Beijing, China: United Nations System in China, UN Women 2014.

Liu, Bohong, Shuo Guo, and Rui Hao. *Research Report on the Retirement Age*. Geneva, Switzerland: Publications Bureau, International Labour Organization, 2011.

Lloyd, Genevieve. "Hume on the Passion for Truth." In *Feminist Interpretations of David Hume*, edited by Anne Jaap Jacobson, 39–59. University Park: Pennsylvania State University Press, 2000.

Ma, Zhongliang, and Lingzhen Yin (马仲良, 尹玲珍主编), eds. *Women's Work and Community Construction* 《妇女工作与社区建设》. Beijing: China Personal Press (中国人事出版社), 2003.

Mao, Zedong. *Selected Works of Mao Tse-tung*. 4 vols. Beijing: Foreign Language Press, 1967.

―――. *Quotations from Chairman Mao*. Peking: Foreign Language Press, 1966.

McRae, Emily. "The Cultivation of Moral Feelings and Mengzi's Method of Extension." *Philosophy East and West* 61, no. 4 (2011): 587–608.

Mengzi (Mencius). *Readings in Classical Chinese Philosophy*. Edited by Philip J. Ivanhoe and Bryan W. Van Norden. 2nd ed. Indianapolis: Hackett, 2005.

Meyers, Diana Tietjens. "Intersectional Identity and the Authentic Self: Opposites Attract!" In *Relational Autonomy*, edited by Natalie Stoljar and Catriona Mackenzie. Oxford: Oxford University Press, 2000.

Miller, Richard W. *Globalizing Justice: The Ethics of Poverty and Power*. Oxford: Oxford University Press, 2010.

Milligan, Christine. *There's No Place Like Home: Place and Care in An Ageing Society*. Burlington, VT: Ashgate, 2009.

Minow, Martha. *Making All the Difference: Inclusion, Exclusion, and American Law*. Ithaca: Cornell University Press, 1990.

Moskop, Wynne Walker. "Book Review: *Caring for Democracy: Markets, Equality, and Justice* by Joan C. Tronto." *American Political Thought* 4, no. 2 (2015): 350–54.

Mou, Bo. "A Reexamination of the Structure and Content of Confucius' Version of the Golden Rule." *Philosophy East and West* 54, no. 2 (2004): 218–48.

Nagel T. "The View from Nowhere." In *Ethics: Selections from Classical and Contemporary Writers*, edited by Oliver A. Johnson and Andrews Reath, 422–34. Boston: Wadsworth Cengage Learning, 2012.

———. *The View from Nowhere*. New York: Oxford University Press, 1986.

Nash, Jennifer C. "Re-Thinking Intersectionality." *Feminist Review* 89 (2008): 1–15.

Nicholson, Linda. *The Second Wave: A Reader in Feminist Theory*. New York: Routledge, 1997.

Nie, Jing-Bao. "The Benevolent Polity: A Confucian Socio-Ethical Vision of Eldercare." *Asian Bioethics Review* 7, no. 3 (2015): 260–75.

Nivison, David S. *The Ways of Confucianism: Investigations in Chinese Philosophy*. Chicago: Open Court, 1996.

Noddings, Nel. *Caring: A Relational Approach to Ethics and Moral Education*. 2nd ed. Updated. Berkeley: University of California Press, 1984, 2003, 2013.

———. "Caring." In *Justice and Care: Essential Readings in Feminist Ethics*, edited by Virginia Held, 7–29. Boulder, CO: Westview Press, 1995.

Okin, Susan M. "Gender Inequality and Cultural Differences." *Political Theory* 22, no. 1 (1994): 5–24.

Oxley, Julinna C. *The Moral Dimensions of Empathy: Limits and Applications in Ethical Theory and Practice*. New York: Palgrave Macmillan, 2011.

Perkins, Franklin. *Heaven and Earth Are Not Humane: The Problem of Evil in Classical Chinese Philosophy*. Bloomington: Indiana University Press, 2014.

Qi, Liang (启良). *Collections of Writing of Qi Liang* (SiXIangZheWenCong). Shanghai, China: XueLin, 1998.

———. *Critique of New Confucianism* (Xin ru xue pi pan). Shanghai, China: San Lian and Xue Lin Joint Publishing, 1995.

Rachels, James. *The Elements of Moral Philosophy*. 3rd ed. New York: McGraw-Hill, 1999.

Raphals, Lisa. *Sharing the Light: Representations of Women and Virtue in Early China*. Albany: State University of New York Press, 1998.

Rawls, John. *A Theory of Justice*. Cambridge, MA: Harvard University Press, 1971.

Reynolds, Jack. *Understanding Existentialism*. Bucks, UK: Acuman, 2006.

Rhode, L. Deborah, ed. *Theoretical Perspectives on Sexual Difference*. New Haven: Yale University Press, 1990.

Robertson, Eleanor. "In Defense of Intersectionality—One of Feminism's Most Important Tools." *Guardian*, December 22, 2013.

Robinson, Fiona. *The Ethics of Care: A Feminist Approach of Human Security*. Philadelphia: Temple University Press, 2011.

———. *Globalizing Care: Ethics, Feminist Theory, and International Relations*. Boulder, CO: Westview Press, 1999.

Sartre, Jean-Paul. *Being and Nothingness*. Cited in Jack Reynolds, *Understanding Existentialism*. Chesham, UK: Acumen Publishing, 2006.

Saul, Jennifer Mather. *Feminism: Issues & Arguments*. Oxford: Oxford University Press, 2003.

Shanahan, Timothy, and Robin Wang. *Reason and Insight: Western and Eastern Perspectives on the Pursuit of Moral Wisdom*. 2nd ed. Belmont CA: Wadsworth, 2003.

Sherman, Nancy. "Recovering Lost Goodness: Shame, Guilt, and Self-Empathy." *Psychoanalytic Psychology* 31, no. 2 (2014): 217–35.

———. *Making a Necessity of Virtue: Aristotle and Kant on Virtue*. New York: Cambridge University Press, 1995.

Shun, Kwong-loi, and David Wong. *Confucian Ethics: A Comparative Study of Self, Autonomy, and Community*. New York: Cambridge University Press, 2004.

Spelman, Elizabeth. *Inessential Woman: Problems of Exclusion in Feminist Thought*. Boston: Beacon Press, 1988.

Stone, Alison. *An Introduction to Feminist Philosophy*. Cambridge, UK: Polity Press, 2007.

Sun, Xi. "4–2-1s Hemmed-in between Two Generations." September 14, 2010. http://www.womenofchina.cn/Issues/Marriage-Family/223429.jsp.

Tao, Jie, Bijun Zheng, and Shirley L. Mow, eds. *Holding Up Half the Sky: Chinese Women Past, Present, and Future*. New York: Feminist Press at the City University of New York, 2004.

Tang, Zongli, and Bing Zuo. *Maoism and Chinese Culture*. Commack, NY: Nova Science, 1996.

Trebilcot, Joyce. "Sex Roles." In *"Femininity," "Masculinity," and "Androgyny": A Modern Philosophical Discussion*. Totowa, NJ: Littlefields, Adams, 1982.

Tronto, Joan C. *Caring Democracy: Markets, Equality, and Justice*. New York: New York University Press, 2013.

———. *Moral Boundaries: A Political Argument for an Ethic of Care*. New York: Routledge, 1993.

———. "Women and Caring: What Can Feminists Learn about Morality from Caring?" In *Gender/Body/Knowledge: Feminist Reconstructions of Being and Knowing*, edited by Alison M. Jaggar and Susan R. Bordo. New Brunswick, NJ: Rutgers University Press, 1989.

Tu, Weiming. "A Confucian Response to the Feminist Critique." In Tasan lecture Korea, November 2001. http://tuweiming.com/lecture7.html.

Van Hooft, Stan. "Caring, Objectivity and Justice: An Integrative View." *Nursing Ethics* 18, no. 2 (2011): 149–60.

Van Norden, Bryan W. "Mencius." In *The Stanford Encyclopedia of Philosophy* (Spring 2017 Edition), edited by Edward N. Zalta. https://plato.stanford.edu/archives/spr2017/entries/mencius.

———. *Virtue Ethics and Consequentialism in Early Chinese Philosophy*. New York: Cambridge University Press, 2007.

Wang, Robin R., ed. *Images of Women in Chinese Thought and Culture: Writings from the Pre-Qin Period through the Song Dynasty*. Indianapolis: Hackett, 2003.

Wang, Yanguang. "The Causes of China's Abnormal Sex Ratio and Improved Approaches." Paper presented at the XXII World Congress of Philosophy: Rethinking Philosophy Today, Seoul, July 31, 2008.

Wei, Guoying. "Gender Comparison of Employment and Career Development in China." *Asian Women* 27, no. 1 (2011): 95–113.

Witt, Charlotte. *The Metaphysics of Gender*. New York: Oxford University Press, 2011.

Wong, David. "Growing Virtue: The Theory and Science of Developing Compassion from a Mencian Perspective." In *The Philosophical Challenge from China*, edited by Brian Bruya, 23–57. Cambridge: MIT Press, 2015.

Wu, Cang-ping. "Family Planning and Population Aging: General Law and the Reality in China." *Chinese Elderly* 5 (1986) (in Chinese). In *Social Policy of the Economic State and Community Care in Chinese Culture*, edited by Sheying Chen. Avebury: Ashgate, 1996.

Yan, Hairong. *New Masters, New Servants: Migration, Development, and Women Workers in China*. Durham, NC: Duke University Press, 2008.

Yang, Bojun (杨伯峻). *Lunyu Yizhu* (论语注释, *Interpretation of Analects*). Beijing: Zhonghua Shuju (中华书局, Chinese Book Bureau), 1996.

Yao, Xinzhong. *An Introduction to Confucianism*. Cambridge: Cambridge University Press, 2000.

Yinhe, Li (李银河). *Women in Hou Village: Power Relations of Gender in Rural Area* (后村的女人们: 农村性别权利关系). Huhehaote: Niemenggu University Press (呼和浩特市: 内蒙古大学出版社), 2009.

Young, Iris Marion. *Justice and the Politics of Difference*. Princeton: Princeton University Press, 1990.

Yu, Jiyuan. *The Ethics of Confucius and Aristotle: Mirrors of Virtue*. New York: Routledge, 2007.

Yuan, Lijun. "Confucian and Feminist Notions of Relational Self and Reciprocity: A Comparative Study." *Journal of East-West Thought* 5, no. 4 (2015): 1–10.

———. *Reconceiving Women's Equality in China: A Critical Examination of Models of Sex Equality*. Lanham, MD: Lexington Books, 2005.

Zeng Y., and L. George. "Family Dynamics of 63 Million (in 1990) to More Than 330 Million (in 2050) Elders in China." *Demographic Research* 2, no. 5 (2000). www.demographic-research.org/Volumes/Vol2/5/. DOI: 10.4054/DemRes.2000.2.5.

Zhang, Shiwei (张师伟). "Rendering and Retrofit: People-Oriented Concept in Process of the Sinicization of Modern Democratic Thought" (濡染与改造：现代民主思想中国化过程中的民本观念). *Journal of Culture, History, and Philosophy* 20163 (2016): 5–15.

Zhang, Xianglong (张祥龙). *Heidegger and Chinese Way of Heaven: Enlightenment and Communication in the Ultimate Envision* (《海德格尔思想与中国天道: 终极视域的开启与交融》). Beijing: Life, Reading, and New Knowledge Press (北京: 生活.读书. 新知 三联书店), 1996.

Zheng, Yefu (郑也夫). *On Prices: A New Perspective from Sociology* (《代价论：一个社会学的新视角》). Beijing: Sanlian Bookstore（北京: 三联书店）, 1995.

Zheng, Zhenzhen (郑真真). "Finding Issues through Phenomenon: Population and Gender Studies" (透过现象看本质: 人口学与性别研究). In *Gender Issues: Multidisciplinary Perspectives* 《他们眼中的性别问题：妇女/性别研究的多学科视野》, edited by Tan Lin and Meng Xianfan (谭琳，孟宪范主编), 66–86. Beijing: Social Sciences Academic Press (社会科学文献出版社), 2007.

Zhou, Yun, "Fertility Control and Women in China." Paper presented at the Women and Gender Research Collaborative Symposium, LBJ Student Center, Texas State University, San Marcos, March 4, 2011.

Index

About the Author

Lijun Yuan is professor of philosophy at Texas State University in San Marcos and author of *Reconceiving Women's Equality in China: A Critical Examination of Models of Sex Equality* (2005).